The Family

UNDER

SIEGE

WHAT THE NEW SOCIAL ENGINEERS HAVE IN MIND FOR YOU AND YOUR CHILDREN

GEORGE GRANT

BETHANY HOUSE PUBLISHERS
Minneapolis, Minnesota 55438

Copyright © 1994
George Grant
All Rights Reserved

Published by Bethany House Publishers
A Ministry of Bethany Fellowship, Inc.
11300 Hampshire Avenue South
Minneapolis, Minnesota 55438

Printed in the United States of America

Library of Congress Cataloging-in-Publication Data

CIP applied for

ISBN 1–55661–350–4   CIP

To Wayne and Mary Jane Morris

Faithful Servants

and

To Jim and Anne Kennedy

Gracious Mentors

Some of the quoted documentation in this book, particularly in Chapters One and Two, is sexually explicit. It is without doubt offensive, but it has been included for the benefit of those who need the material to use as evidence to protect young people from exploitation.

GEORGE GRANT is a nationally known author and speaker who brings a powerful biblical perspective on social, political, cultural, historical, and theological issues. He is Founder of the international charitable relief provider, HELP Services, Vice President of Coral Ridge Ministries, and Executive Director of Legacy Communications. He has written over a dozen books—such as *Grand Illusions*, *Trial and Error*, and *Legislating Immorality*.

CONTENTS

Introduction: Why We Must Do the Work at Hand 15
1. The Enemy in Our Midst 23
2. Abortion Inc.: Planned Parenthood 47
3. Dumb Certainties: National Education Association 73
4. The Sky is Falling: Greenpeace 103
5. Miscarriage of Justice: American Civil Liberties Union ... 131
6. Unnatural Affections: ACT UP 155
7. The Nanny State: Children's Defense Fund 179
8. Medicine Show: World Health Organization 199
9. Old New Age: Tikkun 223
10. Us, Them, and Him 243
Notes 273

Acknowledgments

Nay, misery's blackest night may chance, by fortune's turn, to show a happy dawn.[1]

—Euripides

The darkest hour is that before the dawn.[2]

—Alexander Maclaren

In reflecting on the various wiles and woes of authorship, the great Winston Churchill once said:

Writing a book is an adventure. To begin with it is a toy and an amusement. Then it becomes an infatuation. Then it becomes an amusement. Then it becomes a master and a tyrant. And then in the last phase, just as you are about to be reconciled to your servitude, you kill the monster.[3]

Although I have always considered my calling to write to be a special joy, I must confess there is some truth to what Churchill says. In the case of this book, that is particularly true. It was a hard book to research. It was an even harder book to write. Not because the subject matter is arcane and inaccessible but because it is heart-wrenching and demoralizing. Spending hours on end cataloging the current institutional assaults and abuses against the family is not exactly my idea of fun. Documenting the policies, principles, and programs of the modern social engineers is not particularly uplifting—as you can well imagine.

Why this book then?

Because it is essential not only that we all be aware of the forces

11

at work in our society today but also that we all be aware of God's good providence in the face of such forces. This book is an attempt to provide modern Christians with the background understanding necessary to act wisely and walk righteously in these difficult and complex times.

Knowing that didn't make the taxing work of writing and researching this book any easier, though. Instead, it was a group of *people*—God's gracious provision in my life—that eased me through that process. To them I owe thanks I can never adequately convey.

My fellow workers at Legacy and the Christian Worldview Institute, David Dunham and Mary Jane Morris, were selfless in their care and concern for me. They covered the phones, ran down loose details, encouraged me day after day, and put up with my curmudgeonly ways with good cheer and unswerving friendship. In addition, Jason Craddock—who participated in our first summer internship program—afforded me the keen insights of his legal training and the rich fruits of his pro-life and mercy ministry research.

Robert Huberty and Lisa Lundquist in Washington, and Harley Bellew and Chris Slattery in New York, Carol Novielli and Juanna Estefan in Miami, Tim Murphy and Julie Powjerzki in Chicago, Rasheena Smith and LaRhonda Greer in Detroit, Roy and Beverly MacMillan in Jackson, and Marla Haverty and Miguel de Chavez in Los Angeles, each helped me in identifying and gathering invaluable but obscure primary source documentation.

My students at the Franklin Classical School bore with me patiently during the distracting days of writing—as did the fine scholars at Whitefield Seminary who remained remarkably uncomplaining under my often distracted supervision.

My pastor, James Bachmann; my yokefellow, Steve Mansfield; my graduate school advisor, Ken Talbot; my political plumbline, Howard Phillips; my theology prof, Jim Jordan; my sounding board, Tom Clark; and my mentor, Jim Kennedy, each likewise supported me in innumerable ways.

A small group of intercessors including Dawn Ruff, Bert Ligon, Hafez al Haad, Sharon Hefley, and Joy Lange committed to pray for me during this project. I know just enough about spiritual warfare to know that theirs was a far greater sacrifice than mine.

The audio portion of the project was provided by Pachelbel, Albinoni, Schubert, Enya, Clannad, and Delibes—with much able assistance from Steve Green, Michael Card, Susan Ashton, Charlie Peacock, Buddy Green, and Steve Camp. Muchas gracias, compadres.

David Hazard has been a friend as well as a wise and judicious editor. This book was really his idea and took the shape it did thanks to his unerring professional scrutiny. In addition, all the good folks at Bethany—and particularly Carol Johnson—made this entire process peculiarly unstressful.

But, as always, it was my family—my beloved partner-for-life, Karen, and our blessed brood, Joel, Joanna, and Jesse—that made this book possible.

To all these I offer my sincerest thanks. They made what could have been—and even what should have been—a supremely unpleasant job an extremely satisfying one instead.

Coram Deo.[4]

Introduction

Why We Must Do the Work at Hand

Yet all that is gold is not that which doth golden seem.[1]

—Edmund Spenser

All that glitters is sold as gold.[2]

—Ogden Nash

We are under siege. We cannot deny it any longer. Our families are facing a fierce and unprecedented challenge—one that may threaten their very existence.

None of us are exempt from its ravages. None can avoid its consequences. None can afford to ignore it.

According to the oft-quoted findings of *The Index of Leading Cultural Indicators*:

> The condition of our culture is not good. Over the last three decades we have experienced substantial social regression. Today the forces of social decomposition are challenging—and in some instances, overtaking—the forces of social composition. And when decomposition takes hold, it exacts an enormous human cost.[3]

And that exacting cost has all but devastated the integrity of the family.

We have watched in horror and disbelief as the number of illegitimate births has climbed 400 percent, as divorce rates have quadrupled, as the incidence of domestic violence has increased 320 percent, as the percentage of children either abandoned or left

15

to their own resources has quintupled, and as teen suicides have skyrocketed 200 percent.[4]

Meanwhile, those institutions that have traditionally provided stability, strength, and solace to families in times of crisis—our churches, private associations, and community organizations—have been systematically undermined. Their values have been attacked, their methods have been challenged, and their reputations have been distorted—more often than not at the hands of our own government and the social engineers under its aegis.

Amazingly, this assault was initiated under the pretense of *helping* us, not hurting us. Not only has it hurt us, we have paid for the injury ourselves. Social spending by government has increased five-fold in the last thirty years.[5] Inflation-adjusted spending for the vast plethora of social service programs has increased 630 percent, while spending for its sundry educational programs has increased 225 percent.[6] Sad to say, virtually every dollar poured into those programs has only made matters worse.

In fact, the cure has turned out to be much worse than the disease.

Though the grandiose failure of the modern government-sponsored social engineers has been glaringly obvious for more than a decade—fully documented with reams of empirical data—their desire to utterly supplant and succeed the family remains undeterred. In fact, they are more powerful, more influential, and more determined than ever before. Their organizations, institutions, and endowments have recently entered into a whole host of lucrative new partnerships with government at all levels. "The corridors of power have always been open to us," says Pamela Maraldo, president of Planned Parenthood. "But there is a new sense of energy and a courageous willingness to completely reinvent our society. It's a whole new ball game."[7]

Indeed it is.

This book is not meant to be a comprehensive blueprint for the restoration of the family—much less the nation. Nor is it meant to be a survey of all the woes that modernity has brought to the thresholds of our homes. It is not meant to be an attempt to summarize the empirical data relating to the family's demise in our time. Nor to be a book about politics or sociological mega-trends. It is not even meant to be a woeful wailing at the backslidings of our culture. And it certainly is not meant to be an attempt to hew the sons of Agag in pieces. Instead, it is a quick profile of some of today's most prominent social engineers. It is simply an effort to discover just who they are, what they want, why they want it, and how they intend to get it.

After a brief survey of the contemporary scene in the first chapter, this book examines eight of the organizations and institutions that are helping to define that scene. Thus, in the following chapters, Planned Parenthood, the National Education Association, Greenpeace, the American Civil Liberties Union, ACT UP, the Children's Defense Fund, the World Health Organization, and Tikkun are taken up in turn. Finally, the concluding chapter attempts to help us formulate basic guidelines for a sound and reasoned response.

Obviously, the practical concerns of space and time demanded that I exercise a certain selectivity in choosing which of the plethora of popular organizations and trends warranted our more careful scrutiny. Besides their wide range and representative character, the subjects of this study were each selected because of their special privilege and proximity to the powers-that-be in Washington—as well as in Ottawa and London. Though for the most part they share common philosophies, common methodologies, and common indelicacies, it is their common connections that bring them to our attention here.

Admittedly, this work is a cursory introduction to understanding the popular philosophies of modern social engineers and the ephemeral culture that they dominate. Entire tomes could have been devoted to each of the organizations or topics that I have surveyed over in these few pages.[8] Even so, as G. K. Chesterton has so aptly asserted, "It is necessary to have in hand a truth to judge modern philosophies rapidly; and it is necessary to judge them very rapidly before they disappear."[9]

Like Chesterton, I am grateful for the fact that all of man's follies are little more than wood, hay, and stubble and are undoubtedly impermanent; the gods of the moment last only for a moment. Yet we must live in this moment, and so we must counter it with unremitting doses of sanity.

Although there is an apparently redundant refrain in most of my writing—and that is a heavy emphasis on the lessons of history—this is not mere decoration or illustrative filler. It is essential.

The English author and lecturer John H. Y. Briggs has poignantly argued that a historical awareness is essential for the health and well-being of any society; it enables us to know who we are, why we are here, and what we should do. He says:

> Just as a loss of memory in an individual is a psychiatric defect calling for medical treatment, so too any community which has no social memory is suffering from an illness.[10]

Lord Acton, the great historian from the previous generation, made the same point saying:

> History must be our deliverer not only from the undue influence of other times, but from the undue influence of our own, from the tyranny of the environment and the pressures of the air we breathe.[11]

The venerable aphorism remains as true today as ever: "He who forgets his own history is condemned to repeat it."[12]

It seems that in this awkward new epoch we are afflicted with a malignant contemporaneity. Our morbid preoccupation with ourselves—and thus our ambivalence and ignorance of the past—has trapped us in a recalcitrant present.

Renowned historian Daniel Boorstin has said:

> In our schools today, the story of our nation has been replaced by social studies—which is the study of what ails us now. In our churches, the effort to see the essential nature of man has been displaced by the social gospel—which is the polemic against the pet vices of today. Our book publishers no longer seek the timeless and the durable, but spend most of their efforts in a fruitless search for . . . a la mode social commentary—which they pray will not be out of date when the item goes to press. Our merchandisers frantically devise their new-year models, which will cease to be voguish when their sequels appear three months hence. Neither our classroom lessons nor our sermons nor our books nor the things we live with nor the houses we live in are any longer strong ties to our past. We have become a nation of short-term doomsayers. In a word, we have lost our sense of history. Without the materials of historical comparison, we are left with nothing but abstractions.[13]

History is not just the concern of historians and social scientists. It is not the lonely domain of political prognosticators and ivory tower academics. It is the very stuff of life. And, it is the very stuff of faith. In fact, the Bible puts a heavy emphasis on historical awareness—not at all surprising considering the fact that the vast proportion of its own contents record the dealings of God with men and nations throughout the ages.

Again and again in the Scriptures, God calls upon His people to *remember.* He calls on us to remember the bondage, oppression, and deliverance out of Egypt (Exodus 13:3; Deuteronomy 6:20–23). The graciousness of the commandments (Numbers 15:39–40). To remember the splendor, strength, and devotion of the Davidic Kingdom (1 Chronicles 16:8–36). The valor, forthrightness, and holiness of the prophets (James 5:7–11). The grief of the Babylonian exile (Psalm 137:1–6), and the judgment of the great apostasies (Jude 5–11). The responsibility of the restoration (Ezra 9:5–15). And He calls us to remember the ultimate victory of the Cross (1 Corinthians 11:23–26).

He also calls us to remember the lives and witness of all those who have gone before us in faith—forefathers, fathers, patriarchs, prophets, apostles, preachers, evangelists, martyrs, confessors, ascetics, and every righteous spirit made pure in Christ (1 Corinthians 10:1–11; Hebrews 11:3–40).

When Moses stood before the Israelites at the end of his long life, he did not exhort them with polemics or moralisms. He reminded them of the works of God in history. He reminded them of their duty to remember (Deuteronomy 32:1–43).

When David stood before his family and friends following a great deliverance from his enemies, he did not stir them with sentiment or nostalgia. He reminded them of the works of God in history in a psalm of praise (2 Samuel 22:1–51).

When Solomon stood before his subjects at the dedication of the newly constructed temple, he did not challenge them with logic or rhetoric. He simply reminded them of the works of God in history in a hymn of wisdom (1 Kings 8:15–61).

When Nehemiah stood before the families of Jerusalem at the consecration of the rebuilt city walls, he did not bombard them with theology or theatrics. He simply reminded them of the works of God in history in a song of the covenant (Nehemiah 9:9–38).

When Stephen stood before an accusing and enraged Sanhedrin, he did not confront them with apology or condemnation. He simply reminded them of the works of God in history in a litany of faith (Acts 7:2–53).

Each of these men reminded the men and women of their day that they had a duty to remember.

Remembrance and forgetfulness are the measuring rods of faithfulness throughout the entire canon of Scripture. A family that passes its legacy on to its children will bear great fruit (Deuteronomy 8:2–10). A family that fails to take its heritage seriously will remain barren (Deuteronomy 8:11–14). A people that remembers the great and mighty deeds of the Lord will be blessed (Deuteronomy 8:18). A people that forgets is doomed to frustration and failure (Deuteronomy 8:19–20). In fact, the whole direction of a culture depends on the gracious appointments of memory:

> Wonders cannot be known in the midst of darkness. Righteousness cannot be done in a land of forgetfulness. (Psalm 88:12)

That is why the Bible makes it plain that there are two kinds of people in the world: effectual doers and forgetful hearers (James 1:25). And that is why the ministry of the Holy Spirit in the lives of believers is primarily to bring to our remembrance the Word of Truth (John 14:26).

Philip Schaff, the prolific church historian during the previous generation, argued stridently that we must be eternally vigilant in the task of handing on our great legacy—to remember and then to inculcate that remembrance in the hearts and minds of our children:

> How shall we labor with any effect to build up the church, if we have no thorough knowledge of its history, or fail to apprehend it from the proper point of observation? History is, and must ever continue to be, next to God's Word, the richest foundation of wisdom, and the surest guide to all successful practical activity.[14]

Indeed, in this day when the family is so obviously under siege we dare not neglect our rich legacy. And we dare not keep it to ourselves:

> Listen, O my people, to my instruction; incline your ears to the words of my mouth. I will open my mouth in a parable; I will utter

dark sayings of old, which we have heard and known, and our fathers have told us. We will not conceal them from their children, but tell to the generation to come the praises of the LORD, and His strength and His wondrous works that He has done. For He established a testimony in Jacob, and appointed a law in Israel, which He commanded our fathers, that they should teach them to their children, that the generation to come might know, even the children yet to be born, that they may arise and tell them to their children, that they should put their confidence in God, and not forget the works of God, but keep His commandments. (Psalm 78:1–7, NAS)

Thus the historical sections of this book are not mere nostalgia or sentiment, they are essential to the entire world view formulation necessary to boldly stand in the face of what the new social engineers have in mind for our families.

————

In 1838, James Fenimore Cooper introduced his prescient book of political analysis, *The American Democrat*, saying:

This little work has been written, in consequence of its author's having had many occasions to observe the manner in which principles that are of the least importance to the happiness of the community, are getting to be confounded in the popular mind. Notions that are impracticable, and which if persevered in, cannot fail to produce disorganization, if not revolution, are widely prevalent, and while many seem disposed to complain, few show a disposition to correct them. In those instances in which efforts are made to resist or to advance the innovation of the times, the actors take the extremes of the disputed points, the one side looking as far behind it, over ground that can never be retrod, as the other looks ahead, in the idle hope of substituting a fancied perfection for the ills of life.[15]

The more things change the more they stay the same.
Cooper went on to say:

It is the intention of this book to make a commencement towards a more just discrimination between truth and prejudice. With what success the task has been accomplished, the honest reader will judge for himself.[16]

Frankly, I could not hope for anything more for this little corban volume.

Quaesiti a me, quid ita, si providentia mundus regertur, multa bonis viris mala acciderent. Hoc commodius in contextu operis redderetur, cum praeesse universis providentiam probaremus et interesse nobis Deum; sed quoniam a toto particulam revelli placet et unam contradictionem manente lite integra solvere, faciam rem non difficilem, causam Deum agam.[17]

ONE

THE ENEMY IN OUR MIDST

'Tis the loftiest towers that fall with the heaviest crash.[1]
—Horace

Ever from the higher degree that man falleth, the more is he thrall.[2]
—Geoffrey Chaucer

There is a force at work in our land—a force that has begun to invade the most private areas of home and family. Undoubtedly you have already felt its effects. This force is a part of a greater purpose. It is a part of a plan. Not so much a grand conspiracy, but rather the practical outworking of social engineers who are, even at this moment, hard at work, having gained access to the highest offices of power in this land. Thus, a whole system is being contructed that is at work against you and your best purposes for your family. The irony of it is that this insidious plan is being financed by you and me. If you have somehow been unaware how much ground these new social engineers have gained, what you read next may shock you. These brief, but true stories are retold here only as a warning: The force threatening to take charge of your home and mine is already moving among us. As many Christians are already painfully aware.

Catherine Toleson was terribly unsettled. She was confused and embarrassed. She felt isolated and alone. Second period on Tuesdays and Thursdays was her "Health" class. Her teacher, a matronly woman in her late fifties, often brought in outside speakers to discuss various topics of interest with the students. This week, a representative from a local "women's clinic" had come to talk about sex, contraception, pregnancy, and abortion.

"I was shocked," Catherine told me later. "Not by the facts of life, but by the way those facts were presented. My parents had already had plenty of discussions with me about the birds and bees. I figured I knew just about all a fifteen-year-old should need to know."

Apparently, Catherine's "Health" teacher and the speaker disagreed. "The speaker was so sleek and sophisticated," Catherine recalled. "She was beautiful and soft-spoken. Her clothes were gorgeous. Like a model almost, only really professional-looking. And she was kinda funny and very articulate. When she walked in, she had our attention immediately—I mean, she was so confident and assured and relaxed, the whole class just fell under her spell."

With her disarming presence, she stripped away the youngsters' inhibitions. Sitting on the edge of the teacher's desk, she joked, kidded, winked, and bandied with them.

"At first, I couldn't tell where all this was leading," Catherine said. "But then it became really obvious. She started asking us personal questions. *Very* personal questions. Like about our feelings. About sex. And even about . . . well, about . . . masturbation! It was *so* disgusting. All the boys were kinda giggling. But you could tell, even they were embarrassed."

If that had been all, it would have been bad enough. But the speaker didn't stop with mere titillating and perverse conversation. She pulled a screen down over the dusty blackboard, closed the window shades, and turned off the humming fluorescent lights, then put a short film on the school's wheezing, rattling projector.

"I've never seen pornography before," Catherine admitted. "But this film was worse than what I could have ever imagined hard-core pornography to be."

The film was extremely explicit. An unashamedly brash couple fondled each other in preparation for intercourse. The camera continually zoomed in for close-up shots on sweaty bodies—caressing, kissing, stroking, petting, embracing. At the height of passion, the camera fixed on the woman's hands as she tore open a condom package and began to slowly unroll its contents onto her partner.

"I wanted to look away or cover my eyes, but I couldn't," Catherine said. "I just stared at the screen—in horror."

When the lights came back on, the entire class was visibly

shaken. With wide eyes, the youngsters sat speechless and amazed.

But their guest was entirely unperturbed.

"She began to tell us that everything that we'd just seen was totally normal and totally good," Catherine remembered. "She said that the couple obviously had a caring, loving, and responsible relationship—because they took proper precautions against conception and disease."

At that, the speaker passed several packages of condoms around the room—one for each of the girls. She instructed the boys to hold up a finger so that the girls could *practice* contraceptive application.

Already shell-shocked, the students did as they were told.

But afterwards, several of the girls began quietly sobbing, another ran out of the room and threw up, still another fainted. Mercifully, the class ended just a moment later.

"I have never been more humiliated in all my life," Catherine said. "I felt dirty and defiled after seeing the film. But then, when I had to put *that thing* on Billy's finger—well, it was horrible. It was like I'd been raped. Raped in my mind. Raped by my school."

Layle French also feels violated. When French bought a new home for his family, he decided to rent their former home until the real estate market improved enough that he could sell it. He thought it might even be a good investment for the future and an added source of new income for the family.

He was wrong.

Not long afterwards, he was notified that he was being sued for discriminatory business practices and a violation of the Minnesota Civil Rights Act. And as a result, he and his young family are facing utter financial ruin.

What was the heinous crime that he committed? Very simply, he refused to rent his house to an unmarried couple because of his Christian concerns and convictions about fornication and adultery.

The Attorney General's office had received complaints from an attorney representing a woman and her live-in lover that French had "illegally attempted to enforce his religious prejudices concerning marital status on the marketplace," and was thus "guilty of violating the couple's civil rights."

"They're pretty consistent in telling us that we can't push our religion on somebody else," Layle said. But, in fact, "they are trying to push their beliefs on us."

For Catherine Toleson, the attack was aimed at her mind and soul. For Layle French, his property. For Bill Hargess, the invasion came on another "front."

Hargess is the pastor of a small, but growing, suburban church. Concerned that his congregation faithfully communicate the Gospel in both word and deed he has, in the last couple of years, initiated a number of innovative ministries and outreaches—to the poor, to the homeless, to single adults, to latch-key kids, and to illegal aliens. He has also led the church into active involvement in the anti-pornography and pro-life movements as well.

"I have seen tremendous growth in the lives of our families," he said. "And, I have to attribute it to the fact that we are now, perhaps for the first time, seeing how the Lordship of Christ and the Bible really apply to the everyday dilemmas and details of life."

Now, Pastor Hargess and his congregation have several new dilemmas and details to which they must apply the Lordship of Christ and the Bible. No longer do they have to merely content themselves with the challenges of finding proper medical care for indigent families, or of setting up prenatal care and counseling for pregnant teens, or of securing a mechanic to work on the car of a single mother, or of any number of the other "mundane" tasks that they tackle every week.

Now, they must fight for the very existence of their church.

Some time ago, Pastor Hargess was notified by the Internal Revenue Service that the church's non-profit, tax-exempt status had been challenged by several "community citizen's groups" who had become concerned that the church's "non-religious, politically-motivated activities" violated the "spirit and intent of the law." Particularly of concern to the IRS was the church's pro-life picketing. As a consequence of this concern, the church's bulk mailing permit was revoked, its bank account frozen, and its membership—and "all those working in concert with" its membership—were enjoined from further protests until a full investigation could be launched and a hearing scheduled.

"Even if we did not have solid scriptural warrant," Pastor Hargess said, "or twenty centuries of church history as a precedent for the kinds of mercy ministries that we've been involved in, this kind of blatant persecution and suppression simply cannot be tolerated—at least not here in America where basic civil and human rights are supposed to be protected. I asked the IRS if it was now against the law to practice the Golden Rule. They didn't answer me directly, but they did promise me that they would conduct a thorough investigation."

These days, such investigations leave no good stone unturned. But then, they leave no good turn unstoned either.

Nor is the right to school our children according to the principles we choose exempt from attack.

———

A mood of restless tension filled the room.

It was a meeting of parents. Very concerned parents. They had come together to discuss options and to formulate strategies. But their options seemed few and far between, and when all their strategies appeared impotent, frustrations soared, anxiety rose, and despair prevailed.

"We feel so helpless," said one young father.

"It seems as if there is absolutely nothing we can do," said another.

"All the cards are stacked against us. We don't have the political pull, the connections, the resources, or the savvy to do much of anything except gripe and complain," said still another.

Why such utter dismay?

The State Board of Education had just handed down a series of new regulations severely restricting Christian day schools and home schools. The provisions were written in such a way that there appeared to be no escape clauses, no alternative appeals, and no judicial loopholes. The legislators had done their homework and had come up with an ironclad bill. It would subject all educational programs to state control, attaching severe penalties to churches, families, and schools that failed to comply.

These parents had come together thinking that they could not stand idly by while their children's future and their families' freedom hung in the balance.

But what could they do?

"Oh, I suppose we could write some letters, attend some meetings, and issue some statements," said one frustrated mom. "But what good would that do? They've got us by the throat. How can a few Christian families with few or no resources expect to go up against the monolithic bureaucratic blockade?"

"I hate to just give up," said another, "but no one here has any idea how to address these problems. And I don't know anyone who does. Where do you draw the line? When do you just go along with the crowd?"

———

As diverse as they may appear at first glance, all of these frightening, real, legal scenarios have a number of crucial elements in common:

Each one occurred in the past couple of years.

Each involved ordinary people—like you or me—not powerful political lobbies, affluent commercial interests, or resourceful social movements. Just ordinary people.

Each cost those people a lot of time, money, and heartache.

Each represents a gross miscarriage of justice and a violation of basic Constitutional and human rights.

And each one was perpetrated and plainted by the new social engineers who want to remake society—and your family—by means of manipulation. Most especially by power politics.

Before we look at the organizations that are forcing their way into our lives, it is crucial for us to understand two things. First, we must understand the "game" that is afoot—and that is the game of power politics. There are those who have become adept at the use of politics, and their goal is to remake society—and your family—by means of this powerfully manipulative tool. Second, we must understand that politics was never meant by our founders to be in this place of ascendancy. Unless we see what was intended for our land, we will never understand how far we have moved away from the foundational ideals of our country, nor will we have the firm conviction that it is time to resist the siege that faces us right now.

Politics as Usual—or Unusual

In many ways Lyndon Johnson was a prototype of the modern man-of-the-world. He once satirically quipped, "I seldom think of politics more than eighteen hours a day."[3] The man who would succeed John Kennedy as President of the United States believed that civil government was the most important force in modern life.[4] Thus, political power was everything to him.

How sad.

As syndicated columnist George Will has argued:

> There is hardly a page of American history that does not refute the insistence, so characteristic of the political class, on the primacy of politics in the making of history.[5]

In fact, he says, "In a good society, politics is peripheral to much of the pulsing life of the society."[6]

Certainly, politics is important. But it is not all-important.

Many who live and die by the electoral sword will probably be shocked to discover that most of the grand-glorious headline-making events in the political realm today will actually go down in the annals of time as mere backdrops to the real drama of the everyday affairs of life. But it is so.

So much emphasis is placed on the machinery of politics—on the campaigns, primaries, caucuses, conventions, elections, statutes, administrations, surveys, polls, trends, policies, and programs—and yet the reality is that the importance of fellow workers, next door neighbors, close friends, and family members is actually far greater. Political skullduggery—however much it may or may not upset us—is rather remote from the things that really matter. The affairs of ordinary people who tend their gardens and raise their children and perfect their trades and mind their businesses are, in the end, more important. Just like they always have been, and like they always will be.

That is the great lesson of history.

Through the ages the central message of all the most intriguing figures, of all the most dominating movements, of all the most compelling ideals, has been that ultimately it is the simple things that matter most.[7] It has been that ordinary people doing ordinary things are the force that determines the outcome of human events—not princes or populists issuing decrees. That peasants with pitchforks and *babushkas* with brooms can topple empires and *kremlins* while all the world looks on in awe. Simple folks, doing their mundane chores, can literally change the course of history—because they are the stuff of which history is made.

As G. K. Chesterton aptly observed, "The greatest political storm flutters only a fringe of humanity. But an ordinary man and an ordinary woman and their ordinary children literally alter the destiny of the nations."[8]

Not to say that politics is irrelevant. Far from it. It is just that there are a number of things in life that are *more* significant.

Even Eugene McCarthy, once the darling of the New Left, admitted as much, saying:

> Being in politics is a lot like being a football coach; you have to be smart enough to understand the game, and dumb enough to think it's important.[9]

Intuitively, the man-on-the-street knows that is true.

According to political analyst E. J. Dionne, that is why most of us are wont to approach politics with more than a little indifference:

> Americans view politics with boredom and detachment. For most of us, politics is increasingly abstract, a spectator sport barely worth watching.[10]

He says that since the average person "believes that politics will do little to improve his life or that of his community, he votes defensively," if at all.[11]

As odd as it may seem, that kind of robust detachment is actually close to what America's founding fathers originally intended. They feared on-going political passions and thus tried to construct a system that minimized the impact of factions, parties, and activists.[12] Citizens of the Republic were expected to turn out at the polls to vote for men of good character and broad vision—and then pretty much forget about politics until the next election.[13]

Gouvenor Morris—the man who actually wrote the first draft of the Constitution and who was instrumental in its acceptance—said:

> The Constitution is not an instrument for government to restrain the people, it is an instrument for the people to restrain the government—lest it come to dominate our lives and interests.[14]

Similarly, Patrick Henry stated:

Liberty necessitates the diminutization of political ambition and concern. Liberty necessitates concentration on matters other than mere civil governance. Rather, whatsoever things are true, whatsoever things are honest, whatsoever things are just, whatsoever things are pure, whatsoever things are lovely, whatsoever things are of good report; if there be any virtue, and if there be any praise, free men must think on these things.[15]

Suspicious of professional politicians and unfettered lobbyists—as well as the inevitable corruptions of special interests—the founders established a system of severe checks and balances designed to de-politicize the arena of statecraft, and to contain politics to the very limited realm of government.

Though there was disagreement between Federalists and Anti-Federalists about how much "energy," or "lack thereof," government ought to exercise, there was universal agreement about what John DeWitt called the "peripheral importance of institutional action to the actual liberties of daily life."[16]

Thus the founders worked together to insure that the republican confederation of states was as free as possible from ideological or partisan strife.[17] Though they were not entirely successful, for much of our history American life has been marked by the distinct conviction that what goes on next door is of greater immediate concern than what goes on in Washington.

Sadly, those days are no more.

Perhaps the most distinctive aspect of our age is the subsuming of all other concerns to the predominance of politics. And thus, we have succumbed to a Lyndon Johnson-like dependence upon the power of the state.

The tragic result has been that all of life has become politicized, and if the new social engineers have their way, politics will increase in power—especially in its power to penetrate into our everyday lives and rule our destinies. For in fact politics has become, for many of the political elite, a kind of state religion.

Faith, Hope, and Politics

And now abide faith, hope, and politics, these three; but the greatest of these is politics. This is how far we have moved from the intent of our founders.

In the twentieth century, the smothering influence of ideological politics is everywhere evident. It has wrested control of every academic discipline, of every cultural trend, of every intellectual impulse, even of every religious revival in our time. From Nazism and Stalinism to pluralism and multiculturalism, from liberalism and conservatism to monopolism and socialism, ours has been an epoch of movements beguiled by the temporal seductions of ideological politics.

Nearly every question, every issue, every social dilemma has been and continues to be translated into legal, juridical, or mechanical terms. They are supplied with bureaucratic, mathematical, or systemic solutions. If there is something wrong with the economy then government must fix it. If the health-care system is inefficient then government must reform it. If education is in disarray then government must revamp it. If family values are absent then government must supply them. And if government itself doesn't work, well then, government must reinvent government. Whatever the problem, it seems that government is the solution.

Virtually all social historians agree that this is indeed the indelible mark of our time: the capitulation of everything else to the rise of political mass movements based upon comprehensive, secular, closed-universe, and millenarian intellectual systems. Thus, at one time or another, Henry David Aiken, Karl Dietrich Bracher, Isaac Kraminick, Frederick Watkins, Barbara Tuchman, Antonia Fraser, Paul Johnson, Russell Kirk, and Murray Rothbard have all dubbed this the "Age of Ideology."[18]

The name of the ideological game is power. G. K. Chesterton observes:

> There is, as a ruling element in modern life, a blind and asinine appetite for mere power. There is a spirit abroad among the nations of the earth which drives men incessantly on to destroy what they cannot understand, and to capture what they cannot enjoy.[19]

According to philosopher Eric Voegelin, this awful tendency "is essentially the politics of spiritual revolt."[20] It is, he says, a kind of "psychic disorientation."[21]

But this modern notion is a far cry from the kind of world view the American founders and pioneers maintained. They shared a profound distrust of central governments to solve the grave problems that afflicted individuals, communities, and societies. Certainly they believed in a strong and active civil authority—but only in its proper place. Thus they abhorred every brand of statist ideology.

Thomas Jefferson warned against the danger of "reducing the society to the state or the state to society."[22] Patrick Henry argued, "The contention that the civil government should at its option intrude into and exercise control over the family and the household is a great and pernicious error."[23] Gouvenor Morris insisted that the everyday affairs of society should be designed to avoid what he called the "interference of the state beyond its competence."[24]

Generations later Henry Cabot Lodge would reiterate their warnings:

> Government is but a tool. If ever we come to the place where our tools determine what jobs we can or cannot do, and by what means, then nary a fortnight shall pass in which new freedoms shall be wrested from us straightway. Societal problems are solved by families and communities as they carefully and discriminately use a variety of tools.[25]

Sadly, such warnings have gone unheeded in our day.

Today, there are social engineers who believe that the dilemmas of the modern age are simply too grave to trust to free markets, free communities, and free institutions. And so they have erected a sprawling political and ideological kingdom of Babylonian proportions. Thinking that the foundations of America's great experiment in liberty are no longer sufficient to secure the general welfare, they have expanded the girth of government to the point that there is no aspect of our lives that is left untouched by it.

And still they insist that "Government must do more."[26]

A generation ago Robert Nisbet wrote:

> The real significance of the modern state is inseparable from its successive penetrations of man's economic, religious, kinship, and local allegiances, and its revolutionary dislocations of established centers of function and authority.[27]

Similarly the bestselling Canadian author William Gairdner has said:

> The essence, logic, thrust, and consequence of the modern

state—even when this is not the expressed intention—is the invasion and eventual takeover of all private life by the state.[28]

Try to imagine some aspect of your daily existence that has escaped the invasive regulation of government. If there is one it won't exist for long. Modern politics is promiscuous in its desires: Nothing is beyond its purview any longer. And in forging cozy partnerships with socio-political organizations like Planned Parenthood, Greenpeace, the National Education Association, the Children's Defense Fund, the American Civil Liberties Union, ACT UP, the World Health Organization, and Tikkun—among others—the ideological social engineers of our day continue to stoke the consuming fires of politics-as-usual.

So, why is this bad? Why should we be concerned?

Syndicated columnist Joseph Sobran replies:

> The essence of government is force: whatever its end, its means is compulsion. Government forces people to do what they would not otherwise choose to do, or it forces them to refrain from doing what they would otherwise do. So, when we say *"government should do x,"* we are really saying, *"people should be forced to do x."* It should be obvious that force should be used only for the most serious reasons, such as preventing and punishing violence. The frivolous, improper, or excessive use of force is wrong. We used to call it tyranny. Unfortunately, too many people think that calling for the government to do x is merely a way of saying that x is desirable. And so we are increasingly forced to do things that are not genuine social duties but merely good ideas. The result is that the role of state coercion in our lives grows greater and greater.[29]

In short, the omnivorous politicalization of life is at enmity with liberty. We used to, as Sobran says, call that tyranny.

A century ago Frederick Bastiat predicted the possibility of a time when politically mesmerized busybodies would "place themselves above mankind."[30] He feared that they would "make a career of organizing it, patronizing it, and ruling it."[31] They would "think only of subjecting mankind to the philanthropic tyranny of their own social inventions."[32] Worst of all, he said, they would "confuse the distinction between government and society."[33]

He was right. That time has come.

For less, the founding fathers of democracy launched a revolution. What will we do?

Reluctant Revolutionaries

We forget—though God and those who sacrificed to acquire our freedom would have us remember. Too many of us celebrate our independence with the mere entertainments of colorful pop and dazzle once a year in July, forgetting the very urgent reasons why our freedom was bought with blood. And if we forget our past, we will sleep through the loss of our freedom today.

It is shocking to observe the foundational concepts of Western liberty and to see how we have slipped our moorings and drifted back into political tyranny.

Why did the founding fathers risk and sacrifice all? We must look long and hard. For if we clearly understand their motives, we may better understand our own.

Perhaps the most notable aspect of America's revolutionary period was that its chief protagonists were not particularly revolutionary.

From Samuel Adams and John Hancock to Richard Henry Lee and George Washington, from James Iredell and Patrick Henry to Samuel Chase and John Dickinson, the leaders of the American cause were profoundly conservative.[34] They were loathe to indulge in any kind of radicalism that might erupt into violence—rhetorical, political, or martial. For the most part they were the faithful sons of colonial gentry. They were devoted to conventional Whig principles: the rule of law, *noblesse oblige*, unswerving honor, squirey superintendence, and the maintenance of corporate order.[35] They believed in a tranquil and settled society free of the raucous upsets and tumults of agitation, activism, and unrest.

Their reticence to squabble with the crown was obvious to even the most casual observer. It took more than the Boston Massacre, more than Lexington and Concord, more than Bunker Hill, more than Falmouth, and more than Ticonderoga to provoke the patriots to commit themselves to forceful secession. Even as late as the first week of July 1776, there was no solid consensus among the members of the Continental Congress that "such an extreme as full-scale revolt," as John Dickinson dubbed it, was necessary.[36] That week, the "Declaration of Independence" drafted by a committee composed of Benjamin Franklin, Roger Sherman, Robert Livingston, John Adams, and the young Thomas Jefferson, was defeated twice before it was diffidently adopted—and even then the cautious delegates managed to keep its pronouncements secret for four more days.[37]

The patriots were, at best, reluctant revolutionaries.

Why then did they rebel? What could possibly have so overcome their native conservatism?

It was their traditionalism—their commitment to those lasting things that transcend the ever-shifting tides of situation and circumstance—that finally drove them to arms.

According to John Adams, in his manifesto *The Rule of Law and the Rule of Men*, it is the "duty of all men" to "protect the integrity of liberty" whenever the "laws of God," the "laws of the land," and the "laws of the common inheritance" are "profligately violated."[38] Justice demands, he argued, "a defense of the gracious endowments of Providence to mankind," including "life, liberty, and property."[39] To deny this duty is to insure the reduction of "the whole of society" to the "bonds of servility."[40]

Patrick Henry agreed, asserting that it was only a "grave responsibility" that the leaders held to "God and countrymen" that could possibly compel the peace-loving people of America to fight.[41] Economic mercantilism had politicized and tyrannized matters of commerce. Legislative despotism had politicized and tyrannized matters of conscience. These combined and insured that "an appeal to arms and the God of Hosts" was "all that was left" to the patriots.[42]

According to John Hancock, the Americans had been "denied representation" in either "the taxing authorities of parliament or of the trade boards."[43] In addition, their colonial charters had been "subverted or even abrogated," their "citizenship rights" according to English common law had been "violated," and their "freedom of religious practice" and "moral witness" had been "curtailed."[44] Thus, rule of the colonies had become "arbitrary and capricious"; it had become "supra-legal"; it had become "intolerable."[45] Under such circumstances "a holy duty" demanded "a holy response."[46]

The American patriots reached a consensus—that ideological and political encroachments upon the whole of society could not be ignored any longer. And this was confirmed in American pulpits. The very conservative colonial pastors certainly did not set out to "stir up strife or political tumult at the cost of the proclamation of the Gospel," as Charles Lane of Savannah put it.[47] On the other hand, "The Gospel naturally mitigates against lawless tyranny, in whatever form it may take," said Ebenezer Smith of Lowell.[48] Indeed, as Charles Turner of Duxbury asserted, "The Scriptures cannot be rightfully expounded without explaining them in a manner friendly to the cause of freedom."[49]

Thus, "Where the spirit of the Lord is, there is liberty" was a favorite pastoral text—as were "Ye shall know the truth and the truth shall make you free" and "Take away your exactions from my people, saith the Lord God."[50]

The churches of America were generally agreed that "Where political tyranny begins true government ends," as Samuel West of Dartmouth declared, "and the good Christian must needs be certain to oppose such lawless encroachments, however bland or bold."[51]

It was not the Enlightenment rhetoric of firebrands like Thomas Paine or Benjamin Rush that drove men from hearth and home to battlefield.[52] It was the certainty that God had called them to an inescapable accountability. It was the conviction that they were covenantally honor-bound to uphold the standard of impartial justice and broadcast the blessings of liberty afar.[53] It was the firm conviction that politics was not to consume the whole of their lives.[54]

In the end, the reluctant revolutionaries were forced to act by a recognition of the fact that "resistance to tyrants is obedience to God."[55]

Thus was America's great experiment in liberty begun—in resistance to tyranny. And only thus can it possibly endure.

"Is life so dear," asked Patrick Henry, "or peace so sweet, as to be purchased at the price of chains and slavery? Forbid it, Almighty God! I know not what course others may take, but as for me: give me liberty or give me death."[56]

Where the Spirit of the Lord Isn't

The reason that our founders resisted political tyranny is every bit as valid for us today. But do we fully understand their motives? We should. We must.

The opening refrain of the Declaration of Independence affirms the absolute standard upon which that liberty must be established:

We hold these truths to be self-evident, that all men are created equal; that they are endowed by their Creator with certain inalienable rights; that among these are life, liberty, and the pursuit of happiness. That, to secure these rights, governments are instituted among men, deriving their just powers from the consent of the governed.[57]

Their first appeal was to the Creator. Appealing to the "Supreme Judge of the World" for guidance, and relying on His "Divine Providence" for wisdom, the framers committed themselves and their posterity to the absolute standard of "the laws of nature and of nature's God."[58] A just government exists, they argued, solely and completely to "provide guards" for the "future security" of that standard.[59] Take away those guards, and liberty was simply not possible.

That is precisely why they felt compelled to declare their autonomy from the activist government of the crown. It had become increasingly bureaucratic, intrusive, burdensome, and fickle. Thus the possibility of genuine liberty had been thrown into jeopardy.

As our founders declared, the king's government had "erected a multitude of new offices, and sent hither swarms of officers to harass our people, and eat out their substance."[60] It had "called together legislative bodies at places unusual, uncomfortable, and distant . . . for the sole purpose of fatiguing them into compliance with the king's measures."[61] It had "refused assent to laws, the most wholesome and necessary to the public good."[62] It had "imposed taxes without consent . . . taking away our charters, abolishing our most valuable laws, and altering fundamentally the forms of our government."[63] And it had "plundered our seas, ravaged our coasts, destroyed the lives of our people . . . and excited domestic insurrections among us."[64]

The founders believed that no one in America could be secure under the king, because absoluteness had been thrown out of the now ideologically tainted political vocabulary. Because certain rights had been abrogated for at least some citizens by a smothering, dominating political behemoth, all of the liberties of all the citizens were at risk. The checks against petty partiality and blatant bias had been virtually disabled: The private sector had been swallowed up by the public.

Thus, they acted boldly to "form a more perfect union."[65] They launched a sublime experiment in liberty never before surpassed, never again matched. Sadly, not even today. Was our war to free us from government abuse fought in vain? Judging by the size and intrusiveness of government today, it would seem so.

Author P. J. O'Rourke comments:

> There are twenty-seven specific complaints against the British Crown set forth in the Declaration of Independence. To modern ears they still sound reasonable. They still sound reasonable in large part, because so many of them can be leveled against the present federal government of the United States.[66]

According to recent polls, a full 75% of the citizenry say that they "have little or no confidence in their government."[67] "Our national temper is sour," says Simon Schama, "our attention span limited, our fuse short."[68] We have become more than a little cynical and skeptical.

As H. L. Mencken once said:

> The intelligent man, when he pays taxes, certainly does not believe that he is making a prudent and productive investment of his money; on the contrary, he feels that he is being mulcted in an excessive amount for services that, in the main, are useless to him, and that, in substantial part, are downright inimical to him. He sees them as purely predatory and useless.[69]

And again:

> Men generally believe that they get no more from the vast and costly operations of government than they get from the money they lend to their loutish in-laws.[70]

It is little wonder then that political pundits are now warning of an imminent "second American revolution," a "civil war of values," or perhaps a whole bevy of "culture wars."

Culture Wars

How is imminent culture war possible when, instead, by all counts, we should be enjoying the fruits of a kind of cultural "golden age." For it seems that whatever could go right for us in our generation has.

During the past decade and a half, we have enjoyed the longest peacetime economic expansion in history.[71] The growth alone was greater than the size of the entire German economy; the Japanese fell hopelessly behind in the most critical high technology industries—computer micro-processors, silicon chips, fiber optics, digital displays, and software; inflation dropped from 15% to 3%; interest rates fell from a high of 21.5% to 6%; twenty million new jobs were created; exports surpassed both Germany and Japan; and our share of worldwide manufacturing output rose for the first time in forty years.[72]

Internationally, the American vision succeeded beyond our wildest dreams. The Cold War is over. We have emerged as the sole remaining superpower.

> Despite its historic political and economic triumphs, the American Republic is entering its own time of reckoning, an hour of truth that will not be delayed. It is nearing the climax of a generation-long cultural revolution, or crisis of cultural authority.[73]

Indeed, a veritable panoply of cultural conflicts now worry us—none of them directly related to foreign relations' economic performance. The integrity of the family is sorely threatened, for instance. Educational standards seem to have utterly collapsed. Crime and violence are, in many neighborhoods, raging out of control. Scandal and corruption have compromised the foundational institutions of faith, politics, and charity. Racial tensions have once again erupted in our inner cities. Abortion, environmentalism, radical feminism, AIDS, pornography, drug abuse, and homosexual activism have fragmented and polarized our communities. The basic values of our nation are now persistently called into question. Patriotism has very nearly succumbed to cynicism. And in the midst of this long litany of woe, public distrust of government is epidemic—while public distrust of government officials and wanna-be government officials is pandemic.

This, then, is the fruit of that controversial and oft disputed "Culture War."[74]

Publishing mogul Malcolm S. Forbes, Jr., says our culture is gripped by an "aching angst," the "social equivalent of postpartum blues."[75] Historian Simon Schama believes we are afflicted with "a deep and systemic sickness."[76] According to Henry Kissinger, we are in the midst of a "spiritual void."[77] George Will says we are suffering from "a kind of slow-motion barbarization from within."[78] William Bennett argues that we are witnessing the "de-valuing of America."[79] Zbigniew Brzesinski asserts that we are "out of control."[80] Paul Johnson submits that we are ensnared by a "moral and ethical folly" that we feel "helpless to correct."[81] Similarly, Gertrude Himmelfarb argues that a prevailing demoralization has set in because "We have succeeded in de-moralizing social policy—divorcing it from any moral criteria, requirements, or even expectations."[82]

James Michaels summarized these provocative concerns for *Forbes* magazine:

> It isn't the national debt or the unemployment rate or the current recession that bothers the nation's thinkers. It's not an economic mess that they see. It's a moral mess, a cultural mess. While the media natter about a need for economic change, these serious intellectuals worry about our psyches. Can the human race stand prosperity? Is the American experiment in freedom and equal opportunity morally bankrupt?[83]

Political scientist James Q. Wilson says:

> What frustrates many Americans, I think, is that their hardearned prosperity was supposed to produce widespread decency.[84]

But, it didn't.

The Survival of Our Families Hangs in the Balance

We know what is wrong with our society. For the most part we can agree on the sundry woes that plague our families, our communities, and our institutional structures. We all know what has caused our national malaise. We can quote a litany of statistics documenting rising crime rates, declining educational standards, and the awful prevalence of violence, drugs, sex, corruption, alienation, death, and disaster.

Where we differ is not so much on the problems but on the solutions. We are in harmony when it comes to public abuses. It is concerning public uses that we part company. We can all acknowledge the social evils. It is on the social ideals that we trip over one another. It is not wickedness that we dispute, but righteousness. It is not our society's difficulties that divide us, but its aims.

No one can deny the fact that the government is addressing very real and pressing problems when it expands its authority to attempt health-care reform or AIDS education or what-have-you. No one doubts that the Children's Defense Fund, Planned Parenthood, Greenpeace, the National Education Association, the American Civil Liberties Union, ACT UP, the World Health Organization, and Tikkun have focused the attentions of the socio-political juggernaut on issues of grave importance.

But if moral sense is what we have lost, then the question we must ask of these politically powered social engineering organizations is this: Are their highly ideological solutions the right ones?

William Gairdner describes this stark disparity:

> The legions of well-intentioned but smug, educated elites have agreed in advance to reject thousands of years of inherited wisdom, values, habit, custom, and insight and replace this heritage with their official utopian vision of the perfect society. They are the *progressives*, and they can be found in every political party. Trained as scientific, or logical rationalists, these social utopians haughtily treat all social or moral traditions and conventions as arbitrary, rather than as venerable repositories of indispensable social, family, and religious values. They despise natural authority, especially of a local or family variety, and they want to replace it with a sufficiently homogenous state power to bring about their coercive social dreamland. So with a government wage or grant in one hand and a policy whip in the other, they set about forcibly aligning individuals and customs with their dangerously narrow vision, then clamor after ever greater funding and ever more *progressive* legislation for the *education* or *socialization* of the people.[85]

Ultimately, this is the crux of the modern struggle for the soul of our world. And the survival of our families—to say nothing of our nation and our civilization—depends upon its resolution.

A New World System Is at Our Doorstep

Many Christians are inclined to identify the "culture war" with a greater and far more pervasive "spiritual war"—a war that rages not simply in the corridors of power in Washington or in the shopping malls of our own hometown, but in the heavenlies. All that we see seems to reinforce what pop theologians have been telling us for nigh onto two decades: "Satan is alive and well on planet earth." We recognize that if the siege on our families is to be somehow repulsed, then we will have to engage in that greater conflagration.

But for all our blithe and incidental talk these days of "spiritual warfare," "territorial spirits," "warring factions," and "heavenly contention," most of us have little or no notion of our adversary's real intent. Despite consuming vast quantities of books, tapes, conferences, videos, and sundry spiritual warfare bric-a-brac, we have little or no conception of his ultimate aim and ambition.

So what in the world is Satan doing after all? What is his overall strategy? What does he hope to accomplish?

Many of us might be tempted to answer that his demonic plan has been, is now, and always will be to wreak havoc on goodness, truth, and purity wherever they might be found, and to possess individuals with destructive passions. We think of the devil as an insidious destroyer.

If we become fix-focused on the satanic tendency to tear down godly conventions and mores we will overlook the opposite tendency, and that is to build up his own malevolent ones. He has always nurtured Babel-like aspirations to build a "New World Order" and usher in a "New Age." He is always striving to "make a name" for himself and fill the world with his "glory." In other words, it isn't that he wants to be a fiend but rather to be "like the Most High" (Isaiah 14:14).

Otto Blumhardt, the pioneer Lutheran missionary to Africa in the seventeenth century, wrote:

> The devil's conceit is merely that he might supplant God's providential rule with his own. He is driven by jealousy, not envy. Hence, his grand urge to misworship is but the engendering of fine traditions, magnificent achievements, and beneficent inclinations, yet all apart from the gracious endowments of God's order. Satan is a despot not unlike those that human experience attests: entranced by the false beauties, the false majesties, and the false virtues of independence from the Almighty.[86]

From the time of the temptation in the Garden to the present, the great satanic conspiracy has always been first and foremost to offer some sane, attractive, and wholesome-seeming counterfeit to the Kingdom of God. Satan is not dead set on getting us all to drink blood from roiling cauldrons in debauched occultic rites. This would never work, not on Christians at any rate.

But another, subtler strategy might. One satanic strategy that could work, even on Christians, would be to render us ineffective by distracting us from the high call of the Gospel with some interesting and enticing alternative. Satan modestly aspires to convert men to the "Nice News" as opposed to the "Good News."

As Oswald Chambers has said:

> Satan's great aim is to deflect us from the center. He will allow us to be devoted to the death to any cause, any enterprise, to any- thing but the Lord Jesus.[87]

Scripture is clear that Satan hopes to realize his ambition not merely by plunging individuals into bottomless pools of concupis- cence but by gaining sway over the deepest affections and highest aspirations of this poor fallen world. He thus masquerades as an "angel of light" and even his demonic minions appear as "messen- gers of righteousness" (2 Corinthians 11:13–15).

Again, as Chambers has asserted:

> This is his most cunning travesty . . . to counterfeit the Holy Spirit . . . to make men upright and individual—but seemingly self-governed and with no apparent need of God.[88]

In the process of implementing this credible and proficient alter- native world system, much death and destruction are the result. Defilement and debauchery are inevitable when his wretched game is afoot. But these evils are not Satan's final objective. They are simply the second- and third-order consequences of his cultural coup. They are only the lamentable hazards of warfare with much higher—or lower—aim.

Be assured, though: Satan's revolt innately and intrinsically de- volves into devastating *warfare*.

Throughout the Scriptures the immediate reality and proximity of this fierce spiritual conflict is emphasized. But this is what we must notice: This ever-escalating conflagration of spiritual forces is not merely some invisible war waged solely in the heavenlies. On the contrary, it involves cultures, civilizations, institutions, pow- ers, and principalities. Though we are assured that our principal enemies are not "flesh and blood" (Ephesians 6:12), we are equally reminded that flesh and blood are by no means exempt from the hostilities (Hebrews 11:32–40). Instead, we are told that this fierce warfare—in which we are all commissioned to engage—involves men and nations, not simply hobgoblins and ghouls (Genesis 1:28; Matthew 28:19–20). Indeed, the deleterious effects of Satan's rebellion have gone so far as to directly weaken nations, shake kingdoms, destroy cities, and imprison masses (Isaiah 14:12–17).

Clearly, Satan's strategy has been to undermine both culture *and* spiritual conversion, both sociology and salvation, both reform and redemption. He desires the fealty of whole civilizations not simply of cadres, of cliques, and of covens—however influential they might actually be.

Who Will Rule the Nations?

If he can attain to the rule of nations, Satan's strategy for the rule of citizens is just as surely accomplished. The moral decline of a people thus precedes the moral decline of a person in the overarching plot. This is difficult for us to grasp, so inclined are we to a detached philosophy of individualism. Yet covenantal realities dominate the coursing history of civilizations—and our solitary parts in that coursing are often, therefore, subsumed within the irresistible force of the whole.

So, what in the world is Satan doing after all? What is his overall strategy? What does he hope to accomplish?

Simply put, his grand design seems to include possessing the hearts and souls of individual men, in part, by remaking their nations in his own image. Disingeniously, he seems to believe that if he can somehow win the much-disputed culture wars he can end-run God's providence and at last enthrone himself.

Not surprisingly then, the assaults on the Christian foundations of Western/democratic culture are very real, very powerful, and very calamitous. That is why we are admonished again and again to "put on the full armor of God (Ephesians 6:10–18) and be ready to "suffer hardship as good soldiers of Christ Jesus" because it is inevitable that we will have to "wage war" to "demolish strongholds" and to "tear down fortresses" in this present woe-begotten world (2 Corinthians 10:4–5).

God has called on us to engage in spiritual warfare. But rather than merely hurling our fevered maledictions at "mysterious unseen forces in the spirit realm" we have been afforded the opportunity to engage the enemy—that is, his strategies—on the somewhat more familiar turf of hearth and home, of culture and community, of city and civilization. We can confront his socio-political battlements as we roll up our sleeves and get our hands dirty solving the problems of our day in the context of our ordinary lives, work, and ministries—thus stealing away the moral high ground that many social engineers of today have sought for themselves. Thus, we can foil his incendiary offensives as we build up a righteous heritage for our families rooted in the sovereign work of Christ.

We are prone to think of spiritual warfare in terribly exotic terms. In reality though, it is fought and won at the much more strategic level of ordinary life. It is fought and won as the people of God do their jobs where they are. It is fought and won as we righteously contend for our families in submission to God's sovereignty and providence.

As you read about the organizations profiled in this book—groups whose ideologies and methods are aimed at tearing down the foundational truths of Scripture and bringing us all into bondage to a new order governed by social engineers—remember this: We can fight the good fight as we become what God has called us to become and as we do what God has called us to do. We can stand for the Truth, and in doing so we can unravel Satan's conspiracy by carrying the banner of Christ's consummate victory into our everyday tasks. Beginning right here. Beginning right now.

T W O

ABORTION INC.

PLANNED PARENTHOOD

In the end, all will be revealed and truth will prevail.[1]
—Richard Tavener

Murder cannot be hid long—a man's son may,
but in the end truth will out.[2]
—William Shakespeare

The dance was scheduled for a Friday night. The school gym had been decorated with crepe paper, streamers, and hand-painted banners. The bleachers had been stacked and rolled out of the way to make room for the sound stage with its ancient Marshall speakers and sixteen-track mixer. By all appearances this dance would be no different than any of the others held here over the past thirty-five years.

But appearances can be deceiving. This dance would be very different.

Sponsored by the local Planned Parenthood affiliate, the dance was promoted as "a fun and exciting musical extravaganza guaranteed to keep you dancing while learning about sexuality and safer sex."[3] According to fliers handed out at the school, the "Safety Dance" was intended to be both "educational and entertaining." Featuring "games, crazy condoms, and hot music with sexual messages," plans for the fun-filled evening included "a danceable history of sex and rock 'n' roll, and up to four hours of sexually explicit dance music interspersed with a sex educator's response to *Dirty Dancing.*"[4]

According to a promotional packet given to teachers in the school, the evening event represented a "whole new approach to contraceptive education" based upon "positive images."[5] As an example of this "positive" approach the packet cited the "Puttin' on the Condom" game—one of the most innovative activities scheduled for the dance:

> During the course of the evening each person receives and wears a name tag depicting a different step in condom use. During this activity, participants arrange themselves in a line (or a circle) according to how they think a condom is used (if there are a large number of participants, have several groups perform the activity at the same time, and compare results!) After the line is formed, have the participants read off their tags in order. Acting out the steps can increase the fun of this activity.[6]

According to the packet, the name tags are labeled as follows:
- Physical attraction
- Think about having sex
- Talk about having sex
- Decide to use a condom
- Pool money . . . or more foreplay
- Go to a condom store
- Decide what kind to buy
- Take box off rack
- Pay cashier
- Decide where to store them
- Decide to have sex
- Need to use a condom

Twenty more "steps" spell out in graphic detail the game that was planned as part of the high school dance.[7]

Another sample activity was described as the "Risk Rap." According to the brief instructions,

> Participants tape placards containing a "sexual activity" on a wall ranking them from least risky to most risky for HIV infection.[8]

The placards read as follows:
- Massage
- Slow Dancing
- Fantasy
- Dressing/undressing one another

- Dry Kissing
- Skinny-dipping/moonlight swimming
- French Kissing
- Erotic films and magazines
- Sex toys

And so on, for twenty-seven additional, explicitly sexual activities—from backrubs to masturbation.[9]

The packet listed several more of the "many educational" activities scheduled for the dance including the "Condom Relay Race." It was described as a "fun, competitive activity enabling participants to become comfortable handling condoms." According to the instructions,

> This activity requires one condom (unlubricated, or lubricated with plenty of tissues handy) per participant, and several bananas (firm, not ripe). Divide the group into a comfortable number of teams (8–10 players works best) and have teams form parallel lines. Each player receives one unopened package containing a condom. The first player in each line also receives a banana. When commanded to start, the first player gives the second person in line the banana to hold, opens the package, and rolls the condom onto the banana. The first player then rolls the condom off. The second player then gives the third person in line the banana, and the process continues until the last in line runs to the front of the line and puts the condom on the banana held by the first person in line, who may then eat the banana.[10]

With the enthusiastic support of the school administration, the dance was held as planned. The gym was packed that night.[11]

Needless to say, parents and community leaders were outraged when they discovered what Planned Parenthood and the school had exposed their children to that night. But by the time they found out about it, the dance had already taken place.

The damage was done. Apparently, three girls got pregnant that night.[12] And as if to add insult to injury, all three had abortions at the very Planned Parenthood center that sponsored the dance.[13]

Death and Taxes

Planned Parenthood is the world's oldest, largest, and best-organized provider of abortion and birth control services.[14] From its humble beginnings around the turn of the century, when the entire shoestring operation consisted of a two-room makeshift clinic in a run-down Brooklyn neighborhood staffed by three untrained volunteers,[15] it has expanded dramatically into a multi-billion-dollar international conglomerate with programs and activities in 134 nations on every continent.[16] In the United States alone, it employs more than 20,000 staff personnel and volunteers in 922 clinics and 167 affiliates in every major metropolitan area, coast to coast.[17] Boasting a national office in New York, a legislative center in Washington, regional offices in Atlanta, Chicago, Miami, and San Francisco, and international offices in London, Nairobi, Bangkok, and New Delhi, the Federation showed $23.5 million in earnings during fiscal year 1992 with $192.9 million in cash reserves and another $108.2 million in capital assets.[18] With an estimated combined annual budget—including all regional and international service affiliates—of more than a trillion dollars, Planned Parenthood may well be the largest and most profitable nonprofit organization in history.[19]

Utilizing this considerable wealth, manpower, and influence, Planned Parenthood has muscled its way into virtually every facet of modern life.[20] It now plays a strategic role in the health and social services community—and plans to figure prominently in any health-care reform plan.[21] It exerts a major influence on education—providing the majority of sex education curricula and programs in both public and private schools.[22] It carries considerable political clout through lobbying, legislation, campaigning, advocacy, and litigation—coordinating the substantial efforts of the multi-billion dollar abortion industry.[23] It is involved in publishing, broadcast media production, judicial activism, public relations, foreign aid, psychological research counseling, sociological planning, demographic investigation, pharmacological development, contraceptive distribution and sales, mass advertising, and public legal service provision.[24]

Despite this nearly omnipresent intrusion into family, church, government, and culture, Planned Parenthood generally enjoys popular acclaim for its provision of "effective and professional social services for the needy."[25] It has garnered a "sterling reputation" for its development of "honest and insightful reality-based educational programs" for the young.[26] It has chalked up high approval ratings for its advocacy of "low-cost, universally available counseling and health-care services for women."[27]

Nevertheless, the organization has not escaped scrutiny altogether. Despite its considerable political heft, its seemingly bottomless public relations war chest, its enormous prestige, and its "benign, American-as-apple-pie name,"[28] the organization has managed recently to generate a good deal of very troublesome controversy for itself:

- Parents, outraged at the promiscuous content of the organization's sex education materials, AIDS awareness programs, and community advocacy projects have begun to organize grassroots efforts to bar Planned Parenthood from schools, charitable networks, and civic coalitions.[29]
- Innumerable threats of consumer boycotts have begun to jeopardize its lucrative corporate philanthropy program.[30]
- Dissemination of carefully researched and academically sound information about the organization's militantly partisan programs has further imperiled its funding base in both the private and the public sector.[31]
- Disclosure of the organization's burgeoning profits from contraceptive sales—over $64 million in 1991 alone—has brought new scrutiny to the legality of its state and federal tax-exemption.[32]
- Similarly, the announcement that the organization is exploring ways to "market its own high-quality, name-brand condoms, chemical contraceptives, and other sexual devices" has called into question its charitable status.[33]
- Several punitive lawsuits initiated by Planned Parenthood—filed in an effort to close pro-life adoption agencies and abortion-alternative Crisis Pregnancy Centers—have begun to reinforce a perception that the organization is more concerned with the ideological enforcement of its agenda than it is with the health and welfare of its clients.[34]
- Conflict of interest accusations have begun to circulate in Washington concerning the cozy relationships of certain Clinton administration officials and advisors—including Donna Shalala, Frederico Peña, Richard Edelman, Johnetta Cole, Vernon Jordan, and Joycelyn Elders—with the organization.[35]
- Likewise, questions have arisen concerning the role that the current Planned Parenthood president, Pamela Maraldo, played

in policy development during the time she served in the Clinton campaign.[36]

Perhaps even more damaging to Planned Parenthood have been recent concerns about the quality of the "health care" provided at the organization's affiliated clinics:

- A spate of medical malpractice lawsuits from botched abortions has intensified the organization's already looming insurability crisis.[37]

- The stigmatization of grisly child-killing abortion procedures has dramatically reduced the number of physicians willing to perform them. As a result, Planned Parenthood clinics have been forced to rely on less adequately trained personnel—nurse practitioners and doctors who have failed in private or institutional practices.[38]

- Revelations about deliberately suppressed research data on abortion risks—particularly concerning the established links between abortion and breast cancer—have raised new questions about the organization's medical objectivity and professional integrity.[39]

- Similarly, the bridling of information about alternatives to the organization's clinical, educational, and surgical services has provoked the wrath of a variety of health-care consumer advocates.[40]

According to syndicated columnist Cal Thomas, "Planned Parenthood has enjoyed one of the longest free rides in political history."[41] But now, he says, "their ticket is about to be punched" and "their agenda is about to be exposed as anything but the benign, responsible movement it has portrayed itself to be."[42]

As David Kupelian and Jo Ann Gasper reported in their widely distributed, often-reprinted exposé for *New Dimensions* magazine:

> Thanks to a stunningly effective long-term public relations campaign, Planned Parenthood has succeeded in making a killing off of medicine's *evil twin*, abortion. But the pro-choice movement is starting to lose its luster, as an increasing number of women choosing abortion claim to have been exploited, abused, and destroyed by the nation's number one abortion provider.[43]

Death Culture

Paradoxically, all the controversy surrounding the organization has yet to slow its omnivorous growth or stymie its colossal successes. On the contrary, according to a recent annual report, "While some might think that controversy necessarily results in decreased support, Planned Parenthood has found the opposite to be true."[44] The ruler of most men's minds are not facts or statistics but general impressions, and like other rulers, general impressions are only with the greatest difficulty deposed.

Closely allying itself with the new administration in Washington, Planned Parenthood has only reinforced its teflon resiliency. With an all-too-typical "I'll-scratch-your-back-if-you'll-scratch-mine" political aplomb, several cabinet-level officials have openly endorsed Planned Parenthood's agenda at various conferences and fund-raisers for the organization. AIDS Czar Kristine Gebbie, for instance, told a chipper crowd of Planned Parenthood supporters that she wants the U.S. to follow the organization's lead in "taking a more positive attitude toward sex" and stop being "a repressed Victorian society."[45]

Not surprisingly, Planned Parenthood has wisely cashed in on this newly invigorated influence, winning a string of strategic victories for its cause:

- The organization persuaded the administration to reestablish federally funded family planning clinics as abortion referral agencies.[46]
- It secured reinstatement of funding for abortion providers overseas through the Agency for International Development and other foreign aid bureaucracies.[47]
- It convinced the administration to convert all overseas military hospitals into abortion facilities.[48]
- It won the right to undertake fetal research on aborted babies.[49]
- It was able to get the Food and Drug Administration's importation and testing ban on the French abortifacient drug, RU 486, lifted.[50]
- It secured new tax funding from the American taxpayer for the United Nations Fund for Population Activity's brutal forced-abortion, infanticide, and sterilization programs in China and India.[51]
- It convinced the administration to reestablish tax funding of abortions in the District of Columbia.[52]

But Planned Parenthood's biggest coup came with the announcement of the President's health-care reform plan. According to Pamela Maraldo, the proposed overhaul of the medical industry would give the organization "the chance to broaden its progressive" agenda.[53] "The winds of change are blowing in our favor," she said.[54] "Thus, we must seize the offensive on several fronts and address new challenges."[55] She went on to assert, "We must position Planned Parenthood squarely at the center of the health-care debate."[56]

By all accounts, the organization has done just that:

- Maraldo was tapped to participate in the secretive meetings conducted by Hillary Clinton to hammer out the details of the plan.[57]
- Other key staffers from the organization were appointed to four of the five different "health-care coalitions" and to each of the three committees charged with drafting the actual legislative package.[58]
- The organization secured official designation as an "essential service provider," thus requiring "Health Maintenance Organizations" to contract with Planned Parenthood for certain "specified services" in order to qualify for the newly created "Health Alliances."[59]
- It also obtained a commitment from the administration to link health reform with education reform—thus insuring that Planned Parenthood's near monopoly in the school-based clinic business would be protected.[60]

According to Janice Kavda, a health management consultant for the state of New York, the implications of this symbiotic relationship between Planned Parenthood and the federal government are vast:

> Planned Parenthood has gambled everything on the Clinton health-care plan. If the plan is actually implemented, the organization could easily become the system's most significant private sector general services provider. It would then be free to implement its philosophical agenda in a myriad of ways through a staggering muster of tax-subsidized programs. This transcends the abortion debate—its implications reach much farther than that. The very nature of our culture is facing sweeping change as big business and big government join in an ideological partnership to reinvent society.[61]

That is not a particularly comforting thought—especially in light of the kind of sweeping changes that ideological partnership intends.

Death and Desire

Most moderns hold to a disjunctive view of the relationship between life and work—thus enabling them to separate a person's private character from their public accomplishments. But this novel divorce of root from fruit, however genteel, is a ribald denial of one of the most basic truths in life: What you are begets what you do; wrong-headed philosophies stem from wrong-headed philosophers; sin doesn't just happen—it is sinners that sin. Thus, according to the English historian and journalist Hilaire Belloc, "Biography always affords the greatest insights into sociology. To comprehend the history of a thing is to unlock the mysteries of its present, and more, to discover the profundities of its future."[62] Similarly, Samuel Johnson quipped, "Almost all the miseries of life, almost all the wickedness that infects, and all the distresses that afflict mankind, are the consequences of some defect in private duties."[63]

Or, as E. Michael Jones has asserted, "Biography is destiny."[64]

This is particularly true in the case of the founder of Planned Parenthood, Margaret Sanger. Even the leadership of the organization admits that it is impossible to entirely understand its policies, programs, and priorities apart from her life and work.[65]

Sanger was born on September 14, 1879, in the small industrial community of Corning in upstate New York, the sixth of eleven children. Her father, Michael Higgins, was an Irish Catholic immigrant who fancied himself a freethinker and a skeptic. After raping, killing, and pillaging his way through the South during Sherman's infamous march to the sea at the end of the War Between the States, he worked sporadically as a stone mason and a tombstone carver. Sanger's mother, Anne Higgins, was a second-generation American from a strict Catholic family. She was frail and had tuberculous, but utterly devoted to her improvident husband and her ever-growing brood of children.

The family suffered cold, privation, and hunger. They also suffered scorn, shame, and isolation because of Michael's radical Socialist ideas and activities. Sanger would later describe her family's life together as "joyless and filled with drudgery and fear."[66]

Not surprisingly, she moved away from her unhappy home as soon as she could. Almost immediately she plunged into a life of restless rebellion. She dabbled in the fashionable progressivism of the day: radical politics, suffragette feminism, and promiscuous sex. She went to college for less than a year before dropping out. She then took a job as a kindergarten teacher for a very brief time. Next she tried nursing—but she never finished the short introductory training course.

During this time of listless uncertainty she met William Sanger, a promising young architect who had made quite a name for himself while working on the designs for New York's Grand Central Station. Within just a few months, they were married.

They settled into a pleasant apartment in Manhattan's upper east side and set up housekeeping. But housekeeping appealed to Sanger even less than teaching or nursing. She quickly grew restless again. Her doting husband cast about, trying to find a way to satisfy her passions—buying her expensive presents, indulging in long vacations, and even building an extravagant home in the suburbs—but nothing seemed to suit his temperamental bride.

In short order they had three children, two boys and a girl—Sanger thinking that they would be the keys to her fulfillment. But alas, they too proved to be but temporary diversions. After nearly a decade of undefined domestic dissatisfaction, Sanger convinced William to sell all they had, including their suburban estate, and move back into the Manhattan hubbub.

She renewed her interest in politics and quickly threw herself into the fast-paced maelstrom of progressivism. She attended rallies, meetings, and caucuses, and became acquainted with the foremost radicals of the day: John Reed, Eugene Debs, Clarence Darrow, Will Durant, Upton Sinclair, Julius Hammer, and Bill Haywood. She joined the Socialist Party. She volunteered as a women's organizer for Local Number Five—speaking at labor organization meetings and writing for the Party newspaper, *The Call*. She even helped agitate several strikes and labor protests.

While William was happy that she had finally found a cause that satisfied her restless spirit, he gradually became concerned that she was taking on too much too soon. Their apartment was in a perpetual state of disarray. Their children were constantly being farmed out to friends and neighbors. And their time alone together was non-existent.

But things only went from bad to worse. Sanger soon began attending Mabel Dodge's meetings for radicals in Greenwich Village. Dodge was a wealthy young divorcee, recently returned from France, where she had spent most of her married years. She had a stunning apartment where she started a salon modeled after those in the Palais Royale and Paris's Left Bank. Her series of evenings were opportunities for intellectuals, artists, actors, writers, and activists to gather, mingle, debate, aspire, and conspire.

Sanger's topic of discussion was always sex—she had come to believe that their shared progressive ideals might not be able to win "a martial war of arms," but they certainly could win "a culture war of values."[67] When it was her turn to lead an evening, she held Dodge's guests spellbound, ravaging them with intoxicating notions of "romantic dignity, unfettered self-expression, and the sacredness of sexual desire."[68]

Free love had been practiced quietly for years by the avant-garde intellectuals in the Village.[69] Eugene O'Neill took on one mistress after another, immortalizing them in his plays.[70] Edna St. Vincent Millay "hopped gaily from bed to bed and wrote about it in her poems."[71] Max Eastman, Emma Goldman, Floyd Dell, Rockwell Kent, Edgar Lee Masters, and many others had for some time enjoyed unrestrained sexploits.[72] But no one had championed sexual freedom as openly and ardently as Margaret. When she spoke, the others became transfixed.

Dodge was especially struck by her sensuous didactae. Later she would write in her memoirs:

> Margaret Sanger was a Madonna type of woman, with soft brown hair parted over a quiet brow, and crystal-clear brown eyes. It was she who introduced us all to the idea of birth control, and it, along with other related ideas about sex, became her passion. It was as if she had been more or less arbitrarily chosen by the powers that be to voice a new gospel of not only sex-knowledge in regard to conception, but sex-knowledge about copulation and its intrinsic importance. She was the first person I ever knew who was openly an ardent propagandist for the joys of the flesh. This, in those days, was radical indeed when the sense of sin was still so indubitably mixed with the sense of pleasure. Margaret personally

set out to rehabilitate sex. She was one of its first conscious promulgators.[73]

Everyone seemed to be delighted by Sanger's explicit and brazen talks. Everyone except her husband, that is. William began to see her progressive ideals as "excuses for a Saturnalia of sex." He made one final valiant effort to save the marriage, moving the family to Paris. But it was too late. The marriage was over.

Upon her return to New York, Sanger decided to try her hand at writing and publishing a progressive paper. She called it *The Woman Rebel*. It was an eight-sheet pulp with the slogan "No Gods! No Masters!" emblazoned across the masthead.[74] She advertised it as "a paper of militant thought," and militant it was indeed.[75] The first issue denounced marriage as a "degenerate institution," capitalism as "indecent exploitation," and sexual modesty as "obscene prudery."[76] In the next issue, an article entitled "A Woman's Duty" proclaimed that "rebel women" were to "look the whole world in the face with a go-to-hell look in the eyes."[77] Another article asserted that "rebel women claim the following rights: the right to be lazy, the right to be an unmarried mother, the right to destroy . . . and the right to love."[78] In later issues, she published articles on contraception, several more on sexual liberation, three on the necessity for social revolution, and two defending political assassinations.[79]

Sanger was promptly served with a subpoena indicting her on three counts for the publication of lewd and indecent articles in violation of federal law. If convicted—and conviction was almost certain—she could be sentenced to as much as five years. Frightened, she fled the country under an assumed name. She had her radical friends forge a passport, provide her with connections in England, and take charge of her children.

As a final gesture, just before she slipped away, she had them print and distribute one hundred thousand copies of a contraband leaflet she had written on contraception called *Family Limitation*. It was lurid and lascivious, designed to enrage the postal authorities and titillate the masses. But worse, it was dangerously inaccurate, recommending such things as Lysol douches, bichloride of mercury elixirs, heavy doses of laxatives, and herbal abortifacients.[80] Margaret Sanger's illustrious career as the "champion of birth control" was now well underway.

She spent more than a year in England as a fugitive from justice. But she made certain that the time was not wasted. As soon as she came ashore, she began to make contact with all the various radical groups of Britain. She was especially interested in developing ties with the eugenicists—the practitioners of an odd pseudoscience who sincerely believed that if human civilization were to survive, the physically unfit, the materially poor, the spiritually diseased, the racially inferior, and the mentally incompetent had to be eliminated. While some eugenicists were forthright in recommending such things as "unameliorated plague, pestilence, and putrification," most felt that the subtler approaches of "education, contraception, sterilization, and abortion" were more "practical ways" to accomplish their ultimate aim of "creating the master race."[81]

Most of the eugenicists were armchair revolutionaries—hardly the sort who normally strike fear in the hearts of men. As historian Paul Johnson has shown, the eugenicists "were not men of action."[82] Instead, "they tried to solve the problems of the world in the quiet of their studies, inside their own heads. They produced a new vocabulary of mumbo-jumbo. It was all hard-headed, scientific, and relentless."[83] Even so, their doctrines were immensely appealing to the intellectual elite—and frighteningly deleterious. According to Johnson,

> All the ablest elements in Western society, the trendsetters in opinion, were wholly taken in by this monstrous doctrine of unreason. Those who objected were successfully denounced as obscurantists, and the enemies of social progress. They could no longer be burned as heretical subverters of the new orthodoxy, but they were successfully and progressively excluded from the control of events.[84]

This, despite the fact that the eugenic scientific scheme had been proven by historical verities and the dumb certainties of experience to be utterly obsolete, if not entirely false.[85] G. K. Chesterton asserted that it was little more than the "combining a hardening of the heart with a simultaneous softening of the head."[86] Whereas Darwinism was the doctrine of "the survival of the fittest," eugenicism, he said, was "the doctrine of the survival of the nastiest."[87]

Sanger immediately got on the eugenic bandwagon. She was not philosophically inclined, nor was she particularly adept at political, social, or economic theory, but she did recognize in the eugenicists a kindred spirit. "It is only through applied eugenics," she wrote "that the vast volume of disease and degeneracy which flows through the channels of heredity can be prevented."[88]

At the same time she was securing her philosophical moorings, she was surrendering her moral grapnels. Her bed became a veritable meeting place for the Fabian upper crust: H. G. Wells, George Bernard Shaw, Arnold Bennett, Arbuthnot Lane, and Norman Haire. And, it was then that she began her unusual and tempestuous affair with Havelock Ellis.

Ellis was the iconoclastic grandfather of the Bohemian sexual revolution. The author of nearly fifty books on every aspect of concupiscence from sexual inversion to auto-eroticism, he had provided the free love movement with much of its intellectual apologia. Much to his chagrin, however, he himself was sexually impotent, so he spent his life in pursuit of new and ever more exotic sensual pleasures. He staged elaborate orgies for his eugenicist friends; he enticed his wife into innumerable lesbian affairs while he quietly observed; he experimented with mescaline and various other psychotropic and psychedelic drugs; and he established a network for both homosexual and heterosexual encounters.

To Sanger, Ellis was a modern-day saint. She adored him at once, both for his radical ideas and for his unusual bedroom behavior. The two of them began to plot a strategy for her cause—and for her eventual return to New York. Ellis emphasized the necessity of political expediency. Sanger would have to tone down her proabortion stance. She would, he said, have to distance herself from revolutionary rhetoric. The scientific and philanthropic-sounding themes of eugenics would have to replace the politically charged themes of old-line anarchism and socialism.

Sanger's first task after crossing the Atlantic was, of course, to face the legal charges against her. She connived a brilliant public relations campaign that so rallied public support for her cause that the authorities were eventually forced to drop all charges. Then, in order to capitalize on all the publicity that her victory had generated, she embarked on a three-and-a-half-month, coast-to-coast speaking tour. She was a stunning success, drawing large, enthusiastic crowds. Next, she decided to open a birth control clinic. Following her eugenic first principles, she opened her clinic in the

Brownsville section of New York, an area populated by newly immigrated Slavs, Latins, Italians, and Jews—which according to Sanger were all "dysgenic and diseased races" that needed to have their "reckless breeding" curbed.[89]

But while the world was ready to tolerate her words, it was not quite ready to tolerate her deeds. Within two weeks, the clinic had been shut down by the authorities. Sanger and her sister, Ethel, were arrested and sentenced to thirty days each in the workhouse for the distribution of obscene materials and the prescription of dangerous medical procedures.

Upon her release, Sanger founded a new organization, the Birth Control League, and began to publish a new magazine, *The Birth Control Review*. She was still intent on opening a clinic, but her time in jail had convinced her that she needed to cultivate a broader following before she made another attempt at that. The new organization and magazine would help her do just that.

Although she was now drawing severe public criticism from such men as the fiery revivalist Billy Sunday, the famed social reformer John Ryan, and the gallant former President Theodore Roosevelt, Sanger was gaining stature among the urbane and urban intelligentsia. Money began to pour into her office as subscriptions and donations soared. And the fact that articles from influential authors such as H. G. Wells, Pearl Buck, Julian Huxley, Karl Menninger, Havelock Ellis, and Harry Emerson Fosdick appeared on the pages of the *Review* only boosted Sanger's respectability that much more.

By 1922 her fame was secure. She had won several key legal battles, had coordinated an international conference on birth control, and had gone on a very successful round-the-world lecture tour. Her name had become a household word, and one of her numerous books had become an instant best seller in spite of—or perhaps because of—the tremendous controversy it had caused.

Entitled *The Pivot of Civilization*, it was one of the first popularly written books to openly expound and extol eugenic aims. Throughout its 284 pages, Sanger unashamedly called for the elimination of "human weeds,"[90] for the "cessation of charity,"[91] for the segregation of "morons, misfits, and the maladjusted"[92] and for the coercive sterilization of "genetically inferior races."[93] Published today, such a book would be denigrated as the basest sort of intolerant racism. But writing when she did, Margaret only gained more acclaim.

She was at the height of her celebrity when she married a second time. J. Noah Slee was the president of the Three-in-One Oil Company and a legitimate millionaire. Though their marriage was unconventional, to say the least, he devoted the rest of his life—and his fortune—to Sanger and her cause.

Almost immediately, Sanger set herself to the task of using her new wealth to further her revolution of progressive ideals. She opened another clinic—this time calling it a "Research Bureau" in a ploy to dodge legal tangles. Then she began to smuggle diaphragms into the country from Holland. She waged several successful "turf" battles to maintain control over her "empire." She campaigned diligently to win over the medical community. She secured massive foundation grants from the Rockefellers, the Fords, and the Mellons. She took her struggle to Washington, testifying before several congressional committees, advocating the liberalization of contraceptive prescription laws. And she fought for the incorporation of reproductive control into state programs as a form of social planning.

Sanger also used her new wealth to fight an important public relations campaign to redeem her reputation. Because of her eugenic connections, she had become closely associated with the scientists and theorists who put together Nazi Germany's "race purification" program. She had openly endorsed the euthanasia, sterilization, abortion, and infanticide programs of the early Reich. She published a number of articles in *The Birth Control Review* that mirrored Hitler's White Supremacist rhetoric. She even commissioned Dr. Ernst Rudin, the director of the Nazi Medical Experimentation program, to write for *The Review* himself.

Naturally, as the end of the Second World War neared and the grisly details of the Nazi programs began to come to light, Sanger was forced to backpedal her position and cover up her complicity. Charges of anti-Semitism had been aimed at her since her trial in 1917, but now that Auschwitz and Dachau had become very much a part of the public conscience, she realized she would have to do something, and quickly.

Her first step toward redeeming her public image was to change the name of her organization. "Planned Parenthood" was a name that had been proposed from within the birth control movement since at least 1938. One of the arguments for the new name was that it connoted a positive program and conveyed a clean, wholesome, family-oriented image. It diverted attention from the international and revolutionary intentions of the movement, focusing instead on the personal and individual dimensions of birth control.

Next, she embarked on an aggressive affiliation program that brought hundreds of local and regional birth control leagues under the umbrella of her national organization, and then dozens of national organizations from around the globe were brought under the aegesis of her international federation. This enabled Sanger to draw on the integrity and respectability of grass-roots organizations, solidifying and securing her place at the top.

Finally, she initiated a massive propaganda blitz aimed at the war-weary, ready-for-prosperity middle class. Always careful to hide her illicit affairs and her radical political leanings, her campaign emphasized "patriotism" and "family values."[94]

By the time she died on September 6, 1966, a week shy of her eighty-seventh birthday, Margaret Sanger had nearly fulfilled her early pledge to spend every last penny of Slee's fortune. More importantly though, she had nearly fulfilled her even earlier pledge to wage a "culture war" on the values and institutions of American life and family.

Bad Choices

Margaret Sanger's character and vision are still faithfully mirrored in the organization that she wrought. She intended it that way. And the leaders that have come after her have in no wise attempted to change that.

Dr. Alan Guttmacher, the man who immediately succeeded her as president of Planned Parenthood, once said, "We are merely walking down the path that Mrs. Sanger carved out for us." Faye Wattleton, president of the organization during the decade of the '80s, claimed that she was "proud" to be "walking in the footsteps" of Margaret Sanger. And the current president, Pamela Maraldo, asserts, "Today, Planned Parenthood proudly carries on the courageous tradition of Margaret Sanger."[95]

Thus, virtually everything that she believed, everything that she aspired to, everything that she practiced, and everything that she aimed for is somehow still reflected in the organization and programs of Planned Parenthood.

In 1922, for example, Sanger chided social workers, philanthropists, and churchmen for perpetuating what she called "the cruelty of charity."[96] She argued that organized attempts to help the poor were the "surest sign that our civilization has bred, is breeding, and is perpetuating constantly increasing numbers of defectives, delinquents, and dependents."[97] She went on to write that the most "insidiously injurious philanthropy" was the maternity care given to poor women.[98] She concluded her diatribe by describing all those who refused to see the necessity of severely regulating the fertility of the working class as "benign imbeciles who encourage the defective and diseased elements of humanity in their reckless and irresponsible swarming and spawning."[99]

Her alternative to charity was "to eliminate the stocks" that she felt were most detrimental "to the future of the race and the world."[100] To that end, Planned Parenthood has always targeted minorities, the unwanted, and the disadvantaged for family limitation, contraception, abortion, and sterilization. "More children from the fit, less from the unfit," Sanger opined, "that is the chief issue of birth control."[101]

In 1939, Sanger designed what she called the "Negro Project" in response to requests by "Southern state public health officials"—men not generally known for their racial equanimity.[102] "The mass of Negroes," her project proposal asserted, "particularly in the South, still breed carelessly and disastrously, with the result that the increase among Negroes, even more than among Whites, is from that portion of the population least intelligent and fit."[103]

The proposal went on to say that "Public Health statistics merely hint at the primitive state of civilization in which most Negroes in the South live."[104] In order to remedy this "dysgenic horror story," the project aimed to hire three or four "Colored Ministers, preferably with social-service backgrounds, and with engaging personalities" to travel to various Black enclaves and propagandize for birth control.[105]

Sanger wrote:

> The most successful educational approach to the Negro is

through a religious appeal. We do not want word to go out that we want to exterminate the Negro population, and the minister is the man who can straighten out that idea if it ever occurs to any of their more rebellious members.[106]

Of course, those Black ministers were to be carefully controlled—mere figureheads. "There is a great danger that we will fail," one of the project directors wrote, "because the Negroes think it a plan for extermination. Hence, let's appear to let the colored run it."[107] Another project director lamented, "I wonder if Southern Darkies can ever be entrusted with . . . a clinic. Our experience causes us to doubt their ability to work except under White supervision."[108] The entire operation then was a ruse—a manipulative attempt to get Blacks to cooperate in their own elimination.

To this day, the thrust of Planned Parenthood's literature focuses on the terrible "burden" that the poor place on the rest of us.[109] It continually reminds us of the costs that welfare mothers incur for taxpayers.[110] It constantly devises new plans to penetrate Black, Hispanic, and ethnic communities with its crippling message of eugenic racism.

When, for instance, Planned Parenthood shifted its focus from community-based clinics to school-based clinics, it reaffirmed Sanger's intentions: targeting inner-city minority neighborhoods.[111] Of the more than 300 school-based clinics that have opened nationwide in the last decade, none have been at substantially all-White schools.[112] None have been at suburban middle-class schools.[113] All have been at Black, minority, or ethnic schools.[114]

A racial analysis of abortion statistics is quite revealing in this regard. According to a Health and Human Services Administration report, as many as 43 percent of all abortions are performed on Blacks and another 10 percent on Hispanics.[115] This, despite the fact that Blacks only make up eleven percent of the total U.S. population and Hispanics only about eight percent.[116] A National Academy of Sciences investigation released more conservative—but no less telling—figures: 32 percent of all abortions are performed on minority mothers.[117]

Planned Parenthood's crusade to eliminate all those "dysgenic stocks" that Margaret Sanger believed were a "dead weight of human waste" and a "menace to the race" has precipitated a wholesale slaughter.[118] By 1975, a little more than one percent of the

Black population had been aborted.[119] By 1980 that figure had increased to nearly two and a half percent.[120] By 1985, it had reached three percent.[121] And by 1992 it had grown exponentially to a full four and a half percent.[122] In most Black communities today abortions outstrip births by as much as three to one.[123]

In order to realize Margaret Sanger's eugenic ideal of eliminating the "masses of degenerate" and "good-for-nothing" races, Planned Parenthood has not only emphasized contraception and abortion, it has also carried the banner of sterilization.[124] And, of course, that sterilization vendetta has been primarily leveled against minorities.

The sterilization rate among Blacks is forty-five percent higher than among whites.[125] Among Hispanics the rate is thirty percent higher.[126] As many as forty-two percent of all Amerind women and thirty-five percent of all Puerto Rican women have been sterilized.[127]

Hardly a champion of choice, Sanger often sought mandatory population control measures—measures carefully designed to deny women the freedom to choose. In 1934, she recommended that the government launch a health-care reform plan that would include "parenthood permits."[128] The permits would only be issued to those couples "deemed eugenically fit by public officials."[129] According to her proposal "no woman shall have the legal right to bear a child, no man shall have the right to become a father" without such a permit.[130] And the permits were "not to be valid for more than one birth."[131]

Following in her footsteps, Planned Parenthood has proposed that our government implement similar draconian measures. For instance, the organization has recommended "compulsory abortion for out-of-wedlock pregnancies," federal entitlement "payments to encourage abortion," "compulsory sterilization for those who have already had two children," and "tax penalties" for existing large families.[132]

And in China, Planned Parenthood helped the government launch a brutal, no-holds-barred, one-child-per-couple policy.[133] Nearly 100 million forced abortions, mandatory sterilizations, and coercive infanticides later, Planned Parenthood literature maintains that the genocidal approach to population control is a "model of efficiency."[134] It has fought to maintain United States tax subsidies for the Chinese operation, and has continued to increase its own funding and program support involvement despite the widespread reports of human rights atrocities.[135]

Your Tax Dollars at Work

What makes the travesty of Sanger's ongoing legacy all the more noxious is the fact that a vast proportion of Planned Parenthood's funding at every level—from the local level to the international level—comes right out of the American taxpayer's pocket. It has become for all intents and purposes an unofficial—and thus unrestrained and unrestricted—branch of the federal government.

We're paying Planned Parenthood's bills while it fulfills Sanger's sordid dreams.

It is widely known that Planned Parenthood receives tens of millions of tax dollars through the Title X appropriations of the Public Health Service Act. In fiscal 1987, Title X funds amounted to a whopping $142.5 million.[136] In 1988, that sum was upped to $146 million.[137] And by 1992 it topped $200 million.[138] During the twelve years of supposedly pro-life Republican administrations, funding for Planned Parenthood's lascivious Title X programs actually tripled.[139] For the big-government social engineers now in power, only the sky is the limit—recommendations have ranged upwards of $400 million.[140] Dispensed as a virtual block grant, to be spent in whatever way Planned Parenthood and the other beneficiaries see fit, this Title X money is obviously a major source of income for the abortuaries and birth control clinics of our land.[141]

What is not widely known, however, is that those Title X appropriations represent only a small proportion of Planned Parenthood's taxpayer largesse. There are some eighteen additional federal statutes, as well as hundreds of state and local measures, that authorize public expenditures and support for "family planning" programs, policies, and procedures.[142] And with the health-care reform package, there are more on the way.[143] So, for instance, even during recent Republican administrations, Planned Parenthood clinics, affiliates, and chapters received annual federal funding under the $17 million Title V provision of the Social Security Maternal and Child Health Program.[144] Each year they received federal funding under the $9 million Medicaid appropriations bill.[145] In addition, those clinics, affiliates, and chapters benefitted each year from the government's $8 million contraceptive development splurge, its $3 million expenditure for a contraceptive evaluation project, its $66 million dollar spending spree for "reproductive sciences," its $14 million spent on demographic and behavioral research, and its $27 million budgeted for community services block grants.[146] Internationally, various Planned Parenthood agencies have been able to skim the cream off virtually every United States foreign aid package.[147] This includes a lion's share of the more than $200 million in International Population Assistance funds, and the more than $100 million in contraceptive and abortifacient research appropriations.[148] Additionally, Planned Parenthood gets a larger part of the untold billions in grants, contracts, and cooperative agreements of the United Nations Fund for Population Activities, the World Bank, and the Agency for International Development.[149]

That is a lot of money—a lot of your money and a lot of my money. Margaret Sanger would no doubt approve.

What kind of return are we getting on our hefty investment?

A Bill of Goods

Amazingly, Planned Parenthood's well-heeled programs have failed to make good on the organization's claims. In fact, from a strictly programmatic perspective, Sanger's ideologically driven agenda has completely and utterly backfired.

Planned Parenthood's program of birth control, for instance, has failed to inhibit unwanted pregnancies, and it has increased the risk of severe medical problems for the women who follow it. Ninety percent of the 55 million women of reproductive age in the United States use some form of contraception, including as many as 79 percent of all sexually active teens.[150] Even so, more than three million unwanted pregnancies are reported every year.[151]

How can this be? According to Planned Parenthood's own figures, the annual in-use failure rate for the Pill is as high as 11 percent.[152] For the diaphragm, the normal failure rate is nearly 32 percent.[153] For the intra-uterine device (IUD), it is almost 11 percent.[154] For "safe-sex" condoms, it is over 18 percent.[155] And for the various foam, cream, and jelly spermicides, it can range as high as 34 percent.[156] That means that a sexually active 14-year-old girl who faithfully uses the Pill has a 44 percent chance of getting pregnant at least once before she finishes high school.[157] She has a 69 percent chance of getting pregnant at least once before she finishes college.[158] And she has a 30 percent chance of getting pregnant two or more times.[159] If she relies on "safe-sex" condoms, the likelihood of an unwanted pregnancy while she is in school rises to nearly 87 percent.[160] In other words, the Planned Parenthood system virtually guarantees that women will get pregnant—and that they will then be "forced" to fall back on the birth control lynch pin: abortion.

Safe and effective? Not by a long shot.

Planned Parenthood's battle against sexually transmitted diseases is also a dismal failure. In fact, the organization's efforts have been tragically counterproductive. It has become a veritable Typhoid Mary, actually encouraging the spread of syphilis, gonorrhea, chlamydia, herpes, hepatitis, granuloma, chancroid, and even AIDS at an alarming rate. Besides the fact that it constantly exhorts youngsters to flaunt a ribald and irresponsible promiscuity, it continually promotes an alarmingly "unsafe" exercise of that promiscuity. Instead of affording its fornicating disciples with the slim security of barrier devices, it primarily peddles the entirely unguarded prescription birth control methods. Eighty-three percent of Planned Parenthood's clients receive non-barrier contraceptives,[161] and 88 percent of those who previously practiced "safe sex" are dissuaded from continuing—despite all its rhetoric to the contrary, the organization actually encourages "unprotected" sexual promiscuity.[162]

Admittedly, barrier devices such as condoms offer only limited protection against venereal infection. Due to in-use mechanical failure—leaks, breaks, tears, slippage, and spillage—their effectiveness has been estimated to be at best 82 percent.[163] But the Pill offers no protection whatsoever.[164] Neither does the IUD or the diaphragm or spermicides or contraceptive sponges or any of the other non-barrier birth control devices that Planned Parenthood favors.[165] Worse, recent studies indicate that not only do these methods fail to guard against venereal infection, they may actually enhance the risks.[166] "Apparently," says demographic analyst Robert Ruff, "Planned Parenthood believes that safe sex is a lot less important than free sex."[167]

Planned Parenthood's greatest failure may well be its highly lauded multi-million-dollar, tax-funded education programs. According to its own survey, conducted by the Louis Harris pollsters, teens who have taken their "comprehensive" sex education courses have a 50 percent higher rate of sexual activity than their "unenlightened" peers.[168] And yet the courses had no significant effect on their contraceptive usage.[169] The conclusion, one that even Planned Parenthood researchers have been unable to escape, is that their sex education courses only exacerbate the teen pregnancy problem.[170]

In 1970, fewer than half of the nation's school districts offered sex education curricula and none had school-based birth control clinics.[171] Today more than 75 percent of the districts teach sex education and there are more than 300 clinics in operation.[172] Yet the percentage of illegitimate births has only increased during that time, from a mere 15 percent to an astonishing 51 percent.[173]

According to the Harris poll, the only things that effectively impact the teen pregnancy problem are frequent church attendance and parental oversight, the very things that Margaret Sanger and Planned Parenthood have railed against for three-quarters of a century—the very things that sex education courses are designed to circumvent.[174]

It seems that Margaret Sanger's success is a failure.

Bad Seed

Just as a nation's "head" defines the character and vision of that nation, so an organization's "head" defines the character and vision of that organization. This is a very basic biblical principle. It is the principle of "legacy." It is the principle of "inheritance."

The Canaanite people were perverse and corrupt. They practiced every manner of wickedness and reprobation. Why were they so dissolute? The answer, according to the Bible, is that their founders and leaders passed evil onto them as their legacy, as their inheritance (Genesis 9:25; Leviticus 18:24–25; Amos 1:3–12).

Similarly, the Moabites and the Ammonites were rebellious and improvident peoples. They railed against God's law and God's people. Why were they so defiant? Again, the Bible tells us that their founders and leaders passed insurrection on to them as their legacy, as their inheritance (Genesis 19:30–38; Numbers 21:21–23; Amos 1:13–15; 2:1–3).

A seed will always yield its own kind (Genesis 1:11). Bad seed brings forth bitter harvest (Ezra 9:2; Isaiah 1:4; 14:20). You reap what you sow (Galatians 6:7). A nation or an organization that is sown, nurtured, and grown by deceit, promiscuity, and lawlessness, cannot help but be evil to the core (Hosea 8:7).

Margaret Sanger and the organization she founded, Planned Parenthood, are poignant illustrations of this truth. From fruit to root this principle is unerringly exposited for all the world to behold—if only we would open our eyes to see.

The sage counsel of the incomparable Samuel Johnson is instructive in this wise:

> Let it be remembered, that the nature of things is not alterable by our perception—or lack therein. We cannot remake or unmake truth; it is our business only to find it and then respond accordingly. No proposition can become less certain by being neglected. It is to no purpose to wish, to suppose, that to be false, which is in itself true, and therefore to acquiesce in our own wishes and suppositions; when the matter is of eternal consequence, to doubt obstinately without grounds of doubt, and to determine without examination, is the last degree of folly and absurdity.[175]

SIEGE ALERT

PLANNED PARENTHOOD

Here is what the new social engineers at Planned Parenthood have in mind for you and your children in the weeks and months ahead:

- They want to affect every child. They want to influence every family. In order to accomplish such lofty aims, they know that their number one priority right now has to be a massive new expansion program that would institutionalize Planned Parenthood programs in every community, every school (public and private), and every health-care delivery system in the nation.
- Built upon a $750 million fund-raising program led by a prominent evangelical pastor—a graduate of Wheaton College and Fuller Theological Seminary—the plan is designed to "mainstream" Planned Parenthood and its perspectives of sex, amorality, and abortion as well as to double the size of its services infrastructure.
- Because the plan is national in scope—supported by the various health-care and educational reform implementation bureaucracies—Planned Parenthood will be able to quietly expand in our communities without many of us ever knowing it.
- In addition, Planned Parenthood is looking to expand its overseas interests and activities—which means it will be seeking massive increases in its already considerable tax subsidy.
- Watch particularly for the organization to capitalize on the AIDS crisis and the health-care reform craze to raise their profile—and lay siege on families—in school-based clinics, general services clinics, and walk-in essential care centers in public facilities all across America.

THREE

DUMB CERTAINTIES

NATIONAL EDUCATION ASSOCIATION

*As long as the twig is gentle and pliant, with small force and
strength it may be bent.*[1]

—Alexander Pope

*'Tis education forms the tender mind. Just as the twig is bent
the tree's inclined.*[2]

—Thomas Fessenden

The students sat before me dumbfounded. Incredulity was evident on their faces as I recounted the myriad of ways the basic history of our nation has been rewritten during the past three decades.

I was teaching a graduate-level survey course for a local college. In an attempt to illustrate how even the most fundamental facts about our national life had been ignored, neglected, or even deliberately subverted, I decided to profile the lives of several of the most prominent men of the founding era.

I began with the first fifteen presidents of the United States—the ones before George Washington. The first two served prior to the signing of the Declaration of Independence—Peyton Randolph of Virginia and Henry Middleton of South Carolina. The next six served between the time of the Declaration and the ratification of the first constitution—John Hancock of Massachusetts, Henry Laurens of South Carolina, John Jay of New York, Samuel Huntington of Connecticut, Samuel Johnson of North Carolina, and Thomas McKean of Delaware. The final seven served under the Articles of Confederation prior to the second national constitution—John Hanson of Maryland, Elias Budinot of New Jersey, Thomas Mifflin of Pennsylvania, Richard Henry Lee of Virginia, Nathaniel Gorham of Massachusetts, Arthur St. Clair of Pennsylvania, and Cyrus Griffin of Virginia. Each of these remarkable men led amazing lives of adventure, valor, and sacrifice. Their stories are the very warp and woof of American history.

I then ran through quick biographical sketches of several other founding-era statesmen who like the first fifteen presidents risked their lives and fortunes—the fifteen fighting for independence from England, the latter for several of the other sovereign American republics. There was Thomas Chittenden, the first president of the Republic of Vermont—which later gave up its independence when it joined the United States in 1791 as the fourteenth state. There was John Sevier, the first president of the Republic of Franklin—which likewise joined the Union as a part of Tennessee in 1792. And there was Fulwar Skipwith, the first president of West Florida—which was forcibly joined to the Union when American expeditionary troops conquered the territory from Mobile Bay to the capital city of Baton Rouge in 1810.

While I knew full well that these facts about the founding era would be essentially unfamiliar to my students, I was still unprepared for their response.

Some were simply astonished. They told me that they had never even had a hint that there were presidents before George Washington. And they certainly had never heard that at one time there had been other independent American republics. They stammered out a bevy of questions: How had I discovered all these arcane facts? Why weren't they taught in our schools? What books could they read that would tell them more?

Several of the other students, though, were more than astonished. They were angry that so much had been omitted from their education—throughout their elementary, secondary, college, and graduate schooling.

At the end of the class session one woman complained that though she had a masters degree in American history from a prominent Ivy League school—even with a special focus on the founding era—she had never been exposed to most of the material I'd covered that day. "It's not as if a few minor facts were left out," she said.

"These are fundamental, world-view-shifting basics. They shed an important light on how and why our nation ultimately took the shape it did. I've gotten used to the bias of historians against the influence and impact of Christianity on events. But this is different. It's almost as if the educational elite has deliberately sabotaged our heritage. I feel as if I've been defrauded by somebody: public schools or textbook publishers or tenured academics in their ivory towers. I'm furious."

But not knowing about the eminent life of Peyton Randolph or the portentous conquest of West Florida is trivial compared with the broader failure of American education. About that, we should all be furious.

Suffer the Children

"A nation at risk."[3] That is how the United States Department of Education has described our country's educational crisis.[4] And for good reason.

Public education in this country is a dismal failure.[5] Johnny can't read and Susie can't spell.[6] Willie can't write and Alice can't add.[7] Teacher competency is down.[8] Administrative effectiveness is down.[9] Student advancement is down.[10] Test scores are down.[11] Everything to do with our public school system is down—everything, that is, except crime, drug abuse, illicit sex, and the cost to taxpayers.[12]

As many as 90 million adults in this country are functionally illiterate.[13] An additional 35 million are alliterate—they can read a few basics with difficulty, but that is about all.[14] SAT score comparisons reveal an unbroken decline from 1963 to the present.[15] Average verbal scores have fallen over fifty points and mathematics scores have dropped nearly forty points.[16] Among the 158 member nations of the United Nations, the United States now ranks forty-ninth in its literacy levels.[17]

Nearly 40 percent of all high school seniors cannot draw inferences from written material; only one-fifth can write a persuasive essay; and less than one-third can solve an arithmetic problem requiring multiple steps.[18] Thirty-eight percent cannot locate the Mississippi River on a map of the North American continent; 35

percent cannot find the Rocky Mountains; and 42 percent cannot identify their own home state.[19]

One study found that 25 million high school graduates cannot correctly identify the United States on an outline map of the world; 44 million cannot find the Pacific Ocean; and some 61 million are unable to come within 500 miles of locating the nation's capital.[20]

Another study revealed that nearly one-third of all graduating high school seniors cannot identify the Declaration of Independence as marking the formal break between the American colonies and Great Britain; 28 percent do not know that Columbus discovered America in 1492—believing that the event occurred sometime between 1750 and 1850; and 32 percent are unable to name more than three past presidents.[21]

Nearly half of all Americans are so poorly educated that they can't perform such relatively simple tasks as calculating the price difference between two items at the grocery store or filling out a job application at a fast food restaurant.

A recent National Endowment for the Humanities study ruled these facts as a grave harbinger of national decline and disintegration:

> Knowledge of the ideas that have molded us and the ideals that have mattered to us function as a kind of civic glue. By failing to transmit these ideas and ideals from one generation to the next, we risk dissolution of the bonds that unite us as a nation and as a free people.[22]

Sadly, most Americans are so poorly educated that they don't even know they are poorly educated. According to Education Secretary Richard Riley:

> Such data paints a picture of a society in which the vast majority of Americans do not know that they do not have the skills to earn a living in our increasingly technological society and international marketplace.[23]

It is little wonder then that the public has lost confidence in the government-run school system. One recent *Washington Post* poll showed that only about 14 percent of all Americans have a great deal of faith in public education.[24] As a result, enrollment in private schools has increased more than 60 percent in the past two decades.[25] In fact, the schools have gotten so bad that nearly a quarter of all public school teachers have taken their own children out of the public system.[26]

All this despite one of the most extensive and expensive school systems the world has ever seen.[27] Spending—in inflation-adjusted dollars—has increased some 400 percent per pupil in the past thirty years.[28] Teacher salaries have more than doubled—again in inflation-adjusted dollars.[29] And the per capita number of support personnel has nearly quadrupled.[30] Education has, in fact, become the second largest industry in the nation, spending more than a quarter-trillion dollars every year, with nearly three million teachers and administrators.[31]

And yet, more than 45 percent of all the products of that system cannot even read the front page of the morning newspaper.[32]

According to a report from the National Commission on Excellence in Education:

> If an unfriendly foreign power had attempted to impose on America a mediocre educational system it could not have devised one worse than the one we presently have.[33]

How could this possibly have happened?

State of the Union

According to a recent *Forbes* magazine profile, the National Education Association is "the worm in the American education apple."[34]

The normally sedate business journal went on to say:

> The public may be only dimly aware of it, but the union's growing power has exactly coincided with the dismal spectacle of rising spending on education producing deteriorating results.[35]

Syndicated columnist James Kilpatrick agrees:

> The NEA in recent years has come to embody every single cause that has contributed to the crisis that threatens our public schools.[36]

Founded in 1857 by representatives of several state teachers associations, the National Education Association is today the country's largest labor union. With a membership now approaching three million, an annual combined budget of $500 million, and a standing political war chest of nearly $20 million, the union is one of the most powerful forces in American life today.[37] It is the largest single interest group lobbying in Washington.[38] It has the largest and richest political action committee.[39] It is the biggest broker of group insurance benefits.[40] And it is the major ideological force in more than 90 percent of the some 16,000 local public school districts throughout the nation.[41]

For nearly 30 years, the union has maintained a smothering monopoly over every aspect of America's government-run educational system—from the content of the curriculum to the proposal of budgets, from the design of facilities to the administration of bureaucracies, from classroom methodologies to teacher salaries, from political reform to regulatory control.[42]

But its appetite for new kingdoms to conquer remains unsated. According to author and educator Phoebe Courtney, the union is not satisfied simply controlling public education:

> It wants complete control over all American education—private as well as public. It has vowed to bring private education under its control through teacher certification and state accreditation laws.[43]

To that end, the union has launched a series of initiatives aimed at consolidating its power nationwide:

- It has worked diligently to promote the nationalization of educational standards—to insure complete uniformity in teaching content, methodology, administration, and outcome.[44]
- It has spent millions of dollars fighting against school choice measures that would allow parents to choose the best schooling options for their children according to their own criteria.[45]
- It has fought for either the elimination or the strict regulation of home schooling—in some states even going so far as to establish "enforcement units" to identify and seek prosecution of parents that home school their children without government approval or certification.[46]
- It has attempted to stymie any and all educational reform—particularly when that reform has involved diversifying the educational options available to taxpayers and parents.[47]
- It has lobbied for centralization of control of the financing of ed-

ucation—recommending that the current system of local financing be scrapped for a federal system.[48]

In 1967 Sam Lambert, the union's executive secretary, predicted:

> The National Education Association will become a political power second to no other special interest group . . . we will organize this profession from top to bottom into logical operational units that can move swiftly and effectively and with power unmatched by any other organized group in the nation.[49]

By all counts, that prophecy has been fulfilled.

Initially called the National Teacher's Association, the union was largely a home office for the federated state education associations during its first 75 years or so of existence. It engaged in some modest research; it lobbied state legislators in support of higher pay and better retirement benefits; and it promoted the progressive methodological ideas of such educators as Horace Mann, Bronson Alcott, William Torrey Harris, Zalmon Richards, Edward Thorndike, and John Dewey.

According to educational pioneer Samuel Blumenfeld:

> The NEA was little more than a discussion club for superintendents, state education officers, and college presidents. Its conventions were commercially self-serving, philosophically stimulating, but politically inconsequential.[50]

But all that would change—dramatically.

In 1962, it wed its modest commercial interests and its *haute* educational fashions with the organizational leverage of the labor movement—thus completing its transformation from a loosely affiliated professional association to a full-fledged union. Since that time, the vast proportion of its efforts and expenditures have been focused on the progressive politicalization of the educational system.

As a result, the urgent task of improving the schools has taken a backseat to the promotion and consolidation of the union's power. Today, less than four percent of the union's vast annual budget is actually spent on instruction and professional development.[51] All the rest is poured into maintaining and expanding the union's dominating control over the American educational debacle.[52]

Scott Thompson, executive director of the National Association of Secondary School Principals, has said:

> The NEA no longer contributes to the improvement of teaching and learning for students. It looks after the narrow interests of its members rather than after the broader interests of its constituency.[53]

The union even admits as much:

> The major purpose of our association is not the education of children, it is or ought to be the extension and preservation of our members' rights. We earnestly care about the kids' learning, but that is secondary to the other goals.[54]

Thus Congressman John Ashbrook was hardly exaggerating when he quipped:

> Any observer of the current scene has to realize that the NEA's priorities these days break down like this: power first, politics second, and education last.[55]

Partners in Crime

"If I become president, you'll be my partners," declared candidate Bill Clinton to the National Education Association Candidate Screening Panel in 1991. "I won't forget who brought me to the White House."[56]

Certainly there is no doubt about who in fact did bring him to the White House.

According to Dan Alexander, a Washington-based educational analyst, the union "has become the single most dominant force in the national Democratic Party."[57] Nearly a quarter of the floor delegates at the party's last five national conventions were members or officials of the union.[58] About twenty percent of the delegates Clinton needed for his nomination came from the rank and file of the union.[59] And close to an eighth of his campaign budget came from the union's political coffers.[60]

At the Democratic National Convention, former union president Mary Futrell declared her unequivocal partisanship:

> Whatever flag you wave during the long political spring, we must all wave the same flag this fall, and that must be the flag of

the Democratic Party's team for the White House.[61]

And wave they did.

During each of the past three congressional elections, the union has spent more than $2.5 million supporting various candidates and causes—an overwhelming majority of them from the extreme left of the political spectrum—from Ted Kennedy and Howard Metzenbaum to Henry Waxman and Tom Foley.[62] Despite the fact that two-thirds of all teachers describe their political philosophy as "conservative," militant left-wing political activism has become the *sine quo non* of their union.[63]

According to Samuel Blumenfeld:

> The NEA's stand on most issues is virtually identical with the radical left. In fact, the NEA seems to have become the main channel through which the radical left is exercising its influence. Those of us who still believe in freedom ought to be very worried, for the NEA controls virtually every school in America through its member-teachers, and those who control the schools control the future.[64]

Agreeing, family advocate Phyllis Schlafly has said that the union has "proved again and again" that "it has an ultra-left-wing extremist agenda."[65] Indeed, a survey of its policy positions bears that fact out all too clearly:

- It is at the vanguard of the "political correctness" movement— from multi-culturalism and inclusive language, to speech codes and hate crimes.[66]

- It has embraced the entire feminist agenda—including abortion on demand, value-free K–12 sex education, school-based sex clinics, quota hiring and advancement standards, and passage of the Equal Rights Amendment.[67]

- It has joined forces with militant homosexual groups in pressing for special status legislative protections, condom give-aways in the schools, and massive judgment-free AIDS education programs.[68]

- It has endorsed the radical environmental agenda—from comprehensive industrial re-tooling and property confiscation to eco-awareness curricula and coercive lifestyle adjustments.[69]

- It opposes school prayer—or any other demonstration of faith in the public sector.[70]

- It has consistently pressed for dramatic cutbacks in military defense spending.[71]
- It opposes tuition tax credits.[72]
- It has lobbied for the repeal of the right-to-work provisions of the Taft-Hartley Act.[73]
- It has actively opposed conservative appointments to the Supreme Court—from Clement Haynesworth and Harold Carswell to Robert Bork and Clarence Thomas.[74]
- It lobbied for the creation of a degree-granting "U.S. Peace Academy" to offset the country's military academies.[75]
- It endorsed the most recent gay rights march on Washington.[76]
- It lobbied for passage of the most recent Civil Rights Restoration Act as well as the Americans with Disabilities Act—which despite their benign-sounding names actually include provisions for the breakdown of family authority, private sector independence, and moral integrity.[77]
- It has consistently opposed drug and alcohol sobriety testing for students.[78]
- And it has supported the right of schools to by-pass parental authority in securing sexuality counseling, procedures, and services.[79]
- According to former school principal and conservative educational lobbyist, Michael Harlinson, the union is comprehensive in its ideological bent:

> There is not a single left-wing cause *célèbre* that the NEA has not enthusiastically embraced. If it's liberal, the union is for it. If it's not, the union denounces it as some kind of plot against all decency and honor. The fact is, the NEA is a power-hungry institutional thug for the political left and little else.[80]

And anyone who happens to disagree with its monolithic liberal agenda is labeled by the union as "chronic tax resisters, congenital reactionaries, dangerous witch-hunters, energized superpatriots, wayward dogma peddlers, and vitriolic race-haters."[81] Says Harlinson:

> Though it constantly harps on a gospel of tolerance and diversity, the NEA is fierce in its denunciation of any and all political opposition. It anathematizes and criminalizes its critics with an intensity that even the Mafia could admire.[82]

When advocates for school choice attempted to place a modest compromise initiative on the ballot in the state of California, for example, the union used what *Forbes* magazine called "unprecedented tactics" to disrupt the petition effort.[83] Members attempted to block would-be signatories' access to the petition in shopping malls.[84] They sabotaged the petitions with fake names and addresses.[85] They attempted to bribe a signature-collecting company with $400,000 to decline the account.[86] And they pledged to spend as much as $10 million in the campaign to defeat the initiative at the ballot box.[87]

"I want each and every one of you to know with certainty," announced the union's president Keith Geiger, "that when you stand up to the privatizers and the voucher pushers, you'll have behind you every bit of support that this organization can muster."[88]

That kind of faithful zealotry for the liberal Democratic party line was rewarded in 1978 when Jimmy Carter created the massive Department of Education—a goal of the union since its establishment more than a century earlier.[89] Afterward, one official boasted, "We are the only union with our own Cabinet department."[90]

It was rewarded again with the first Clinton budget—which pledged a 22 percent increase in the federal funding and control of local schools.[91]

According to Phyllis Schlafly, the union is hardly interested in serious issues of education. Instead, its words and deeds point to "an arrogance of power, a compulsion to control the minds and behavior of children, and a pervasive hostility toward parents."[92]

No wonder our schools are in such awful shape.

The Little Red Schoolhouse

The National Education Association's primary philosophical guru was John Dewey, a Columbia University educator. Dewey believed that the primary purpose of education was the promotion of "socialization." Thus he wrote, "Not knowledge or information, but self realization is the goal."[93] He believed that "the mind is not the property of the individual, but of humanity."[94]

The educational methodology that he worked out thus mitigated against what he called "abstract learning" and encouraged "social skills" through "social studies" instead.[95] Schools thus became "psycho-therapeutic socializers for the harmony of the wider community."[96]

Because the union threw its full weight behind this approach to teaching and learning, the entire government-run educational system gradually turned its attentions away from academic achievement and toward what Richard John Neuhaus has called "fatuously bouncy self-help—the unvarnished egoism of self-esteem, the occult, radical feminist ravings, gay advocacy whinings, and related effluents of ruined souls."[97]

The union thus worked diligently to insure that objective standards of academic excellence and time-honored educational techniques were summarily dispatched in favor of a bevy of methodological fads and fashions:

- It helped to replace phonics with the "look-say" method of teaching reading—which has greatly contributed to the nation's precipitous decline in literacy.[98]
- Its emphasis on "socialization" has resulted in decreased requirements in math and the sciences—again contributing to plunging student competency rates.[99]
- Its attempt to transform teachers into "equippers" has resulted in a massive exodus of qualified teachers from the public school ranks.[100]
- Its opposition to merit raises, teacher competency testing, and recertification standards has resulted in a system that harbors incompetency but fails to reward achievement.[101]
- Its insistence on tenure protections for all government school positions has resulted in incompetent teachers and administrators securing job immutability.[102]

Even the overtly liberal *New Republic* magazine was forced to admit, "Nearly every necessary step to high quality American public education is being fought by the NEA."[103]

But it gets worse. The union's most recent fascination is called "Outcome-Based Education." Though the rhetoric of this "school restructuring" plan sounds good enough, the reality is abominably subversive. According to Michael Harlinson:

> Every parent wants to achieve certain goals or outcomes for their children at school—they want them to learn to read, to acquire certain math and science skills, and to develop logical and deductive disciplines. But this is not at all what Outcome-Based

Education is about. Instead it is a series of social experiments designed to turn out a certain set of social outcomes—self-esteem, tolerance, sexual responsibility, and value-free consciences. In other words, what the union means by *outcomes* and what the parents mean by *outcomes* are quite likely two entirely different things.[104]

As presently constituted the plan is a nightmare of liberalism run-amuck:

- The plan is woefully expensive—involving a dramatic growth of bureaucracy and administration.[105]
- The plan calls for tightened government controls from both the federal and the state level.
- It calls for a least-common-denominator kind of egalitarian scheme that stifles individual achievement and obscures individual needs.[106]
- Objective academic disciplines are replaced by subjective feelings, attitudes, and values.[107]
- Though hundreds of schools have already introduced the restructuring plan, there is as yet no empirical study, no replicable research, and no pilot data to demonstrate that it works—the program has been launched entirely "on faith."[108]
- It offers absolutely no method of accountability to students, parents, teachers, or taxpayers—essentially because it includes no objective standards.[109]

As Harlinson has said:

> With its latest hobby-horse, Outcome-Based Education, the National Education has given up all pretense of trying to educate public school children in favor of propagandizing them with pop-psycho-therapeutic pap. Instead of teaching them the three 'R's—reading, writing, and arithmetic—it is enthusiastically indoctrinating them with the four 'R's—reversionism, revisionism, reprobation, and radicalism.[110]

Professor Thomas Sowell, in his remarkable book *Inside American Education: The Decline, the Deception, the Dogmas*, writes:

> Like many other people, I have long been appalled by the low quality and continuing deterioration of American education. However, after doing much research, I am frankly surprised that the results are not even worse than they are. The incredibly counterproductive fads, fashions, and dogmas of American education—

from the kindergarten to the colleges—have yet to take their full toll. . . . Much has been said about how our young people do not meet the academic standards of their peers in other countries with which we compete economically. While this is both true and important, their academic deficiencies are only half the story. All across this country, the school curriculum has been invaded by psychological conditioning programs, which not only take up time sorely needed for intellectual development, but also promote an emotionalized and anti-intellectual way of responding to the challenges facing every individual and every society. Worst of all, the psycho-therapeutic curriculum systematically undermines the parent-child relationship and the shared values which make society possible.[111]

Whose Values?

The opponents of the Christian world and life view are well aware of the importance of the family. To change the nature, character, and function of the family in our society is absolutely essential if they are to succeed. As a result, Outcome-Based Education is often an overt assault on basic family values. For example, one teacher's guidebook for New York's controversial Outcome-Based Education restructuring plan states:

> Teachers of first-graders have an opportunity to give children a healthy sense of identity at an early age. Classes should include references to lesbians and gays in all curricular areas and should avoid exclusionary practices by presuming a person's sexual orientation, reinforcing stereotypes, or speaking of lesbians and gays as "they" or "other." If teachers do not discuss lesbian and gay issues, they are not likely to come up. Children need actual experiences via creative play, books, visitors, etc., in order for them to view lesbians and gays as real people to be respected and appreciated. Educators have the potential to help increase the tolerance and acceptance of the lesbian and gay community.[112]

An article in the homosexual *Advocate* magazine entitled "Why Johnny Can't Learn About Condoms" vilified "fundamentalist Christians" for opposing homosexual content in Outcome-Based public education:

> Public education epitomizes the religious right's problem with non-Christian society. Public schools serve the function of main-

streaming people—making them into decent, tolerant adults. For certain fundamentalists, that makes public schools the enemy, and they have been able to make this case to a lot of other parents.[113]

So there you have it. Your children must be "mainstreamed" by the government through the educational establishment and its attendant bureaucratic machinery. Your taxes are being used to purposefully raise children in values alien to the Christian faith. And if you object, you are guilty of "censorship."[114]

As James Bennett and Thomas DiLorenzo, authors of the stunning book *Official Lies: How Washington Misleads Us*, have said:

> Public schools in America are essentially monopolies. They are financed by compulsory taxation, enjoy a captive audience of students thanks to compulsory-attendance laws, and—in most cities—assign students to schools according to where they live. Parents who are dissatisfied with the quality of education their children are receiving must either move to an affluent area, where schools are often better, or send their children to private schools. If they choose the latter, parents must pay twice for their children's education: once in property taxes and again in tuition.[115]

This fundamental incongruity in the American tradition of freedom is not some new development in public education. Horace Mann, who is universally recognized as the father of the American public education system, admitted that public schools were needed "as a means for the state to control people."[116] He said, "Great care must be taken to inform and regulate the will of the people."[117] Newton Bateman, a late-nineteenth-century advocate of public education, echoed Mann's sentiments, claiming that:

> Government has a right of eminent domain over the minds and souls and bodies of us all; therefore education cannot be left to the caprices and contingencies of individuals.[118]

Thus, the National Education Association's tactic of getting at children through the public education system is as old as government-run schools are. Indeed, Horace Mann was originally a reformer who wished to "improve" his society through legislation.[119] To his dismay, however, he found adult individuals too resistant and recalcitrant for his designs. Eventually he hit on a new idea: Aim for the children. In 1837, he wrote a friend explaining his new strategy:

I have abandoned jurisprudence, and betaken myself to the larger sphere of mind and morals. Having found the present generation composed of materials almost unmalleable, I am about transferring my efforts to the next. Men are cast-iron, but children are wax.[120]

The proponents of Outcome-Based Education are not merely concerned about passing out tidbits of immoral information, but wish to instill moral—or, more accurately, immoral—beliefs. As one union official forthrightly admitted, "Mere facts and discussion are not enough. They need to be undergirded by a set of values."[121]

Again, this is nothing new. American public education has always been driven by moral values. Horace Mann's arguments for the public school had almost nothing to do with reading, writing, and arithmetic, but with inculcating children with his version of morality:

The germs of morality must be planted deeply in the moral nature of children, at an early period of their life. . . . If we should have improved men, we must have improved means of educating children. . . . Of all the means in our possession, the common school has precedence, because of its universality.[122]

Indeed, Mann wanted religion taught in the public schools. He exhorted teachers to:

Keep children unspotted from the world, that is, uncontaminated by its vices; to train them up to the love of God and the love of man; to make the perfect example of Jesus Christ lovely in their eyes; and to give to all so much of religious instruction as is compatible with the rights of others and the genius of our government.[123]

Though he wanted religion in the public school, he was opposed to orthodox Christianity, and instead wished to promulgate Unitarianism. He did not do this by calling for Unitarianism to be recognized as the official state religion; rather, he simply called for the religious teaching in the schools to be "nonsectarian."

The director of Equal Educational Opportunity for the Commonwealth of Massachusetts, Charles Leslie Glenn, Jr., writes:

Thus, although Mann and the other education reformers may not have intended to promote Unitarianism as a denomination, they were deeply concerned to assure that "liberal religion" would, through the common schools, replace "fanaticism." Were the normal schools some sort of Unitarian conspiracy, then? Only in the sense that they represented the most effective means for the education reformers (themselves mostly but not exclusively "liberal Christians") to develop a supply of teachers who would share their own views about the "pure religion" appropriate to offer as religious instruction in common schools. . . . Orthodox beliefs were not confronted directly, but they were relativized, marginalized. It was by a selective emphasis upon certain elements of Christianity, in a vocabulary familiar from childhood, that the idea was conveyed that these were the real essentials of the faith.[124]

Furthermore, according to Glenn, Mann pioneered subtle methods of centrally controlling education which are still used today:

The collection and interpretation of educational statistics, ostensibly a perfectly neutral activity, had and continues to have the power to define perceptions of the salient strengths and weaknesses of the schools. The recommendation of reading material—and the banning of other material—had and continues to have the power to shape the range of topics that may be taught or discussed, and the framework in which they will be understood. The training—and eventually the certification—of teachers had and continues to have the power to determine what will occur in the classroom, far more than any system of regulation and prescription.

But if the public education system pioneered by Mann and others was so biased, why did Christians, who ostensibly made up a majority of the citizenry at the time, not resist it. Well, according to Glenn, at first some Christians did resist:

Those who—more clear-thinking, perhaps—did not fully agree with Mann insisted that what was presented was in fact a false religion, worse than no mention of religion at all, since it took no account of sin as a corruption of human nature, cutting man off from God and from his own happiness, or of God's plan of salvation through Jesus Christ. By retaining only those aspects of Christianity with which Unitarians agreed, the proposed religious teaching was in fact identical with Unitarian teaching. Thus it was sectarian in the fullest sense.[125]

The eminent theologian Charles Hodge, for example, strongly questioned the right of the government to interfere in the curriculum decisions of local districts—even in the name of nonsectarianism:

What right has the State, a majority of the people, or a mere clique, which in fact commonly control such matters, to say what shall be taught in schools that the people sustain? What more right have they to say that no religion shall be taught, than they have to say that Popery shall be taught? Or what right have the people in one part, to control the wishes and convictions of those of another part of the State, as to the education of their own children? If the people of a particular district choose to have a school in which the Westminster of Heidelberg catechism is taught, we cannot see on what principle of religious liberty the State has a right to interfere, and say it shall not be done. . . . This appears to us a strange doctrine in a free country . . . unjust and tyrannical, as well as infidel in its whole tendency.[126]

According to Glenn:

Hodge's view was shared by many of his fellow Presbyterians, and a brief effort was made to establish a system of Presbyterian elementary schools . . . this effort collapsed under the perceived threat of the schools that immigrant Catholics actually were establishing.[127]

Roman Catholics saw more readily than most orthodox protestants—indeed, they blamed the orthodox protestants—the threat posed by the religiously generic training that took place in the public schools.[128] Though Charles Hodge and other knowledgeable protestant theologians were admirable exceptions, most protestants decided that they had more in common with Unitarians than with Catholics—and willingly began supporting public education against Catholic efforts to build their own schools.[129]

"At some point," says Christian educator Richard Catherwood, "we are going to have to face the fact that the entire public education scheme was and is flawed. We are going to have to go back to square one—in repentance—and essentially learn how to learn all over again."[130]

A Lifetime of Learning

The English novelist and etymologist J. R. R. Tolkien once told his students that all true education is actually "a kind of never-ending story—a matter of continual beginnings, of habitual fresh starts, of persistent newness."[131] Similarly, his great friend C. S.

Lewis said that education is "like a tantalizingly perpetual ve-
randa—the initiation of unending beginnings."[132]

That paradoxical perspective was likewise shared by E. M.
Bounds, the Southern pastor and theologian of the last century renowned for his many fine books on prayer. Shortly after he was captured by Northern partisans at the Battle of Franklin during the
late lamentable War Between the States, Bounds asserted that "All
of life is but preparation for what comes after."[133] Though slightly
wounded, ravenously hungry, bitterly cold, and now made servile
at the hand of unwelcome invaders, Bounds understood that the
past is but a prelude to the future and that the present is necessarily tutelage in an unending process and thus not to be chaffed at.
He went on to say:

> The primer of faith is never closed for the child of God. It's les-
> sons never end. No matter what circumstances may bode, we re-
> main under the bar of instruction forever. Every incident builds
> upon the last and anticipates the next.[134]

For many, it is sad to say, this uniquely Christian perspective is
an entirely foreign world view—an alien notion, an arcane paradox,
an unfathomable mystery. Minds dulled by the smothering con-
formity of popular culture cannot plumb the depths or explore the
breadths of the distinctively Christian virtue of hopeful content-
ment in the face of perpetual tasks. Thus they rush toward what
they think will be the termination of this, that, or another chapter
in their lives. They cannot wait to *finish* school. Thus, for instance,
graduation is not a *commencement* for them, but a *conclusion*. Afterward they hurry through their lives and careers: They plod im-
patiently through their workweek anxious for the weekend; they
bide their time until vacation and plod on toward retirement—always coming to the end of things until at last things come to an
end.

But within the Christian world-view framework, hopeful con-
tentment in the face of never-ending responsibilities is a virtue that
continually breeds in us anticipation for new beginnings not old
resolutions. It is a virtue that provokes us to a fresh confidence in
the present as well as in the days yet to come. That is simply because it is a virtue rooted in an understanding of God's good providence and in the covenant fortunes of His grace.

We above all people—who were brought from death to life, from the end of ourselves to the threshold of eternity—understand this. This is, in fact, the very essence of the Gospel. The crucifixion is not the termination of Christ's mediatorial work, rather it is the conjunction of two beginnings: the Incarnation and the Resurrection. It is the pivot of civilization demarcating a new creation:

> Old things are passed away; behold all things are become new (2 Corinthians 5:17, KJV).

Thus we are now innately an optimistic people, forever starting anew, affirming our faith in full accord with the patriarchs and patristics:

> Now faith is the substance of things hoped for, the evidence of things not seen. (Hebrews 11:1–2, KJV)

Thus, for example, all talk of education is for us a reminder that we have only begun to learn how to learn. It is an affirmation that though our magnificent heritage has introduced us to the splendid wonders of literature and art, music and history, science and ideas in the past—we have only been *introduced,* and a lifetime adventure in these vast and portentous arenas still awaits us.

Indeed, the most valuable lessons that education can convey are invariably the lessons that never end. That is actually at the heart of the Christian philosophy of education.

The prince of preachers Charles Haddon Spurgeon once said:

> I would have everybody able to read and write and cipher; indeed, I don't think a man can know too much; but mark you, the knowing of these things is not education; and there are millions of your reading and writing people who are as ignorant as neighbor Norton's calf.[135]

Those ignorant masses of whom Spurgeon speaks are not those who failed to finish their lessons. They are instead those who *did* finish—or rather those who naively thought that lessons were the sorts of things that *could* be finished.

Education does not have a terminus, a polar extreme, a finish line, an outcome. Instead it is a deposit, an endowment, a promise, and even a small taste of the future. Again, that is the root of the Christian philosophy of education—a philosophy that once provoked the unprecedented cultural flowering in Western civilization and will again if we would but adhere to its principles once again.

The question is, how do we reclaim that glorious heritage? How can we both preserve it and then pass it on to the next generation? How do we go about beginning a lifetime of beginnings?

In his introduction to John Henry Newman's brilliant *The Idea of a University*, the renowned educator Leo Brennan asserts that "though we don't have much to show for it, we Americans are enthusiasts for education."[136] He's right. Though there is perhaps an underlying "anti-intellectualism" in a few isolated circles, by and large we Americans—and particularly we American Christians— place a heavy emphasis on the education of our children. We demand good teachers. We demand good textbooks. We demand good facilities. We demand good supplemental resources. We demand the best and the latest and the snazziest of everything academia has to offer. Which makes our profound lack of it—even within the Christian community—all the more ironic.

The problem, says Brennan, is that "we engage in the eminently dubious process of what is barbarously known as standardization." As a result, "we lower our ideals and we smear our philosophy" by playing "the sedulous ape" to popular, uniformitarian, educational fads and fashions.[137]

The only solution, he argues, is to "restore the basic educational ideals and principles" that provoked Christendom's great flowering of culture in the first place: a strident emphasis on serious and diverse reading, the use of classical methodologies, and all this integrated into the gracious environs of Christian family life.[138]

Sadly, that is not a particularly popular perspective these days. Serious reading, classical content, and familial superintendence are simply not in vogue. They represent archaisms—long since left in the dust of time by the newfangled gadgetry of industrial contemporaneity and progressive modernity.

Take reading for instance:

Long before the bane of television invaded our every waking moment, C. S. Lewis commented that while most people in modern industrial cultures are at least marginally *able* to read, they just *don't*. In his wise and wonderful book *An Experiment in Criticism* he said:

The majority, though they are sometimes frequent readers, do not set much store by reading. They turn to it as a last resource. They abandon it with alacrity as soon as any alternative pastime turns up. It is kept for railway journeys, illnesses, odd moments of enforced solitude, or for the process called *reading oneself to sleep.* They sometimes combine it with desultory conversation; often, with listening to the radio. But literary people are always looking for leisure and silence in which to read and do so with their whole attention. When they are denied such attentive and undisturbed reading even for a few days they feel impoverished.[139]

He goes further admitting that there is a profound puzzlement on the part of the mass of the citizenry over the tastes and habits of the literate:

It is pretty clear that the majority, if they spoke without passion and were fully articulate, would not accuse us of liking the wrong books, but of making such a fuss about any books at all. We treat as a main ingredient in our well-being something which to them is marginal. Hence to say simply that they like one thing and we another is to leave out nearly the whole of the facts.[140]

All this is not to imply any hint of moral turpitude on the part of modern bohemianism, rather it is to recognize the simple reality of the gaping chasm that exists between those who read and those who don't, between the popular many and the peculiar few. It is to recognize that education demands the latter while maintaining steadfast incompatibility with the former.

And there's the rub. We want to *have* our cake and *eat* it too—a prospect as improbable as an Elvis sighting, a Beatles reunion, or a good piece of legislation coming out of Washington.

The problem with serious reading is part and parcel with virtually all the other problems of modernity—serious reading is often laborious work requiring unflinching discipline, and if there is anything that we moderns have an aversion to, it is disciplined work. In this odd to-whom-it-may-concern, instant-everything day of microwavable meals, prefab buildings, drive-through windows, no-wait credit approvals, and predigested formula-entertainment, we tend to want to reduce everything to the level of the least common denominator and the fastest turnaround—which seems to be getting lower and lower and faster and faster with every passing day.

Even the church has fallen prey to this "spirit of the times." If we really had our druthers we wouldn't want worship to be too terribly demanding. We wouldn't want doctrine that challenges our pet notions. We really only want music that we're comfortable with. We only want preaching that reassures us, that reinforces our peculiar preferences, that affords us a sense of serenity—and all in record time. We want *quick* change; *cheap* grace; inspirational platitudes; bumper sticker theology; *easy* faith. We want *Christianity Lite.* We want the *Nice News*, not necessarily the *Good News.*

For the same reasons, when we read we'd really prefer literary junk food. The predigested factoids of *USA Today* are much easier to swallow than Cotton Mather's *Magnalia Christi Americana.* Face it, John Grisham, Danielle Steele, and Tom Clancy are easier to digest than William Shakespeare, John Milton, and G. K. Chesterton. Reading is a discipline—and all discipline is difficult. But then, that is the way it is with anything worthwhile.

In his remarkable book entitled *The Moral Sense*, James Q. Wilson drives home that point with great clarity. He says "the best things in life" invariably "cost us something."[141] We must sacrifice to attain them, to achieve them, to keep them, even to enjoy them.

That is one of the most important lessons we can learn in life. It is the message that we know we ought to instill in our children: patience, commitment, diligence, constancy, and discipline will ultimately pay off if we are willing to defer gratification long enough for the seeds we have sown to sprout and bear fruit.

A flippant, shallow, and imprecise approach to anything—be it sports or academics or the trades or business or marriage—is ultimately self-defeating. It is not likely to satisfy any appetite—at least not for long.

Now, you may be thinking to yourself, "Gee, this is all rather obvious, isn't it? Serious reading as an essential element of educational excellence? Of course."

But in fact, all evidence points to the fact that such a notion is anything but obvious. Just look at the agenda items on any proposal for educational reform—secular or Christian, day-schooling or home-schooling. You'll find recommendations on interactive media, computer software technology enhancements, comprehensive correlative curricula, outcome-based objectives, trade affinity matrices, life skills development, and turn-key textual exercises.[142] But nothing—or next to nothing—about Chaucer, Mandeville, Coleridge, Cervantes, Melville, Hawthorne, Longfellow, Wordsworth, Dickens, Twain, and Warren.

The brilliant men and women who wove the fabric of Western civilization knew nothing of correlative curricula or programmed outcomes or software enhancements—but they were *educated*. And they were educated in a way that we can only dream of today despite all our nifty gadgets, gimmicks, and bright ideas. They were steeped in Augustine, Dante, Plutarch, and Vasari. They were conversant in the ideas of Seneca, Ptolemy, Virgil, and Aristophanes. The notions of Athanasius, Chrysostom, Anselm, Bonaventure, Aquinas, Machiavelli, Abelard, and Wycliffe informed their thinking and shaped their world view. They thus were able to preserve and then to pass on to their progeny a heritage of real substance.

They read—widely and seriously.

Like serious reading, classical methodologies have also fallen into disfavor with us moderns. They have been relegated to the place of museum reliquary.

Supposing that they know better, educational service providers and textbook publishers at the behest of the National Education Association have dispensed with the centuries-long experience of the West and reduced the educational process to a feeble series of failed social experiments. Thus, not only is an awareness of the classics—in history, literature, art, music, philosophy, economics, and applied sciences—utterly lost to today's students, even the awareness of that lost awareness is lost to them.

The incomparable Dorothy Sayers has thus argued:

> Somehow, our whole approach to teaching and learning has gone awry. Do you sometimes have an uneasy suspicion that the product of modern educational methods is less good than he or she might be at disentangling fact from opinion and the proven from the plausible? Although we often succeed in teaching our pupils *subjects*, we fail lamentably on the whole in teaching them how to think. They learn everything except the art of learning.[143]

The now carelessly discarded traditional medieval *Trivium* on the other hand—emphasizing the basic classical scholastic categories of grammar, logic, and rhetoric—equipped generations of students with the tools for a lifetime of learning: a working knowledge of the timetables of history, a background understanding of the great literary classics, a structural competency in Greek- and

Latin-based grammars, a familiarity with the sweep of art, music, and ideas, a grasp of research and writing skills, a world view comprehension for math and science basics, a principle approach to current events, and an emphasis on a Christian life paradigm. Isn't that worth a second look?

The methodologies of this kind of classical learning adhere to the time-honored principles of creative visual, auditory, and tactile learning: an emphasis on structural memorization, an exposure to the best of Christendom's cultural ethos, a wide array of focused reading, an opportunity for disciplined presentations, an experience with basic academic skills, and a catechizing for orthopraxy as well as orthodoxy.

It was the modern abandonment of these classical standards that provoked G. K. Chesterton to remark:

> The great intellectual tradition that comes down to us from the past was never interrupted or lost through such trifles as the sack of Rome, the triumph of Attila, or all the barbarian invasions of the Dark Ages. It was lost after the introduction of printing, the discovery of America, the coming of the marvels of technology, the establishment of universal education, and all the enlightenment of the modern world. It was there, if anywhere, that there was lost or impatiently snapped the long thin delicate thread that had descended from distant antiquity; the thread of that unusual human hobby: the habit of thinking.[144]

Serious reading and classical methodologies: such things hardly represent the kind of whiz-bang razzle-dazzle doohickeries that excite the educational reformers, social planners, and political prognosticators of the National Education Association these days.

Intensive reading? It sounds all well and good, but kids today, they just won't do it, they explain. Latin? It's a dead language, they argue. Thucidides, Bacon, Marlborough, and Toynbee? Why, they're just subjective narratives, they complain. Josephus, Eusebius, Methodius, Foxe, and Cabasilas? Long forgotten, unimportant details, they carp. Aristotle, Pythagoras, Copernicus, Newton, Pascal, and Bonarotti? They can just as easily be surveyed and anthologized, they patronizingly remonstrate. Scott, Thackery, Meredith, Carlyle, Burke, Johnson, and Belloc? How do they prepare a student for the job market? they query.

Oh no, these old throwbacks will never do in this sophisticated environment we now find ourselves in, they harangue. We must be realistic.

But then, who *asked* them anyway? They're the ones who got us into the current designer disaster of cultural disintegration and disarray—where all the profundities of a civilized moral order have become so much rubbish.

If we are to buck the trend of malignant modernity, if we are going to recover our Christian heritage in education, if we are going to be able to pass that heritage on to our children and grandchildren, if we are to undertake the initiation of unending beginnings, then we must return to the dumb certainties of Christendom's experience.

And that experience begins at home.

The Hope at Home

The church, the state, and the family are all providentially entrusted with certain institutional and governmental stewardships. God has established each of them as trustees over specific jurisdictions within a society.

Interestingly, of these three interrelated divine institutions, the family is actually the most basic government. It is not the most important, mind you, just the most basic. The fact is, the church and the state cannot succeed if the family fails to fulfill its tasks. In that regard, the family is the primary agent of stability in a society.

It is the family that is charged with the primary responsibility of infusing children with the principles of God's Word (Deuteronomy 6:6–7), of upbraiding, restraining, and rebuking unrighteous behavior and thus instilling the principles of self-government in the next generation (Proverbs 23:13–14). It is the family that is charged with the responsibility of balancing liberty with justice, freedom with responsibility, and license with restriction (Deuteronomy 11:18–21), of being culture's basic building block, transferring the precepts and parameters of our civilization from one age to the next (Psalm 78:1–7).

The family is central to virtually every societal endeavor under God: from education (Proverbs 22:6) to charity (1 Timothy 5:8); from economics (Deuteronomy 21:17) to individual discipleship (Ephesians 6:1–4); from the care of the aged (1 Timothy 5:3–13) to the subduing of the earth (Genesis 1:26–28).

In that light, an interesting scenario is played out in the life of the prophet Samuel to which Christians in our day had best pay heed. It seems that the failure of his family life actually brought the entire nation of Israel to the brink of disaster (1 Samuel 8:1–3).

Samuel was a very busy and important man. As the judge over Israel, he was forced to make the long and arduous "circuit from Bethel to Gilgal to Mizpah" (1 Samuel 7:16). His duties left little time for the diligent oversight of his home life in Ramah. He apparently attempted to instruct, disciple, and rule his family from afar, but the result of that course, so sincerely undertaken, was nothing short of disastrous.

Samuel's neglect of family affairs was exposed in his sons after he had appointed them to be judges succeeding him. They failed to walk in a manner befitting righteousness. They turned aside after dishonest gain and accepted bribes and perverted justice. From their judicial seat in Beersheba, they exasperated the people and defiled judgment (1 Samuel 8:3).

Though they apparently had had the benefit of the best resources, the finest opportunities, and the greatest legacies, they were deprived of direct parental superintendence and thus did not take up their heritage.

This personal tragedy, as awful as it was for Samuel, was just the beginning of his woes. The citizens of Israel, seeing the wickedness of Samuel's family and the senescence of Samuel himself, began to panic. They feared for the future. They began to fret over the stability of their cultural and political order (1 Samuel 8:4–5).

The elders of the nation came together in Samuel's home to confront the aged leader with their fears and to present him with their demands. Samuel's family failure had undermined national security. Thus, they wanted him to take immediate political action in order to preserve life and liberty in the land. They wanted a king—like all the other nations around them.

Samuel was grieved. His entire life's work had been committed to preserving the standard of biblical law and justice in Israel. Now it seemed that his undersighted neglect at home was nullifying his every accomplishment (1 Samuel 8:6–18). In desperation, Samuel attempted to warn the people of the inherent dangers of their scheme. There would be taxation. There would be conscription.

There would be coercion. There would be tyranny. It was inevitable—when the biblical heritage of goodness, truth, and justice are not nurtured in the home, and thus passed from one generation to the next, disaster results.

But the people could not be swayed (1 Samuel 8:19–20). The prospect of tyranny looked much better to the people than an eroding social and cultural order under Samuel's debauched family. A king and his tyranny then, it would be (1 Samuel 8:21–22).

Throughout his life, Samuel worked hard, traversing the countryside, weaving a social and political fabric impervious to the rending attacks of lawlessness, godlessness, and truthlessness. He poured himself into this work to the exclusion of all else—only to discover late in life that his sorely neglected family was unraveling every stitch.

When the family fails to undertake its task, the entire social and political system suffers. No experts are sufficient, no brilliant ideas or clever methodologies are adequate, no nifty new programs from the National Education Association or any other group or organization can suffice in the face of a supplanted family.

Done With

In the center of Bedford, England, there stands a statue of John Bunyan. It marks the place where that great Puritan spent years in a prison cell for the offense of teaching and preaching without proper state certification. At the foot of the statue is a little bronze plaque. On it are engraved the words of the prosecutor—the Lord Judge Magistrate of Bedford—spoken at Bunyan's sentencing in 1673. The judge said,

> At last we are done with this tinker and his cause. Never more will he plague us: for his name, locked away as surely as he, shall be forgotten, as surely as he. Done we are, and all eternity with him.[145]

Of course, it is not Bunyan that is forgotten. Instead, it is the Lord Judge Magistrate of Bedford that remains unnamed and unremembered. Bunyan foiled the plans of the powers and the principalities by holding fast to that which was once and for all delivered unto the saints: a world and life view rooted in the grace of a

Sovereign God and the unbending disciplines of a Christian walk.

Today the educational sophisticates of the National Education Association would wish upon us the judge's intention for Bunyan: done with; locked away; forgotten. But we, like he, can foil that intent if we too will hold fast to the dumb certainties of truth delivered unto us in the form of a long and glorious heritage.

SIEGE ALERT

NATIONAL EDUCATION ASSOCIATION

Here is what the new social engineers at the National Education Association have in mind for you and your children in the weeks and months ahead:

- They want a complete monopoly over American schools. They want to determine what is taught, how it is taught, and by whom. They want to make education a "closed shop." In order to accomplish such lofty aims, they know that their number one priority right now has to be the implementation of a national educational standardization program that would put ultimate control of curriculum, administration, and accreditation of all schools—public, private, and parochial—in their hands.

- The plan will focus on teacher competency and certification—meaning that the union will attempt to eliminate all private day-school teachers and home-schoolers who do not have state educational training, licensing, and certification.

- The plan will also emphasize the "social skills" or "values" content of the curriculum rather than the traditional "academic skills." This "outcome-based" approach exploiting the social disarray in most government schools—with its attendant environment of violence and rebellion—will then be used to reshape the "feelings" and "attitudes" of children in a uniform effort to help them "fit in" with the National Education Association's utopian vision of the world.

- In addition, the union is looking to continue to flood the federal legislative docket with "reform" bills designed to tighten top-down accountability—in most cases reducing the authority and impact of local school boards, principals, and classroom teachers. Thus even the few isolated cases where good schools remain or where high academic standards are still emphasized are in danger of being swallowed up by an increasingly intrusive nationalization plan.

- Watch particularly for new "family-life," "life-skills," "decision-making," or "social values" curricula requirements—noble-sounding subjects that all too often are the means educators use to reshape the thought and morals children are taught at home.

FOUR

THE SKY IS FALLING

GREENPEACE

Men freely believe what they wish.[1]

—Julius Caesar

I can believe anything provided it is incredible.[2]

—Oscar Wilde

Ian Matten is not allowed to go in his backyard anymore.

It has been designated by the national Fish and Wildlife Service as a prime habitat for the endangered Kanab Ambersnail. Utilizing the sweeping powers authorized by new environmental legislation, federal agents barricaded his two-acre lot and posted it as a "protected preserve."

Matten's children can no longer play on their swing set. The family can no longer have backyard barbecues. They are not allowed to sit on their patio. They can't even mow their lawn in the summer.

"This is a horrible mess," the amazed homeowner said. "We used to have a beautiful backyard. My wife and I are both avid gardeners. Neighbors used to love to come and take walks around our pond—it was landscaped with wild flowers and herbs. We've even had several friends request to have their weddings here. It was idyllic."[3]

But no more.

The area is overgrown with weeds. The once carefully pruned fruit trees are dying. The pond is covered in algae. And the flowers and herbs have practically been choked out all together. Property values in the once stable middle-class neighborhood have plummeted. "I feel like a prisoner here," Matten complained. "The government has taken our dream home and turned it into a slum. And I can't do a thing about it."[4]

It all began innocently enough. A college student from down the block was canvassing the neighborhood for the environmental group Greenpeace. He was explaining to residents the grave dangers that the Kanab Ambersnail faced in that part of the country. When he stopped at the Matten household, Ian happened to offhandedly mention the fact that he had a number of the snails living in his pond.

Big mistake.

A week later, federal officers invaded the Matten backyard—taking samples of the soil and water, driving vehicles across the well-manicured lawn, and tramping through well-tended gardens. Two days later, they were back. The area was fenced off and Matten was told that people were no longer allowed within a hundred yards of the pond. In addition, he was told that the geese that sometimes swam in the pond must be kept out of the area—lest they eat the snails. He faced a $50,000 fine for each snail eaten.

Matten began to look for a lawyer.

Meanwhile, it seems that the local Greenpeace group decided to ensure enforcement of the new restrictions. When the migratory geese flew in and began to swim in the pond—as they had each of the fourteen winters the Mattens had lived there—members of the group notified the authorities that Matten was not properly protecting the preserve.

The federal officers ordered the state Department of Wildlife Services to send someone out to the pond to shoot the geese, remove their stomachs, and bring the contents to a local lab so that they could determine how many snails had been eaten.

Matten caught wind of the scheme and called the local news media. When a state trooper and wildlife agent arrived, they were met with a whole slew of cameras and noisy inquisitive reporters. The officers wisely decided not to kill the geese with so many witnesses gawking at their every move. Instead they trapped three of the hapless birds, induced vomiting, and returned to their offices with specimen bags brimming. Lab analysis revealed no contraband snails, but Matten received a terse warning nevertheless.

Greenpeace has since chalked up the whole episode as one more "important victory for the environment."[5]

A spokesman for the Justice Department defended the state's handling of the incident saying, "Think of the kind of attack we'd face from the hard-core environmentalist groups like Greenpeace if we didn't prosecute these cases. There would be outrage."[6]

Ian Matten is outraged. But apparently his outrage doesn't count.

Myth Statements

The preeminent English historian of our day, Paul Johnson, has sagely observed:

> The environmental movement began as an ecological panic, and thus from the beginning lacked the sense of balance and proportion that is associated with a movement of reform.[7]

The movement's lack of balance and proportion is manifest in a myriad of ways, shapes, and forms—as the frighteningly strident pronouncements of its leading spokesmen makes all too obvious.

The movement is, for example, adamantly anti-human:

- Paul Watson, a Greenpeace staffer bemoaning the existence of the human race, has asserted, "We, the human species, have become a viral epidemic to the earth."[8]

- Dave Foreman, founder of the Greenpeace splinter group, Earth First, likewise makes no bones about his scorn for humanity: "The human race could go extinct and I for one would not shed any tears."[9]

- Ingrid Newkirk of People for the Ethical Treatment of Animals, another Greenpeace splinter group, argued that: "We humans have grown like a cancer. We're the biggest blight on the face of the earth."[10]

- James Lovelock, a respected NASA consultant, best-selling author, and longtime hero to Greenpeace legions has said: "Humans on earth behave in some ways like a pathogenic micro-organism, or like the cells of a tumor or neoplasm. We have grown in numbers and in disturbance to Gaia, to the point where our presence is perceptibly disabling, like a disease."[11]

- Lynn Marguilis, a distinguished biology professor at the University of Massachusetts, popular environmentalist author, and enthusiastic direct action team-leader has said: "Those who speak only for the special interests of human beings fail to see how interdependent life on earth really is. We cannot view evolutionary history in a balanced manner if we think of it only as a four-billion-year preparation for *higher* organisms, like humans. Most of life's history has been microbial. We are recombinations of the metabolic processes of bacteria that appeared during the accumulation of atmospheric oxygen some 2,000 million years ago. Like rats, we have done well separating ourselves from and exploiting other forms of life, but our delusions will not last."[12]

- David M. Graber, a Park Service employee describing his affections toward his fellow man has said: "I know social scientists who remind me that people are a part of nature, but it isn't true. Somewhere along the line—at about a billion years ago, maybe half that—we quit the contract and became a cancer. We have become a plague upon ourselves and upon the earth."[13]

- Merton Lambert, spokesman for the Rockefeller Foundation, explaining corporate philanthropy's lucrative support for groups like Greenpeace has said: "The world has cancer—and that cancer is man."[14]

- But perhaps the most stunning indictment of environmentalism's animosity to mankind is David Foreman's assertion that: "We see AIDS not as a problem, but as a necessary solution."[15]

Besides its antipathy to mankind in general, radical environmentalism is at enmity with the progress of civilization as well:

- Rene Dubos: the premier back-to-nature enthusiast described the environmental impetus to *go all the way* back-to-nature: "For the Greeks, it is Prometheus, stealer of fire, who is chained to the rock. Nemesis in the shape of shrieking, destroying harpies follows the steps of the overmighty. In the Bible, it is the proud who are put down from their seats; the exalted are those of humble spirit. At the very beginnings of the scientific age, in the Faustian legend, it is the man of science who sells his soul to secure all knowledge and power. . . . It is a primordial truth: science is the source of evil."[16]

- According to Ted Turner, the cable TV mogul: "Chain saws are more destructive than the atom bomb."[17]

- In a similar vein, Al Gore has said: "We know that the automobile's cumulative impact on the environment is posing a mortal threat to the security of every nation that is more deadly than that of any military enemy that we are again likely to confront."[18]
- Merlin Stone, the famed feminist-theologian, likewise has said: "Industrial civilization is acne on the face of Gaia."[19]
- In 1962, Margaret Mead, the eminent anthropologist, explained why Western civilization had little chance of surviving another thirty years: "Not war, but a plethora of man-made things . . . is threatening to strangle us, suffocate us, bury us, in the debris and by-products of our technologically inventive and irresponsible age."[20]
- Once again: David Foreman, the foremost advocate of eco-terrorism, was presuppositionally in sync with the rest of the movement when he issued his now-infamous challenge: "Are you terminally ill with a wasting disease? Don't go out with a whimper; go out with a bang! Undertake an eco-kamikaze mission. The possibilities for terminally ill eco-warriors are limitless. Dams from the Columbia and the Colorado to the Connecticut are crying to be blown to smithereens, as are industrial polluters, the headquarters of oil-spilling corporations, fur warehouses, paper mills. . . . To those feeling suicidal, this may be the answer to your dreams. . . . Don't jump off a bridge, blow up a bridge. Who says you can't take it with you?"[21]

But it gets worse. Besides opposing the advancement of civilization and harboring misanthropic maledictions, the movement has also proven itself to be a consistent foe of civil and social liberties:

- Audubon Society President Peter A. A. Berle—who is lauded as an environmental "moderate" compared to the radical minions of Greenpeace, has stated: "We reject the idea of property rights because everybody has property rights and one's property rights affect another person's."[22]
- According to Paul Ehrlich, the famed population-bomber, nothing short of a totalitarian system is sufficient to save the planet: "The proportions of the current crisis call for . . . apparently brutal and heartless decisions . . . the creation of a powerful

government agency which would . . . research and impose such solutions as compulsory birth regulation, the addition of temporary sterilants to water supplies or staple food, financial rewards and penalties designed to discourage reproduction, luxury taxes . . . placed on layettes, cribs, diapers, diaper services."[23]

- Barry Commoner, the famed biologist from Washington University agrees, saying: "The problems that we face are so profound that they call for . . . not a new legislative base, but a new constitutional one."[24]

- Again, according to Commoner: "Our society will have to repudiate its present productive system and substitute a system organized in harmony with the global ecosystem using the second law of thermodynamics as its guiding standard . . . it may be time to view the faults of the U.S. capitalist economic system from the vantage point of a socialist alternative."[25]

- According to Greenpeace enthusiast Murray Bookchin: "Modern society is literally undoing the work of organic evolution. If this process continues unabated, the earth may be reduced to a level of biotic simplicity where humanity . . . will no longer be able to sustain itself as a viable human species. . . . This centuries-long tendency finds its most exacerbating development in modern capitalism: a social order that is orchestrated entirely by . . . the plundering of the human spirit by the marketplace."[26]

- Similarly, Al Gore has said: "I believe the central organizing principle in the post-Cold War world must become the task of saving the earth's environment. We are close to the time when all of humankind will envision a global agenda that encompasses a kind of Global Marshall Plan, if you will, to address the causes of poverty and suffering and environmental destruction all over the earth."[27]

Not surprisingly, the environmental movement adds a distinctly anti-Christian bias to its toxic dose of anti-human, anti-progress, and anti-liberty presuppositions:

- According to Lewis Mumford, a much-quoted Greenpeace philosopher: "Nothing less than a profound re-orientation of our vaunted technological way of life will save this planet from becoming a lifeless desert. . . . For its effective salvation mankind will need to undergo something like a spontaneous religious conversion."[28]

- Revealing the New Age orientation of the movement, Edmund Schofield has said: "From birth the individual is coerced by institutions and custom into false relationships . . . thus . . . liberate yourself from illusion . . . abolish the shams . . . explore your own higher latitudes. Get right with yourself and all these things will be added unto you; get right with yourself and perforce you will develop at last the proper relationship with others, with Nature, and so with divinity."[29]

- Al Gore in his best-selling tome *Earth in Balance* detailed how the mono-cultural imperialism of Christianity set back the cause of Gaia's New Age harmonics: "The spiritual sense of our place in nature predates Native American cultures. . . . The prevailing ideology of belief in . . . much of the world was based on the worship of a single earth Goddess who was the fount of all life and who radiated harmony with all living things. . . . A Goddess religion was ubiquitous throughout much of the world until the antecedents of today's religions—most of which still have a distinctly masculine orientation—swept out of India and the Near East, almost obliterating belief in the Goddess. The last vestige of Goddess worship was eliminated by Christianity."[30]

- Another influential environmental New Age devotee, William Anderson, has said: "Our remote ancestors said to their Mother Earth: *We are yours.* Modern humanity has said to Nature: *You are mine.* The Green Man has returned as the living face of the whole earth so that through his mouth we may say to the universe: *We are one* . . . The Green Man is the mouthpiece of the inspiration of the Divine Imagination. In art and science we express and explore the works of the Divine Imagination through our own imaginations. . . . The Green Man is the threshold of the imagination between our outer natures and our deepest selves and, as he is so closely connected with the Great Goddess, we must also ask, *What is the Great Goddess in ourselves?* In ancient teachings she is Sophia or Wisdom, the wisdom we so sorely need and which the Green Man is waiting to transmit to us."[31]

- According to Lynn White, another of the widely read and highly regarded Greenpeace philosophical mentors: "More science and more technology are not going to get us out of the present eco-logic crisis until we find a new religion, or rethink our old one. The beatniks, who are the basic revolutionaries of our time, show a sound instinct in their affinity for Zen Buddhism."[32]

• And David Brower, the environmentalist godfather, has said: "I would like to go back to the time of Moses and say, *Go back up and bring back down the other tablet.* The Ten Commandments just talk about how we're supposed to treat each other. There's not a bloody word about how we're supposed to treat the earth. It must be up there still. Go find that tablet. . . . I've come to the conclusion that the religions—every one of them—have been de-vised by us to rationalize how things work or things we can't un-derstand."[33]

• Even Prince Charles, the future king of England and temporal head of the Anglican church has said: "One of the underlying factors which may have contributed to the desire to dominate Nature rather than live in harmony with it on a sustainable ba-sis is to be found in the book of Genesis. . . . By contrast, the Koran specifically mentions that the natural world is loaned from God."[34]

Myth Begotten

When the ecology craze first hit college campuses during the heyday of the '60s radicalism, bizarre New Age mysticism, and flower-power activism, there were already a large number of envi-ronmental groups working to preserve wilderness areas, protect endangered species, and clean up industrial pollution. Conserva-tionism had been an important aspect of American policy-making for a century—ever since the pioneering work of John Muir and Theodore Roosevelt gave us our national park system. But like so much of the rest of the "establishment," these organizations were simply not radical enough for the left-wing zealotry of the hippies, yippies, and war protesters.

And so they started their own groups.

Within just a few short years the first of those radical groups had so grown in both size and stature that it actually dwarfed all its precursors in the movement. Its founders, who embraced direct ac-tion and civil disobedience as a cure for environmental ills from the start, chose a paradoxically tranquil name: the Don't Make a Wave Committee.

It was formed in 1969 by a small cadre of Quaker peace activists, including a number of expatriate Americans who had moved their families to western Canada to avoid the Vietnam draft. The group's initial aim was quite limited: to protest the testing of nuclear weapons by the U.S. at Amchitka Island in the Aleutian Islands off the coast of Alaska. Along with the threat of radioactive leakage into the environment, the group feared that a nuclear detonation of between 50 and 250 times the size of that which leveled Hiroshima would set off earthquakes, which in turn would cause tidal waves all around the Pacific Rim. They hatched the idea of sailing to Amchitka during a test in hopes of getting close enough to a detonation to stop it. Just before its first voyage, the group renamed its rented boat the *Greenpeace.*

The direct-action idea was based on the old Quaker principle of protest-pacifism called "public witness."[35] According to Quaker tradition this tactic was "a sort of passive resistance that involves going to the scene of an objectionable activity and registering opposition to it simply by one's presence there."[36]

The group's first attempt to bear "public witness" was canceled in September of 1971, when the U.S. postponed its nuclear test. The protesters were more than 1,000 miles from the island when another test took place during their second attempt. Just by making the effort, however, they somehow created a sensation in the media. Despite never even coming close to meeting its objectives, the group claimed a stupendous victory.

Shortly afterward, the group renamed itself after their *ersatz* protest vessel and set out on its next mission: to halt above-ground nuclear testing by the French in the Mururoa Atoll, near Tahiti in the South Pacific. It was the start of a long, violent, and ultimately tragic relationship between the growing environmental group and the hubris-filled French government. In 1972 the French Navy rammed a Greenpeace vessel owned and commanded by former Canadian badminton champion David McTaggart. The next year French sailors savagely beat McTaggart and another protester as they attempted to halt a bomb test.

Again, though the group failed to meet its objectives, it cashed in on a deluge of sympathetic media exposure. Almost overnight,

Greenpeace was thrust into the forefront of the burgeoning ecology movement.

Having earned its radical anti-nuclear credentials the group next focused on broader environmental issues: particularly the protection of endangered species. It determined that it was up to them to "save the whales." So in 1973 it sponsored a concert to raise money for "whale awareness education" in Japan and the Soviet Union—the world's largest consumers of whale products and the bane of environmental concern for the giant ocean cetaceans. Eighteen months later Greenpeace activists set sail on a historic journey to confront the Japanese and Soviet whaling fleets in the North Pacific. The crew brought home dramatic photographs and film of activists steering outboard motor-driven rubber dinghies, called "Zodiacs," between harpoon-firing ships and the whales. Soon, evening news audiences were watching in astonishment as the protesters zoomed and swooshed in front of the menacing harpoons, taunting the whalers and "guarding" the whales. The protesters became media icons and were canonized by environmentalists the world over.

Flushed with their photo-op successes, the daring radicals launched similar protests wherever they could find evidence of whaling. Even the harpoons shot over their heads were not enough to deter the activists in a later battle against Icelandic whalers. Then, and again off the coast of Spain, it took a full military mobilization to stop their acrobatic shenanigans.

Whales and Greenpeace quickly became synonymous. At considerable personal risk, activists compiled a portfolio of illegal whaling incidents by a handful of unscrupulous operators—thus concocting a blanket condemnation against the venerable whaling industry. As a result, in 1986 the International Whaling Commission approved a comprehensive ban on commercial whaling. Greenpeace had its first genuine victory. And what a victory it was.

Myth Directed

Without question, the group's approach to environmental issues, from nuclear tests to whales to the seals it fought to protect, was unlike anything the mainstream of the movement had ever seen. According to environmental journalist Rik Scarce, the group's protesters were *"active* activists."[37] They not only sailed, climbed, and hiked to the sources of environmental problems, he said, but they became daredevils who constantly created new tactics:

> They bolted shut effluent pipes leading from chemical plants and skydived off power plant smokestacks to publicize pollution. These media stunts held no hope of stopping a particular environmental ill in and of themselves, much less of ending all poisoning of the water or air. Rather, hugging seals and hanging banners were screams for attention, the cries of individuals, and of a rapidly growing organization, that disdained the suit-and-tie conventionality of the mainstream.[38]

The Earth was dying, they thought, and it was time to do something drastic and dramatic to stop it. It was time to use the graphic power of television. It was time to captivate and anger the public. It was time to tug heart-strings, pressure governments, and overwhelm industry. It was time to launch a full-scale social revolution to save the environment.

As is so often the case with radical reform movements, the Greenpeace revolution quickly became institutionalized and bureaucratized. The tendency of all social engineers to concentrate the apparatus of change in the hands of a few "enlightened experts" leads inevitably to an authoritarian centralization of power and a uniformitarian dogmatization of organization.

Before long the radical activists had transformed Greenpeace from a rag-tag collection of hippies and drop-outs into a vast and sprawling mega-corporation. With McTaggart at its helm, the organization rapidly grew and then went international, eventually establishing more than fifty offices from London to East Lansing and from Seattle to Sydney. According to Scarce:

> Because the web of life includes all ecosystems and all individuals, Greenpeace reasoned that only by making its presence felt throughout the world could it bring pressure to bear on environmental problems. In so doing it assumed the role of the most ambitious environmental protection organization in the world.[39]

Among its many international operations, Greenpeace has established beach patrols in French Guyana to protect sea turtle eggs; protested Japan's use of drift nets, forty mile-long curtains of death that indiscriminately kill sea life; hung the international sign for "radiation" from U.S. and Soviet warships; and investigated the flow of toxic wastes from developed nations to the Third World.[40]

Perhaps the most ambitious of its far-flung exploits is the establishment of a scientific research base in Antarctica. Several governments have similar stations there, but Greenpeace is the only nongovernmental presence on the barren icy continent. Not surprisingly, the group has attracted media attention by revealing the "extensive and literal trashing" of the region by the very researchers who are there studying it.[41] Claiming that "huge waste dumps" litter the landscape, and "untreated sewage is dumped directly into the ocean, threatening fragile ecosystems" the organization has proposed that all of Antarctica be declared a "World Peace Park."[42]

According to Scarce, Greenpeace classifies its campaigns into four general categories—nuclear, toxics, ocean ecology, and atmosphere and energy:

> Its nuclear program may be best known for its 1989 run-ins with the U.S. Navy. Greenpeace repeatedly attempted to halt testing of the submarine-launched Trident II nuclear missile by sailing a ship into an area off-limits to all vessels. Shades of McTaggart's first run-in with the French, the U.S. Navy rammed the boat to make clear its displeasure at the interference. Its toxics programs are likely the most grassroots based of Greenpeace's efforts—they have helped organize numerous neighborhoods fight garbage and hazardous waste incinerators, which spew toxic pollutants and threaten human health. In its ocean ecology work, Greenpeace lists as among its accomplishments the 1987 ban on the disposal of plastics at sea by the U.S. and the federal government's requirements that shrimp fishing boats, which kill thousands of endangered sea turtles each year, be equipped with "Turtle Excluder Devices," reverse trap doors that let as many as ninety percent of the turtles caught in shrimp nests escape. And as part of their atmosphere and energy campaign, Greenpeacers have occupied metal boxes placed across train tracks leading into several Du Pont factories to protest that company's continued manufacture of ozone layer-depleting chlorofluorocarbons.[43]

And what does it hope to accomplish? What is the ultimate aim of these direct action environmental protests? The answer is nothing less than a total transformation of our society—from the lifestyles we lead and the products we consume to the laws that govern our families and define our communities, from the control we maintain over our private possessions and the influence we have over our children to the freedoms we exercise and the liberties we enjoy.[44]

Myth Conception

Greenpeace has grown from a cadre of a few committed activists into the largest environmental organization in the world. It is a multi-national conglomerate headquartered in Amsterdam with gross revenues of about $125 million.[45] Its nearly one thousand full-time employees work out of offices in twenty-three nations; in the U.S. alone there are thirty-five field offices. Greenpeace membership in the U.S. numbers just over three million, about half of the world total.[46]

In 1987 Greenpeace spun off a lobbying arm called "Greenpeace Action." It takes its case door-to-door throughout the nation and sponsors three lobbyists who buttonhole members of Congress and haunt the halls of the bureaucracies. But Greenpeace's approach is different than most advocacy groups, insists Executive Director Peter Bahouth:

> We are multi-media in the sense that we are not a lobbying group or a research organization or a litigation house or a grass-roots activist movement, but we are a bit of all of those things. So, when we formulate campaigns or projects, we combine all those things in what we do.[47]

Bahouth says that the people developing and carrying out Greenpeace actions are committed to the cause and are not swayed by the traditional political enticements of money, power, or prestige.[48]

What really sets Greenpeace apart from other mainstream environmental organizations is its direct action and civil disobedience approach to ecological issues. The idea "is to go to the site of the problem," says Bahouth, "whether it's the middle of the Pacific Ocean . . . or in Washington . . . or in Antarctica, we want to expose things that certain institutions want to keep secret. And we work internationally to break down boundaries that have been set up by institutions or political powers that limit our ability to relate to the environment."[49]

Bahouth feels that "people are motivated to support us because they are moved to action. We are rewarded because we create a bond with the public by virtue of doing something that they do not necessarily have the ability to do themselves."[50] In its campaigns Greenpeace takes what he calls an "ecological approach" to environmentalism. "We see that things are connected to one another very directly." Thus he says:

> If you're going to talk about declining salmon stocks, for example, you can talk about the fact that salmon are being caught in drift nets, about deforestation, which is ruining the streams, agricultural runoff, toxic pollution into streams and rivers, and in some cases you could probably talk about oil production and spills. We see that as an organization you can paint yourself into a corner if you do not draw these things together and act on them.[51]

Capitalizing on this broad-brush approach, Greenpeace has been able to generate hundreds of letters or telephone calls on such seemingly remote and esoteric issues as drift-net fishing or agrarian crop dusting. And as a result, it has been able to radically reshape the environmental agenda of policy makers.

But of course, there is a paradoxical cost to that kind of clout: Spending hundreds of thousands of dollars each year on junk mail, even if the paper is recycled, is hardly the kind of image that an environmental organization likes to cultivate—especially when it is certain that 90 percent or more of the "direct mail solicitations" will go unanswered or even unopened, dumped into the trash, and taken to a landfill. That, many say, is "wildly hypocritical,"[52] perhaps even "ecological heresy."[53]

But then hypocrisy or heresy has never stopped modern social engineers before. It is not likely to stop them now.

Myth Behavior

Perhaps the most impressive accomplishment of the massive Greenpeace organization during its nearly twenty-five-year history has been its ability to sell itself not only as a mainstream environmental organization, but as a "global green conscience" whose self-described nonviolent activities are somehow beyond reproach.[54]

Thus when Denmark's state-owned television network broadcast an hour-long documentary claiming that the organization has funnelled millions of dollars into private bank accounts, bribed politicians, and encouraged ecological terrorism, even many opponents of radical environmentalism were surprised.[55]

The program, entitled *The Crack in the Rainbow*, documented the existence of private international bank accounts, containing more than $20 million skimmed from public contributions to campaigns such as *Save the Rainforests, Save the Ozone Layer,* and *Save the Whales.* The secret accounts were for "shell holding companies" or "fake fronts" accessible only to top Greenpeace leaders.[56] The program also sent shock waves into the political world of the European economic community, the United States, and Canada revealing that Greenpeace used a $5 million slush-fund to buy the International Whaling Commission votes necessary to ban commercial whaling.[57]

The program also alleged close ties between Greenpeace and several radical splinter groups including Earth First—a self-styled "eco-terrorist" group responsible for industrial sabotage and vandalism.[58] In addition it exposed how Greenpeace "faked footage" of animal torture to encourage a ban on seal-skin, perpetrated fundraising fraud, and used tax-exempt dollars to support various partisan political campaigns—including those of Jimmy Carter, Al Gore, and Bill Clinton.[59]

Supported by the testimony of former Greenpeace chief accountant, Frans Kotte, the allegations were collaborated by several journalistic investigations—including in *Forbes* magazine, the *Washington Times*, the *Calgary Herald*, the *21st-Century Technology Report*, the *British Columbia Report*, and *The Economist*.[60]

According to Canadian journalist Brian Kieran, the program revealed what many had known for quite some time: Greenpeace activists are little more than "garden variety thugs." Patrick Moore, one of the organization's co-founders—now alienated from the group—went so far as to say, "There is no question Greenpeace has moved from spreading disinformation to spreading hate."[61]

Even if the program's allegations prove to be slightly exaggerated, there is substantial evidence that Moore's indictment is not exaggerated in the least. All you have to do is read what Greenpeace leaders have to say to see that.

Myth Information

Leaving aside its philosophical and financial scandals, the most glaring problem with radical environmentalism is not just *what* it wants to do but *how* it intends to do it. No one can legitimately object to protecting the environment, exercising wise stewardship over resources, or preserving wilderness recreational areas. But to falsely manufacture crises—especially when we are thereby diverted from genuine needs—is inexcusable.

According to Larry Abraham and Franklin Sanders in their remarkable book *The Greening*, environmentalists are masters of just such deceit.[62] Why? So that they are able to "justify their sweeping social and cultural reforms."[63] In other words, they actually invent "ecological disasters" *ex nihilo* in order to bias their political position.

Stephen Schneider, an environmental catastrophist, admitted as much, saying:

> We have to offer up scary scenarios, make simplified, dramatic statements, and make little mention of any doubts we may have. This double ethical bind we frequently find ourselves in cannot be solved by any formula. Each of us has to decide what the right balance is between being effective and being honest.[64]

That odd "double ethical bind" is evident in almost all of the movement's hot-button issues—thus highlighting the vast difference between Christian conservationism and modern environmentalism.

Global warming, for instance, is often held up by environmental activists as the ultimate ecological nightmare. Aaron Wildavsky, a political scientist for the University of California at Berkeley, states:

> Global warming is the mother of environmental scares. In the scope of its consequences for life on planet Earth and the immense size of its remedies, global warming dwarfs all the environmental and safety scares of all time put together.[65]

Al Gore concurred, saying,

> We should begin with the debate over global warming, because while it is only one of several strategic threats, it has become a powerful symbol of the larger crisis and a focus for the public de-

bate about whether there is really a crisis after all.[66]

But the actual scientific evidence concerning global warming belies such wild-eyed environmental rhetoric on the subject:

• The commonly held belief that most scientists believe in global warming is false. There is no scientific consensus on the subject. Environmentalists in the media and politics who claim that such a consensus exists are simply not telling the truth. And they know it.[67]

• The empirical evidence for global warming is quite incomplete. In fact, in some regions of the world—such as North America—temperatures appear to be dropping not rising. Meanwhile the average global temperatures are neither rising nor falling a significant amount.[68]

• Most of the global warming scare is based on computer-generated models of the earth's climate. These models cannot even explain our present temperatures, let alone be trusted to predict future temperatures. These models are only as accurate as the information fed into the computers.[69]

• Interestingly, many of the people now screaming of the threat of global warming were the same ones who were warning us about the dangers of global cooling in the early seventies.[70]

According to environmentalists, global warming is primarily caused by the release of carbon dioxide into the atmosphere through industrial pollution. The carbon dioxide supposedly traps heat in the earth's atmosphere, causing rising world temperatures—thus, the legendary "greenhouse effect." The only way to combat the greenhouse effect, they say, is to eliminate the artificial production of carbon dioxide.

According to environmentalist author David Day:

> Although greenhouses work on a slightly different principle, the idea is that increased carbon dioxide brought about by air pollution and forest destruction will result in a heating-up of the earth's temperatures. This shift in the overall world temperature would result in a dramatic shift in climates. It is believed that North America's grain belt, for instance, would suffer from permanent drought and become a vast desert. Other major agricultural areas would become either too wet or too dry for crops. The most dramatic effect, however, would probably be the melting of sections of the polar ice-caps. It is thought that the release of these huge reservoirs of frozen water would result in the planet's sea-lev-

els rising by ten to twenty feet. This would cause massive flooding that would put the cities and lands of nearly half the world's population under water.[71]

Again, the scientific reality seems to be a far cry from the rhetoric:

- The commonly held belief that most scientists believe in the greenhouse effect is simply unfounded. There is no scientific consensus whatsoever on the subject.[72]
- Even if there was global warming, it would not necessarily be caused by greenhouse gases. The global climate has changed considerably over the millennia without any interference from human civilization.[73]
- Though there have been some hot years in the eighties, there has been a slight cooling trend over North America during the past forty years—when greenhouse gases were supposedly increasing. If those gases are responsible for global warming, why did the temperature go down?[74]
- Carbon dioxide is produced in massive quantities by nature itself. Relative to the carbon dioxide from natural sources, the amount of artificially created carbon dioxide is actually quite minute.[75]

Next to global warming, the ozone layer is environmentalism's highest priority. In theory, ozone in the stratosphere protects the earth from the sun's ultraviolet radiation. If the ozone layer is weakened—and environmentalists insist that it has indeed been weakened—then thousands of people around the globe will be more susceptible to various kinds of skin cancer, wildlife and agriculture will also be adversely affected, and eventually the earth will become uninhabitable. Andrew Rees, an environmental activist and author, argues:

> A one-percent reduction in ozone could cause an estimated fifteen thousand new skin cancers annually in the U.S. and seventy thousand worldwide. Already, cases of malignant melanoma have doubled in the last ten years and are increasing by five percent a year globally. In 1989, 27,300 Americans suffered from skin cancer, six thousand died from it. In Australia, the incidence of skin cancer is up five hundred percent in the last twenty years. Cataracts and other eye diseases will increase, and genetic mutations are possible.[76]

Once again, the scientific evidence is far from conclusive:

- Ozone depletion is supposed to increase the amount of ultraviolet radiation reaching the earth. But the amount of measurable ultraviolet radiation is currently going down, not up.[77]
- In fact, there is no proof of ozone depletion at all. The amount of ozone in any given area varies naturally, but the overall amount appears to have remained quite stable for the past several decades.[78]
- Ozone is not a nonrenewable resource—it is continually being produced by the interaction of ultraviolet radiation and oxygen.[79]
- The much vaunted "hole" in the ozone layer over Antarctica is actually only an atmospheric thinning which always develops during the six-month polar winter in which there is no sunlight. Once the South Pole faces the sun the ozone thinning is replenished. Just like always.[80]

According to the current environmental common wisdom, ozone depletion is caused by chlorofluorocarbons—artificially produced chemical substances. These chemicals supposedly release chlorine into the upper atmosphere creating near catastrophic conditions. According to Al Gore, "Like an acid, it burns a hole in the earth's protective ozone shield above Antarctica and depletes the ozone layer worldwide."[81] As a result, chlorofluorocarbons have been virtually banned worldwide beginning around the turn of the century.

Amazingly there is a dearth of evidence to support this kind of drastic decision.

- There is absolutely no proof that chlorofluorocarbons are depleting the atmosphere—because there is absolutely no proof that anything is depleting the atmosphere.[82]
- Chlorofluorocarbons are heavier than air—so heavy that they can be poured from one container into another. There is no reason to believe therefore that the chemicals are able to travel into the upper atmosphere to destroy ozone.[83]
- The chlorine from chlorofluorocarbons is only an infinitesimal fraction of the chlorine that is released into the atmosphere from natural sources such as sea water and volcanoes. So even if all chlorofluorocarbons released chlorine into the stratosphere, they would not significantly increase the natural chlorine content of the atmosphere. While the estimated amount of chlorine

from chlorofluorocarbons is less than 7,500 tons annually, the estimated amount from other sources is over 649,000,000 tons.[84]

- The so-called "ozone hole" over Antarctica could not have been caused by chlorofluorocarbons because the seasonal thinning of the ozone was noted in 1956—before the use of the chemicals was widespread.[85]

- Chlorofluorocarbons are an important component of refrigeration and air conditioning. Replacing the chemicals will not only cost billions and billions of dollars, it will cost human lives. In fact most experts believe that raising the cost of refrigerated food will probably cost 20 to 40 million deaths in third-world countries.[86]

Acid rain—allegedly caused by sulfur oxide emissions from factories that burn fossil fuels—is another environmental ill described in almost apocalyptic terms by environmental extremists. In 1989, David Day wrote:

> Acid rain is one of the most volatile environmental issues of the decade. It is an issue that has had wide public exposure and the destruction it has caused in the nations of the northern hemisphere is extraordinary. Yet both the governments of Britain and America—despite the howls of outrage from their neighbors— claim that the case against acid rain has not been proved to them. There is a logic to this sort of defiant stupidity. It stems from the fact that both America and Britain are massive exporters of airborne pollution and acid rain, and both wish to avoid the financial burden of cleaning up their industries. They would rather allow their industries to continue to profit by dumping their pollution on their neighbors.[87]

The fact is, the published data on the acid rain problem is inconclusive at best, contradictory at worst. The commonly accepted idea that acidic water evaporates from polluted lakes and streams and then, through the process of precipitation, rains down death and destruction on unsuspecting neighbors is not entirely warranted by the facts:

- Acid rain is not destroying forests, as the environmentalists claim. Rather, global forestation is increasing faster than at any other time in human history.[88]

- Lakes and rivers that have increased in acidity have done so in large part because of a lack of soil alkalinity.[89]

- That kind of soil acidity is all too often caused by decaying vegetation. Because forests are not being harvested as much as they once were, more trees are dying and decaying. Before the timber industry began harvesting in these regions, the lakes and streams were naturally acidic.[90]
- The reduction of sulfur dioxide emissions to federally mandated and environmentally safe levels during the last decade has not reduced the acidity imbalance at all—in fact, as sanctions have been imposed, the problems have only worsened.[91]
- There may be a much simpler solution: The acid content of lakes and streams could be reduced simply by putting lime into the water. This would cost a tiny fraction of the amount it would cost to reduce sulfur dioxide emissions.[92]

The real boogeyman of modern environmentalism is the automobile. According to Ezra J. Mishan, an environmental economist:

> The private automobile is, surely, one of the greatest, if not *the* greatest, disasters that ever befell the human race. For sheer irresistible destructive power, no other creation of man—save perhaps the airliner can compete with it. . . . One could go on, for the extent of its destructive power is awesome to contemplate.[93]

Again, the hyperbolic panic of environmentalism plays fast and free with the facts:

- The worst of the many ills of automobiles is that they supposedly contribute to the greenhouse effect and ozone depletion—but in fact there is no greenhouse effect or ozone depletion.[94]
- Automobiles supposedly cause smog, but smog is also caused by vegetation. Most of the cities that have reduced auto emissions have found smog continues to be a problem. Evidence indicates that smog levels were the same before the invention of the automobile as they are today.[95]
- Despite the common notion that smog is unhealthy and even deadly, there is no statistical health differential between Los Angeles—a high-smog city—and other urban areas in the West.[96]
- Before the widespread use of automobiles, cities had much worse pollution and health problems as a result of horse manure. A car is actually cleaner than a horse.[97]
- Although there is no doubt that some automobiles contribute to poor air quality, high-polluting cars can be spotted by modern

technology and made to reduce the toxic content of their emissions without inconveniencing all drivers.[98]

- On average, both air and water are getting cleaner, not dirtier in America and other developed nations.[99]

According to environmentalists we are running out of . . . well, almost everything. Andrew Rees writes, "The developed world is squandering the world's resources at colossal rates, as though they were in infinite supply."[100] We are told horror stories of endangered species, rain forest depletion, and nonrenewable resources.

Thus Andrew Rees asserts that "the West—the twenty percent who consume eighty percent of resources and energy—must reduce its enormous appetite and recycle all it can."[101] This is to be accomplished by tax-manipulation and new legislation prohibiting what the government deems to be wasteful and mandating what the government deems to be efficient.

In fact, the situation warrants no such panic:

- The number of endangered species is falling dramatically, and wilderness wild lands are increasing just as dramatically.[102]
- Almost all reserves of nonrenewable resources are becoming less scarce, not more scarce—including fossil fuels. This is because resources do not simply exist for the taking but must be discovered. As we get better at locating natural resources our reserves go up.[103]
- Environmentalists constantly tell us that our natural resource reserves will only last a few decades. But reserves have never provided for more than a few decades—even a hundred years ago. When known reserves begin to dwindle, then people have an incentive to find new reserves.[104]
- Environmentalists constantly call for government-imposed rationing and conservation schemes. But in a free market, scarce resources cost more than plentiful resources, forcing people to conserve the scarce resources and find substitutes.[105]
- If recycling is profitable, then people will be paid for their trash. If recycling is not profitable, then it will waste resources. By forcing people to recycle, environmentalists are hurting the environment.[106]

According to Larry Abraham and Franklin Sanders, "Error may not be eternal, but certain errors are awfully persistent."[107] But for those of us who are genuinely concerned about the preservation of the creation, what alternative do we have? Where can we look for guiding principles that will enable us to care for the earth?

The answer is deceptively simple.

For the Beauty of the Earth

Who owns the earth?

Clearly, the answer to that question is God owns it. But God chose in the beginning of time to turn over the stewardship of the earth to humanity. He told Adam and Eve, "Rule over the fish of the sea and the birds of the air and over every living creature that moves on the ground" (Genesis 1:28, NIV).

Not only would humanity rule over everything in the world, but we would also have the right to make use of everything the world produces: "I give you every seed-bearing plant on the face of the whole earth and every tree that has fruit with seed in it. They will be yours for food" (Genesis 1:29, NIV).

God started Adam off in the Garden of Eden and told him to dress it and to guard it. To *dress* means to beautify and enhance. Adam was to take hold of the beautiful garden and work with it, bringing it from glory to glory while guarding it against enemies.

The Garden of Eden was the center of the world, so whatever Adam did in the Garden would ultimately determine the condition of the entire world. Consummate responsibility rested with him.

But these happy circumstances were suddenly and drastically transformed by the Fall. Though the world was made inherently good, it was changed for the worse in a tragic moment of universal import (Romans 8:19–22).

God allowed Satan to come into the Garden in the form of a serpent, and there he challenged Eve to disobey God. Although Adam was standing right next to her, he kept silent and failed to guide her (Genesis 3:6). Instead, when she ate of the forbidden fruit he joined her.

By listening to Satan's word, Adam made himself subject to Satan. Originally Adam had been God's steward; now he had given the world over to Satan and become his steward. Satan had acquired a kind of legal claim to the entire world—which explains why the devil tried to tempt Jesus with all the kingdoms of the earth, saying, "I will give you all their authority and splendor, for it has been given to me, and I can give it to anyone I want to" (Luke 4:6, NIV).

Thankfully, God had no intention of letting Satan run His world. He announced right away to Adam and Eve that the "Seed of the woman" would one day crush the serpent's head and restore the fallen world (Genesis 3:15). God assured Adam and Eve and their descendants that anyone who trusts Him would be redemptively protected from Satan's domination of the earth.

Throughout His dealings with fallen man, God reiterated that eternal promise in terms of temporal restoration.

When Israel came out of Egypt and God established the Mosaic covenant with them, for example, He instituted a new law of Jubilee (Leviticus 25). One of the major purposes of this Jubilee was to show people that someday the world would revert to its true owners—God's covenant children—and that Satan and his legions are actually only temporary squatters. It thus beautifully illustrated the spiritual truth of the Gospel in what were essentially environmental terms.

God told the people when they came into the Promised Land to mark off plots of land for every family, which would be held permanently and never sold. If an Israelite leased his property to someone else, God's law stated that in the fiftieth year it would revert to its original owner.

A man might lose his land for any number of reasons: A man might prefer to dwell in a town and lease his land to a friend; he might become poor and be forced to lease out part or even all of his land. But one thing was certain: God would restore the land to its original owners.

The point was obvious: Because of sin and judgment, men have a tendency to lose their grip on the world, and just as Adam turned the whole world over to Satan because of his sin, so sinners tend to lose their land to others.

The book of Joshua describes how the land of Israel was originally divided among tribes, clans, and families. Because of sin, however, the people kept losing their land. The book of Judges shows how the people would fall into sin and foreigners would take over. Although God gave the land back to them repeatedly, the people's sins finally brought them into captivity in Assyria and Babylon.

Nevertheless, the prophet Isaiah predicted the people would return from exile. It would be like a Jubilee, he said, in which the land would revert to its true owners:

> The Spirit of the Sovereign Lord is on me, because the Lord has anointed me to preach good news to the poor. He has sent me to bind up the brokenhearted, to proclaim freedom for the captives and release for the prisoners, to proclaim the year of the Lord's favor. (Isaiah 61:1–2, NIV)

As momentous as it was, however, the return of Israel to the Promised Land after the Exile was only a picture of a greater Jubilee to come.

In inaugurating His earthly ministry, Jesus announced the ultimate year of Jubilee (Luke 4:17–21). Satan had previously offered the world to Jesus if only He would worship him, but Jesus refused. Instead, He said a new world was coming, one to which Satan never had any claim. The new world of the kingdom of God would begin with a Jubilee, and the world would thereafter revert to its true owners. In the synagogue of Nazareth, Jesus read from the scroll of Isaiah, and then said, "Today this scripture is fulfilled in your hearing" (Luke 4:21). He was announcing that the Jubilee had arrived; the world was going to be taken from Satan and given to a New Adam; and the true owners, the saints, would possess the Kingdom.

According to the original Jubilary legislation, the beginning of the Jubilee was to be ceremonially demonstrated: "Then have the trumpet sounded everywhere on the tenth day of the seventh month; on the Day of Atonement sound the trumpet throughout your land" (Leviticus 25:9). Just so, it was the Atonement wrought by Jesus Christ at Golgotha that ushered in the ultimate Jubilee. On the Day of Atonement, the death of the innocent sacrifices banished sin and Satan (Leviticus 16). Thus at Calvary the death of the innocent Lamb of God stripped Satan of his claims to the world.

The Jubilee's arrival was thus announced on the Day of Pentecost, when the Holy Spirit came upon Peter and he proclaimed the Good News (Acts 2). As in the prophecies of Isaiah and Luke, the Spirit comes in power to proclaim the redemptive release of the new Jubilee.

After Pentecost, we find the Jerusalem believers "had everything in common. Selling their possessions and goods they gave to anyone as he had need" (Acts 2:44–45). This is not a picture of "Christian communism." Rather, the first believers were affirming the year of Jubilee had arrived, the earth had reverted to God, and He was now parceling it out to the new owners. Thus, they sold what they had and gave it to the church and started new lives in the kingdom.

But if the ultimate Jubilee was ushered in on the Day of Pentecost, why does the earth still "groan and travail" waiting for the redemption of God? (Romans 8:22). The fact is, though the kingdom has come in essence, it will not be until the advent of the New Heavens and New Earth that we shall experience the completion of Christ's great Jubilee. On that day the earth will belong fully to the Lord and His people, and Satan and his demons will entirely be dispossessed.

Nevertheless, the basic principle of the Jubilee still stands. Wherever the kingdom goes, the physical world God made in the beginning starts to revert to its true owners. This happens peacefully but it happens all the same. The Jubilee reminds us the world is God's gift to His children. We must therefore be careful to nurture and preserve it.

The humanist culture around us, however, presents two possible alternatives to this Christian view of stewardship. While appearing to be opposites, they are actually identical.

The first asserts that we must live for today. "Eat, drink, and be merry," we are tempted, "for tomorrow we may die." We are told the world is ours to do with as we please. Thus we can consume, pollute, and exploit—all that matters is our present personal peace and affluence. Of course, such an egoistically hedonistic world view can only make life on earth miserable, as everything we need to live is profligately wasted for the pleasure of the moment with no thought for the future. By idolizing self, we will turn our world into a polluted wasteland.

The second alternative asserts that we must preserve nature and make certain that the world remains unaffected by us. We are told the world is a fragile system we are duty-bound to preserve and protect for its own sake—as if it had intrinsic value. Such an altruistically environmental world view can likewise only make our life on earth miserable as every resource we need to live by is declared off-limits for the sake of that jealous goddess, "Mother Earth." Our idolization of nature will also turn our world into a howling wilderness.

Thus, in the end, the philosophy of Greenpeace is no less destructive than the polluters and exploiters it so adamantly opposes. Yet it presses forward with its sweeping agenda for social change nonetheless. To the detriment of us all.

As the great reformer of Scotland John Knox once said:

> Those who pose as the saviors of mankind are all too often more dangerous than the very ills they purport to remedy. There are often simple answers to the woes of society, just no easy ones. Messiah always offer both. Beware of such men.[108]

SIEGE ALERT

GREENPEACE

Here is what the new social engineers at Greenpeace have in mind for you and your children in the weeks and months ahead:

* They want to "save" the planet. And in order to do that, they want to control industrial policy, property rights, and even "multi-cultural sensitivity and awareness" in America's schools. In order to accomplish such lofty aims, they know that their number one priority right now has to be an all-out media blitz to make the average citizen "think green." Through every avenue of pop-culture—television, movies, radio, music, comics, and magazines—the plan is to inundate Americans with the idea that the current "ecological crisis" must take precedence over all other concerns or needs.

* The plan would thus mobilize wide public support for a number of what otherwise would be very unpopular political and economic moves—including the complete coercive overhaul of the refrigeration, transportation, and heavy manufacturing industries.

* Public awareness programs, and special ecology units would become standard fare in all of America's schools—public and private—as well as in all government social or welfare services programs. The goal, of course, is not simply to get kids to conserve energy or recycle paper, plastic, and glass—commendable stewardship activities in and of themselves—but to change their vision of the world.

* In addition, the plan would reinforce the idea that individual families or the private sector simply cannot be trusted to act responsibly on their own in ecological matters—rather, the force of government coercion must be brought to bear in order to conform behaviors.

* Watch particularly for a radical redefinition of property rights in both the courts and the legislatures—measures designed to yield ultimate sovereignty of all inheritance, land, and development to the federal government.

FIVE

MISCARRIAGE OF JUSTICE

AMERICAN CIVIL LIBERTIES UNION

Some excel at promising in words the best things, but doing in deeds the opposite.[1]

—Aesop

Some talk in quarto volumes and act in pamphlets.[2]

—John Pym

"A man can't regret a right decision," Bishop Knox said. "And I made the right decision."[3]

Apparently that's not just his opinion. An overwhelming 97 percent of the residents of his community agree that Knox did indeed make the right decision—but that may not be enough to save his job.[4]

Knox, the principal of Wingfield High School in Jackson, Mississippi, was fired when he allowed a prayer to be broadcast over the intercom system one day following the regular morning announcements at the public school. No matter that the prayer was entirely nonsectarian. No matter that the prayer was student initiated. No matter that the prayer was approved by the student body—with a vote of 490 to 96. No matter that recent Supreme Court rulings have held that such prayers are fully within current constitutional parameters. No matter.

Saying that broadcasting the prayer was "coercion for those students who did not wish to have prayer in the school," the local affiliate of the American Civil Liberties Union persuaded the Jackson

School Board to discipline Knox and put an immediate halt to the "unwarranted and illicit behavior."[5]

Needless to say, the firing has caused a furor in this normally quiet, conservative southern town. The School Board came under immediate and intense fire. The local media was deluged with calls and letters of protest. Yellow ribbons appeared all over town—and all around the school grounds—supporting Knox. And students boycotted classes—risking suspension by the interim administration. Support has flooded in from other parts of the state—and even from the Governor's office.[6]

Jackson is a bustling city of warm Southern hospitality in the heart of Mississippi. Sometimes called the "Buckle of the Bible Belt," its skyline is dotted with steeples and its culture is heartily seasoned with grace. Though it is rich with Gothic Revival and Second Empire homes as well as several magnificent antebellum public buildings, the lively character of the city owes as much to the present as to the past. It has what local author Eudora Welty calls "a confident rootedness that gives genesis to a strong sense of family and community."[7]

According to Michael Lerenstein, an attorney from nearby Vicksburg, it is just that sense of family and community that has made the suspension of Knox so noxious to local parents, teachers, students, and community leaders. "This whole issue boils down to a small group of ideologues from the ACLU trying to impose their peculiar notions of separation of morality and public life on an entire community," he told me. "And they do this even though they have little or no support here. That is the kind of arrogant elitism that'll make a close-knit community really rise up and show its true colors." We stood at the crest of Le Fleur's Bluff on the Pearl River overlooking the Beaux Arts capital grounds and beyond, toward the crenelated clock tower in the center of downtown. He fixed a steely gaze of determination on me and said, "We don't need outsiders coming in here and telling us that our schools ought to conform to the standards of New York or Washington or Los Angeles or some other urban nightmare. Why don't they just leave us alone?"

Why don't they indeed?

For its part, the ACLU has staked its position on the moral high ground of the Constitution. "The Bill of Rights is not up for a popularity contest," says the local director Lynn Watkins.[8] But the supporters of Knox also base their argument on First Amendment principles. "The law says freedom *of* religion," asserts student Adam Watson, "not *from* religion."[9] Watkins claims that the ACLU is merely "championing the cause of liberty."[10] But Joe Bellamy, another student, counters that, "Our liberty is hardly served by high-powered lawyers threatening us with lawsuits, bureaucrats firing our principal, and reporters sermonizing about what we ought and ought not be allowed to say or think."[11]

"Any constitutional scholar would be hard pressed to say who is right and who is wrong in this case," says legal analyst Marvin Callum. "We essentially have an unresolvable clash of absolutes—it is one presupposition against another. This case will not be easily settled. The battle lines are drawn."

Saying that he had no intention of creating a legal bruhaha, Knox incredulously protested that the prayer was actually quite "innocuous, innocent, and inoffensive."[12] Indeed, it could hardly have been more discreet and still have remained a prayer. It simply said: "Almighty God, we ask that you bless our parents, teachers, and country throughout the day. In your name, we pray. Amen."[13]

That's it. Nothing more.

But even that insignificant of a demonstration of faith was too much for the ACLU to bear. It is, after all, an organization that has always left no good stone unturned in an effort to insure that no good turn goes unstoned.

Trial and Error

The American Civil Liberties Union advertises itself as an advocate of "truth, justice, and the American way."[14] It advertises itself as the "lone defender" against prejudice, tyranny, and brutality.[15]

Philosopher George Santayana has said, "Advertising is the modem substitute for argument; its function is to make the worse appear the better."[16] Certainly, that appears to be the case with the ACLU. What it advertises itself as and what it actually is are two entirely different things.

"Modern men and movements," Jean Paul Sartre often argued, "ought not be adjudged by what they say, but rather by what they do."[17] Similarly, Frederick Nietzsche asserted that, "If you wish to understand men and movements, do not merely ask what they say, but find out what they want." Although neither Sartre nor Nietzsche had sound philosophies, in this case, their cautious discretion is a point well taken. The fact is, what the ACLU *wants* and ultimately *does* utterly belie what it *says*.

That discrepancy then is the key to properly adjudging and understanding the organization.

The ACLU says, for instance, that it "has only one client: the Bill of Rights."[18] It advertises itself as doggedly impartial, caring only about the integrity of the Constitution itself.[19] But, the facts say otherwise.

The radical labor and social dissent movements have always been the ACLU's primary clients. In its very first annual report, the ACLU described itself as "a militant, central bureau in the labor movement for legal aid, defense strategy, information, and propaganda."[20] It went on to assert that along with the International Workers of the World and the Communist Party, it was the "center of resistance" for radical groups in America.[21] In its advertising flier it argued that, "The union of organized labor, the farmers, and the radical and liberal movements, is the most effective means . . . whereby rights can be secured and maintained. It is that union of forces that the American Civil Liberties Union serves."[22] Thirteen years later, the organization reaffirmed its commitment to the radical cause stating that, "The struggle between capital and labor is the most vital application of the principle of civil liberty."[23]

In 1976, Aryeh Neier, then the Executive Director of the ACLU, broadened the client base of the organization saying that it was "the legal branch of the women's movement."[24] In fact, as the years went by, the ACLU would identify with virtually every subversive dissent movement that appeared on the national scene: communists, anarchists, socialists, terrorists, homosexuals, lesbians, pornographers, Nazis, abortionists, and atheists.[25]

Even a cursory glance at the official *Policy Guide* of the ACLU demonstrates that it is far more interested in pursuing its ideological agenda than it is in defending the Constitution.

Indeed, it is a sobering lesson in contrasts:

- The ACLU supports the legalization of child pornography[26] while it opposes voluntary school prayer.[27]
- It supports legalization of drugs[28] while it opposes sobriety checkpoints.[29]

- It supports tax exemptions for Satanists[30] while it opposes tax exemptions for churches.[31]
- It supports legalization of prostitution[32] while it opposes religious displays in public.[33]
- It supports abortion on demand[34] while it opposes medical safety regulation and reporting.[35]
- It supports mandatory sex education[36] while it opposes parental consent laws.[37]
- It supports busing[38] while it opposes educational choice or home schooling.[39]
- It supports automatic entitled probation[40] while it opposes prison terms for criminal offenses.[41]
- It supports public demonstrations for Nazis and communists[42] while it opposes public demonstrations for direct action pro-lifers.[43]
- It supports legalization of polygamy[44] while it opposes teaching "monogamous, heterosexual intercourse within marriage" in the public schools.[45]

The militant bias of the ACLU is especially evident in the record of the organization in dealing with Christianity. When it comes to faith, the spokesmen, policy makers, and attorneys for the ACLU have made their position painfully clear: They're against it. No ifs, ands, or buts about it.

Although they have fought for the free speech and expression "rights" of pornographers, witches, abortionists, homosexuals, convicted criminals, child molesters, occultists, communists, lesbians, Nazis, illegal aliens, AIDS patients, and Satanists, they have resolutely attempted to deny those same privileges to Christians.[46] As a result, according to Richard and Susan Vigilante, they have effectively reduced "the place of religion in American life" and have restricted religious speech "in a way they would never allow other forms of speech to be restricted."[47]

Their discriminatory intolerance is a matter of record. In recent years, they have sought to

- Halt the singing of Christmas carols like "Silent Night" and "Away in a Manger" in public facilities;[48]
- Deny the tax-exempt status of all churches—yet maintaining it for themselves as well as for various occult groups;[49]
- Disallow prayer—not just in the public school classrooms, but

in locker rooms, sports arenas, graduation exercises, and legislative assemblies;[50]
- Terminate all military and prison chaplains;[51]
- Deny Christian school children access to publicly funded services;[52]
- Eliminate nativity scenes, crosses, and other Christian symbols from public property;[53]
- Repeal all blue law statutes;[54]
- Prohibit voluntary Bible reading in public schools—even during free time or after classes;[55]
- Remove the words *In God We Trust* from our coins;[56]
- Deny accreditation to science departments at Bible-believing Christian colleges and universities;[57]
- Prevent the posting of the Ten Commandments in classrooms;[58]
- Terminate all voucher programs and tuition tax credits;[59]
- Prohibit census questions about religious affiliation;[60]
- Purge the words *under God* from the Pledge of Allegiance.[61]

As Patrick Buchanan has all too obviously pointed out, "That is not a record of tolerance."[62]

Interestingly, the ACLU is led into this absurd contradiction of its purported purpose because it sees the Christian faith as "an almost irresistible persuasive force."[63] Gadfly liberal columnist Nat Hentoff has said that the ACLU seems to be "afraid of making religious speech first-class speech, the way all other speech is" because it really ascribes "extraordinary powers to religious speech."[64] In other words, the ACLU fears Christianity in a way that it fears nothing else.

Of course, its fear is cloaked in high-sounding Constitutional concerns—its bigotry is not overly blatant. It makes much ado over the principle of "separation of church and state."[65] It brandishes the idea of "the wall of separation" like a saber. And it fixates on the "establishment clause" of the First Amendment. According to Barry Lynn, once the ACLU's Legislative Director:

> There is clearly a distinction made between religious speech and activity and any other speech and activity. There is an establishment clause which limits and tempers only religious speech and activity. There is no establishment clause which in any way limits economic, cultural, historical, or philosophical expression. Thus, the state may embrace any economic, political, or philo-

sophical theory; it may not embrace or enhance any religious activity.[66]

Thus, according to the ACLU, the Christian faith is so powerful, so dangerous, and so intrusive that the founding fathers had to design the Constitution in order to protect us from it. Despite the fact that such a reading of history is convoluted at best, the ACLU has been very successful in pressing it upon our courts, schools, and communities all across the country. For all intents and purposes, says Russell Kirk, it has been able to "harass out of existence" public expressions of faith.[67]

Combined with its animosity for tradition, family integrity, and common moral values, its disdain for faith makes the ACLU a frightening threat to the fragile fabric of freedom in this culture. It is all too evident, as legal analyst Mark Campisano has argued, that the organization's policies, positions, and programs have "a pernicious underlying theme: hostility to the processes of constitutional democracy."[68] This appears, he says, "in three basic forms: first, in attempts to override democratic processes and replace them with judicial decrees, in ever larger spheres of public life; second, in attempts to expand individual rights without regard for countervailing public interests; and third, in attempts to prevent certain viewpoints from being heard in the public arena."[69]

It seems that the organization illustrates all too vividly James Madison's warning about the American Constitution when he wrote, "Liberty may well be endangered by the abuses of liberty as well as the abuses of power."[70]

The Long Arm of the Law

The ACLU is the world's oldest, largest, and most influential association of lawyers, political activists, and social reformers.[71] For more than seventy-five years it has claimed a single-minded devotion to protecting the Constitutional rights of every citizen in the United States through lobbying, legislation, and, most especially, litigation.[72]

It is organized as a carefully decentralized grass-roots network of fifty-one separately incorporated affiliates, over four hundred local chapters, and approximately five thousand volunteer lawyers from coast to coast.[73] The national office provides a number of crucial support services—coordinating national efforts, providing technical research, managing publicity and fund-raising programs, spearheading publishing efforts, focusing affiliate vision, maintaining a legislative and lobbying presence, developing long-range goals, launching special educational projects, and pooling resources for federal appellate cases—but by and large, each of the local chapters and affiliates is free to choose which civil liberties issues it will stress, which cases it will take to court, which political campaigns it will actively participate in, and which local legislation it will either support or oppose.[74] Each elects its own governing boards, hires its own staff, and develops its own budget.[75] Thus, even though all of the affiliates share common goals, common policy directives, and common resources, they are driven by the engines of local concern and the exigencies of local issues.[76]

Despite this carefully cultivated grass-roots profile, the organization remains supremely unpopular. Public opinion polls have consistently shown that the American Civil Liberties Union has a negative rating with the American populous ranging anywhere from fifty-six to eighty-three percent.[77] Though recent turns of political events have ensured the placement of its key leadership in strategic positions of influence throughout the federal bureaucracy, by its own accounting, the ACLU is "the most hated organization in America."[78]

Nevertheless, the organization has achieved a number of remarkable successes—more often than not, dramatically transforming the nature of America's legal and judicial system. With only 250,000 contributing members, seventy staff lawyers, and a budget of approximately fourteen million dollars, it has established more standing court precedents than any other entity outside the Justice Department, and it has appeared before the Supreme Court more often than anybody else except the government itself.[79]

Some of its landmark cases include:

- The Palmer Raids Case of 1920: The ACLU combated Attorney General Mitchell Palmer over the deportation of a number of resident aliens who had been convicted of violent labor disruptions or who had been proven to be actively involved in various communist subversive activities throughout the country.
- The Draft Amnesty Campaign of 1921: The ACLU launched a

nationwide drive to release draft objectors and convicted subversives following the First World War.

- The Patterson Strike Case of 1924: The ACLU defended a group of textile union members and other social activists—including the ACLU's own founder, Roger Baldwin—who launched a large-scale strike and illegally occupied private property.

- The Scopes Monkey Trial of 1925: The ACLU launched its "manipulated test case" strategy against the state of Tennessee's education standards, locating a small town biology teacher to act as a plaintiff and a showcase lawyer to focus national attention on the issue. Despite the fact that the ACLU and its high profile defender, Clarence Darrow, lost to the state's attorney William Jennings Bryan, the publicity proved to be invaluable.

- The Sacco and Vanzetti Case of 1927: The ACLU defended two notorious anarchists who had been charged with first-degree murder following a payroll robbery. With a long list of ties to the subversive socialist underground, Sacco and Vanzetti sealed the ACLU's reputation as a radical instrument of the Left for some time to come.

- The Gastonia Case of 1929: The ACLU defended seven striking workers who had been convicted of murdering a North Carolina police chief during a particularly violent confrontation. After declaring their anti-Christian and communist beliefs, the seven defendants jumped bail and fled to the Soviet Union.

- The Scottsboro Case of 1931: The ACLU and the communist-led International Labor Defense worked together to overturn the convictions of nine black men who had been found guilty of raping two white women on a freight train. Sentences for all nine were reduced or reversed.

- The *Ulysses* Case of 1933: The ACLU led the anti-censorship battle over a novel by Irish author James Joyce, which had been banned because of U.S. obscenity laws.

- Japanese Internment Case of 1942: The ACLU failed to respond at first but later was persuaded to take up the cause of Japanese-Americans who had been improperly detained in isolation camps just after the Pearl Harbor attack launched U.S. involvement in the Second World War.

- Hollywood Blacklisting Campaign of 1952: The ACLU led the

crusade against what it called "Red Baiting" by Congress in the entertainment industry.

- Smith Act Reversal of 1957: The ACLU supported the defense of fourteen men convicted of conspiracy to violently overthrow the government of the United States. Lawyers argued on First Amendment free-speech grounds.

- Nativity Scenes Ban of 1960: The ACLU launched several legal initiatives to prohibit Christmas decorations or the singing of carols in public schools or on public property.

- Regent's Prayer Case of 1962: In this case—one of several anti-prayer suits that the ACLU was involved in—lawyers argued that a prayer recited each day in the New York public schools constituted an unlawful "establishment of religion."

- The Tinker Case of 1969: The ACLU won the right of public school students to protest against the Vietnam War by wearing black arm bands.

- Doe v. Bolton of 1973: In this "manipulated test case," the ACLU led the legal fight in a case that—with the companion Roe v. Wade ruling—eventually overturned the restrictive abortion laws in all fifty states.

- The Watergate Hearings of 1974: The ACLU abandoned its facade of political neutrality by pursuing, in both the media and through legal channels, the impeachment of President Richard Nixon.

- Christmas Pageants Ban of 1976: The ACLU has long fought against any form of public demonstration of religious faith. In this case they brought suit in New Jersey in an effort to prohibit Christmas pageants in the public schools.

- The Skokie March of 1978: The ACLU shocked its liberal support by defending the right of American Nazis to march through a predominantly Jewish suburb of Chicago.

- Newark School Board Case of 1981: The ACLU took this case in an attempt to prohibit the Gideons from distributing Bibles to students in the public schools on the grounds that such programs constitute a violation of the "separation of church and state."

- Arkansas Creationism Case of 1982: Fifty-six years after it had argued against educational exclusionism in the Scopes Trial, the ACLU reversed itself, fighting against the right to teach various views of origins in public school classrooms.

- The Akron Case of 1983: The ACLU successfully fought to over-turn the right of localities to regulate the medical safety and the proper disclosure of abortion-related businesses.
- Civil Rights Restoration Act of 1984: The Washington office of the ACLU led the four-year-long legislative battle to overturn the Supreme Court's Grove City decision, thus requiring institutions receiving federal grants to extend privileged service access to homosexuals, abortionists, and drug abusers.
- Jager v. Douglas County of 1986: The ACLU was able to forbid religious invocations before high school football games. For the first time, the lawyers successfully used "endorsement" language instead of the traditional "establishment" language—the implication being that the government is not only forbidden to establish or institutionalize religion, it is even forbidden to endorse or condone it.
- The Bork Confirmation of 1987: Once again abandoning all pretense of political neutrality, the ACLU led the smear campaign designed to deny Judge Robert Bork confirmation to the Supreme Court.
- Equal Access Act of 1991: The ACLU was successful in making voluntary student prayer or Bible study meetings before or after school the one exception to the federal Equal Access Act of 1984. So, while students may gather in public schools to discuss Marxism, view Planned Parenthood films, play "Dungeons and Dragons," listen to heavy metal rock music, or hold gay activist club gatherings, they are not allowed to pray or read the Bible together.
- The Americans with Disabilities Act of 1991: The ACLU was able to convince a Republican White House to open its doors to homosexual activists and AIDS extremists—and then to sign into law the most comprehensive preferential policy pronouncements in our nation's history.
- The Gays in the Military Hearings of 1993: The ACLU took the lead in the fight to lift the historic ban on aberrant sexual proclivities in the American armed forces as well as the implementation of a liberal and preferential recruitment and promotion policy.

By any standard this long list of achievements is remarkable.

And, considering the fact that the ACLU no longer has to take many of its cases before the bench—its influence is so great that even a *threat* of a lawsuit is often enough to change policies, reshape legislation, and redirect priorities in case after case—those achievements are even more remarkable.[80]

Despite its unpopularity with average citizens, the legal influence of the organization has been quickly translated into political influence. In fact, the ACLU practically controls the legal functions of the vast federal bureaucracy and overwhelmingly dominates appointments to the courts:

- Ruth Bader Ginsburg, the most recent addition to the Supreme Court, formerly served as the ACLU's chief legal counsel.[81]
- Morton Halperin, the former director of the Washington, D.C. chapter of the ACLU, now serves as the number-two man at the Pentagon.[82]
- Ninety-two percent of the management-level appointments to the Justice Department during the Clinton administration have been drawn from the ranks of the organization's membership.[83]
- Eighty-eight percent of the Federal Court nominees have likewise come from the membership rolls.[84]

As Calvin Eldridge has said, "It is amazing that an organization as despised by the American people has come to so completely dominate American government. It is almost as if there has been a bloodless coup in Washington. The ACLU has taken over."[85]

True Confessions

The ACLU actually grew out of the vision and passion of a single man, Roger Baldwin.[86] He was a blue-blooded Boston Brahman, raised in an esteemed radical tradition. He was born in 1884 and thus came of age during a period of dramatic social upheaval and progressive change.

Following his graduation from Harvard, Baldwin spent a gentlemanly year in touring Europe. But the life of the idle rich—spending long, aimless hours gazing out at the Mediterranean from the marbled portico of an Italian palazzo or compulsive shopping in the exclusive shops of Paris, London, and Vienna—did not suit him well. Throughout his life he had an insatiable appetite for adventure. He was a restless man of action with little time for either rest or relationships. And so, upon his return to Boston, he sought out "mountains to climb, rivers to ford, and giants to kill."[87]

Through his family connections, he was offered a job in St. Louis managing a neighborhood settlement house and teaching sociology at Washington University—despite never having taken a course in social ethics.

Immediately after he arrived in the city, he launched into a blind flurry of activity. He became a faithful and devoted member of the Civic League—an old-line grassroots reform organization in the city. He helped to organize the famed St. Louis City Club—a luncheon group that was the focal point for political discussions—and brought a number of prominent suffragettes, socialists, anarchists, and communists to town to speak. He attended meetings of the IWW—the International Workers of the World—a violent labor movement with a marked Marxist flavor. He participated in local politics and helped reformulate St. Louis municipal government. And, of course, he also busied himself with his classes at the University and with the youngsters at the settlement house.

It was his work there at the settlement house that led him to invest more and more of his time in the juvenile court, and after a year, he was appointed chief probation officer. This was Baldwin's first introduction to the judicial system, and he quickly was consumed with its intricate details and seemingly unlimited possibilities. It soon became his chief passion.

At the time, the court was little more than a criminal bench. Not content with that, he marshaled his radical heritage and resources to pioneer the concept of *in loco parentis*—the court in the place of the parent—a concept that is still very much a part of our judicial system. Seeing his Progressive ideals implemented by the courts revolutionized Baldwin's thinking. It was the beginning of a growing conviction that perhaps society could one day be fundamentally altered without violent insurrection, utilizing the courts to bypass conservative families, communities, and democratically elected institutions. He would recall later in life that it was then that he was "converted" to "judicial supremacy."[88]

But all this was mere dabbling in radicalism compared to what would follow. In 1917 he received an invitation to move to New York to go to work for the American Union Against Militarism—the AUAM.

The AUAM was a pacifist lobbying group organized by Lillian Wald, Jane Addams, Paul Kellog, and other prominent liberals to counter the growing chorus of voices calling for American involvement in the First World War. Their strategy was calm and reasoned, based on their contacts and rapport with the Wilson Administration in Washington. But, their effort proved to be too little too late.

Baldwin left St. Louis on April 2. On April 6, America officially joined the Allies in the "war to end all wars," in the "war to make the world safe for democracy." By May 18, the Selective Service Act had been railroaded through Congress and signed into law.

Suddenly, the complexion of the AUAM's task had changed dramatically. At Baldwin's behest, and under his leadership, it turned its attention toward war resistance. Thus, the Bureau of Conscientious Objectors was founded on May 19, 1917. Set up in order to help draft dodgers develop practical strategies of resistance and to provide them with financial and legal support, the Bureau became the most active and the most visible branch of the AUAM.

Immediately, the Bureau caused a storm of controversy. The *New York Times* criticized it, saying that Baldwin, and others working with him, were "antagonizing the settled policies of the government, resisting the execution of its deliberately formed plans, and gaining for themselves immunity from the application of laws to which all other good citizens willingly submit."

In an attempt to quell the fears of the AUAM board and to duck some of the heat, Baldwin made a few superficial structural changes in the organization and renamed it the Civil Liberties Bureau. But the ruse didn't help. Since Baldwin refused to tone down his rhetoric and calm down his activity, the AUAM decided on October 1, 1917, to sever all ties with both him and the Bureau. So, once again the organization was renamed and reincorporated—this time as the National Civil Liberties Bureau.

But that was just the beginning of Baldwin's troubles. One of the first pieces of literature that he wrote for the new Bureau was declared "unmailable" by the Post Office because of its "radical and subversive views."[89] A short while later the Bureau's offices were raided by the FBI and its files confiscated. And if that wasn't enough, twelve days later Baldwin was called to register for the draft.

True to form, he decided to resist the draft, and he was promptly arrested and brought to trial. Before the bench, he unashamedly professed his commitment to anarchism, his association with the IWW, and his allegiance to socialistic reform. And though his forthrightness won for him the admiration of the judge, it did not clear him of his offense. He was sentenced to a year in the penitentiary. The radical anarchist leader Emma Goldman said then that he had "proved himself the most consistent" of all the reformers, and that she was "prouder of him" than of anyone else.

Upon his release, Baldwin set about trying to salvage what was left of his Civil Liberties Bureau. It had struggled along without him for more than a year and was virtually inoperative. On January 20, 1920, he moved it into new offices on West Thirteenth Street in New York—shared with the Communist Party's *New Masses* tabloid. He also reincorporated and renamed the fledgling group for the third and final time.

The new American Civil Liberties Union was to serve the various subversive and revolutionary labor movements to which Baldwin had dedicated his life. There was no pretense of objectivity. "The cause we now serve is labor," he wrote in a memo at the time. "We are frankly partisans of labor in the present struggle."[90]

The ACLU was not Baldwin's only contribution to radicalism, however. In 1920 he also launched the Mutual Aid Society to offer financial help to Leftist intellectuals, trade unionists, and the radical fringe. "He started the International Committee for Political Prisoners to provide counsel and support to anarchist and communist subversives who had been deported for their criminal activities. He helped to establish the American Fund for Public Service—with two million dollars donated by Charles Garland, a rich young radical from Boston—in order to pour vast sums of money into revolutionary causes. And finally, he developed close institutional ties with the Communist movement and the Socialist International.[91]

Baldwin had by this time moved fully into the orbit of Soviet admirers, and he earnestly desired to see a Bolshevik insurgency in America. He wrote that Lenin's totalitarian regime was "the greatest and most daring experiment yet undertaken to recreate society in terms of human values."[92] He went on to say that it was "a great laboratory of social experiment of incalculable value to the development of the world."[93]

In his book *Liberty Under the Soviets*, written after a blissful visit to Russia, Baldwin admitted that the government there had instituted "complete censorship of all means of communications and the complete suppression of any organized opposition to the dictatorship or its program."[94] He went on to state that "no civil liberty, as we understand it in the West, exists for the opponents of the regime."[95] Despite this, he lauded the Soviet state for the "far more significant freedom of workers," the "abolition of the privileged classes," the "revolution in education," and the "liberty won for anti-religion."[96]

How did this "champion" of civil liberties justify such seeming contradictions in his values? Very simply, he baptized the facts with his ideology:

> Such an attitude as I express toward the relation of economics to civil liberty may easily be construed as condoning in Russia repressions which I condemn in Capitalist countries. It is true that I feel differently about them, because they are unalike. Repressions in Western Democracies are violations of professed constitutional liberties, and I condemn them as such. Repressions in Soviet Russia are the weapons of struggle in a transition period to socialism.[97]

Like so many liberals, Baldwin had twenty-twenty vision in his right eye, but was blind in his left. In an article he wrote for *Soviet Russia Today*, he again utterly contradicted his professed concerns with civil liberties for the sake of ideology, saying, "When the power of the working class is once achieved, as it has been only in the Soviet Union, I am for maintaining it by any means whatever."[98] And again, "No champion of a socialist society could fail to see that some suppression was necessary to achieve it."[99]

To work in solidarity with his comrades, Baldwin joined scores of "United Front" organizations. Many years later, he would admit that they were essentially "recruiting centers" for the Communist Party where "lists could be taken, sympathizers spotted and enrolled, and funds could be siphoned off for Party purposes."[100] He said:

> I joined. I don't regret being a part of the Communist tactic which increased the effectiveness of a good cause. I knew what I was doing. I was not an innocent liberal. I wanted what the Communists wanted and I traveled the United Front road to get it.[101]

The work of the ACLU naturally reflected this Sovietization. Of the ACLU Board and National Committee members elected during the first 60 years of the organization, almost 80 percent had Communist affiliations. A full 90 percent of the cases that it defended involved Communists.[102] And as a result, it was stigmatized as a "Communist Front" organization itself.[103] It came under investigation of the House Committee on Un-American Activities.[104] And it was even isolated from the mainstream labor movement and the more moderate liberal reform organizations.[105]

Baldwin seemed entirely unconcerned with the controversy. In a letter to Emma Goldman he wrote, "I see so much to be said for the destruction of privilege based on wealth that I will stand for Russia against the rest of the world."[106]

His edenic allegiance was suddenly and dramatically tempered with a healthy dose of reality when Josef Stalin signed the infamous nonaggression pact with Adolf Hitler. Nevertheless, the radical leftist bent of the organization stayed intact—and remains to this day.

During the Second World War, Baldwin made a herculean effort to legitimize the work of civil liberties in the eyes of the establishment. He focused once again on the courts—as opposed to international politics—as the best and surest path to radical reform. Instead of subverting the moral order of the nation and its institutions openly through revolution, he draped his subterfuge in the rhetoric and aura of constitutionalism, liberty, and patriotism. He explained this new strategy in a letter to his communist friend Louis Lochner:

> We want to look like patriots in everything we do. We want to get a lot of flags, talk a great deal about the Constitution and what our forefathers wanted to make of this country and how that we are the fellows that really stand for the spirit of our institutions.[107]

This new moderated public relations image proved to be a very effective strategy. Of course, the fact that under Franklin Roosevelt the government was actively sponsoring a variety of Leftist causes didn't hurt either. By the end of the war, the ACLU was accepted into the mainstream. One of its members—Felix Frankfurter—was elevated to the Supreme Court, and another—Francis Biddle—became the U.S. Attorney General. Later, the Truman, Eisenhower,

Kennedy, Johnson, Carter, Bush, and Clinton administrations would literally be filled with high-level ACLU members and supporters.[108]

In short order, the ACLU and its founder were lionized and tenured in the hallowed halls of the American Establishment. In one of his final actions as President in 1981, Jimmy Carter awarded Baldwin the Medal of Freedom—the nation's highest civilian honor.

"We learn from experience," George Bernard Shaw said, "that men never learn anything from experience."[109]

Order in the Court

G. K. Chesterton once quipped, "A liberal may be defined approximately as a man who, if he could, by waving his hand in a dark room, stop the mouths of all the deceivers of mankind forever, would not wave his hand. And a liberal organization is any society of liberals intent on holding back the benevolent waves of others."[110]

By that standard the ACLU is the very epitome of liberalism; it is the quintessential liberal organization.

Though it halfheartedly protests that it is "neither liberal nor conservative," but rather "an objective public interest organization devoted exclusively to protecting the basic civil liberties of all Americans," the facts belie the pose.[111] The ACLU seems to have co-opted the entire save-the-starving-third-world-co-dependent-lesbian-whales agenda of contemporary liberalism for itself. Indeed, as Reed Irvine has asserted, "ACLU is a four-letter word meaning liberal."[112]

Liberalism has actually been the unswerving heart and soul of the ACLU from its earliest days. John Haynes Holmes, one of the organization's original board members, confessed that the organization was only "using the civil liberties issue," and that its real interest was "the cause of radicalism."[113] He went so far as to say that the ACLU was "manipulating" cases "as a means toward certain ends; namely, the advancement of labor and the revolution." Roger Baldwin said, "Civil liberties, like democracy, are useful only as tools for social change."

Conservative scholar William Donohue has argued that, "Social reform, in a liberal direction, is the *sine qua non* of the ACLU. Its record, far from showing a momentary wavering from impartiality, is replete with attempts to reform American society according to the wisdom of liberalism."[114] Similarly, Mark Campisano, former Supreme Court clerk for Justice William Brennan, has asserted, "An accounting of the ACLU's case load suggests that the organization is an ideological chameleon—that beneath the protective coloration of civil liberties, the ACLU is pursuing a very different agenda—a very liberal agenda."[115]

Thus, the apparent inconsistency of the ACLU—its failure to defend religious liberties, for instance—is actually a fierce consistency. It is a forthright adherence to its liberal-first principles. The civil liberties that the ACLU constantly bleats about are clearly less "rights" to be protected than "weapons" to be wielded for the cause of liberalism.

Roger Baldwin freely admitted the partisan nature of his agenda saying:

> I am for socialism, disarmament, and ultimately for abolishing the state itself as an instrument of violence and compulsion. I seek social ownership of property, the abolition of the propertied class, and sole control by those who produce wealth. Communism is the goal. It all sums up into one single purpose—the abolition of dog-eat-dog under which we live.[116]

This attitude has marked the ACLU, to one degree or another, throughout its long history, so that William Donohue could accurately argue that:

> Social reform, in a liberal direction, is the *sine qua non* of the ACLU. Its record, far from showing a momentary wavering from impartiality, is replete with attempts to reform American society according to the wisdom of liberalism. The truth of the matter is that the ACLU has always been a highly politicized organization.[117]

In recent years, the ACLU has revealed its blatant partisanship time after time: It vehemently opposed the Vietnam War.[118] It demanded unilateral nuclear disarmament.[119] It called for disinvestment in South Africa.[120] It violated its own policy in order to stymie the nomination of William Rehnquist to the Supreme Court.[121] It steadfastly opposed the Nixon Administration and was the first organization to call for his impeachment following Watergate.[122] During the eight years of the Reagan Administration, it blasted the

President with one invective after another.[123] It led the fight to defeat the confirmation of Robert Bork to the Supreme Court.[124] It frequently writes speeches for left-wing candidates that it likes.[125] And it even issues scorecards on legislators evaluating their performance according to the ACLU's own ideological yardstick.[126]

As Donohue has said, "Quite simply, the ACLU has a politics, and that politics is liberalism."[127] According to constitutional lawyer Michael Palin, it is "completely out in left field."

The perception that it has a diverse portfolio of cases scattered all over the ideological map is, very simply, a myth of its own creation. Although the organization has occasionally ventured out of the Left's territorial waters to defend such groups as the Ku Klux Klan, the John Birch Society, and even the Jews for Jesus, without exception those cases have been carefully contrived either as public relations "showpieces" or as "back door precedents" for their own agenda. In other words, they have been little more than a means to an end.[128] Roger Baldwin admitted as much when he wrote:

> All my associates in the struggle for civil liberties take a class position, though many of them don't know it. I too take a class position. It is anti-capitalist and pro-revolutionary. I champion civil liberty as the best of the non-violent means of building the power on which the workers' rule must be based. If I aid the reactionaries to get free speech now and then, if I go outside the class struggle to fight against censorship, it is only because those liberties help to create a more hospitable atmosphere for working-class liberties. The class struggle is the central conflict of the world; all others are incidental.[129]

So, the incidental case that the ACLU might deign to undertake for a non-radical, a conservative, a Christian, or an ordinary citizen—in Baldwin's parlance a "reactionary"—is little more than an "incidental" means to "create a more hospitable atmosphere" for its pet leftist causes.[130]

Rights and Responsibilities

A brash and cavalier attitude to America's goodness and moral stalwartness is perhaps the single most distressing trait of the ACLU. In the name of civil liberties, it has pressed forward a radical agenda of moral corruption and ethical degeneration.

Ironically, its brazen disregard for decency and its passionately undeterred defense of perverse impropriety has actually threatened our liberties because it has threatened the foundation of those liberties.

The ACLU wants the privileges of America bestowed upon the citizenry as an unearned, undeserved, and unwarranted entitlement. Apart from the grace of God, though, there simply cannot be any such entitlement in human societies. Great privileges bring with them great responsibilities. Our remarkable freedom has been bought with a price. And that price was diligence, sacrifice, and moral uprightness. The legal commitment of the ACLU to the fanatically twisted fringe of American culture—pornographers, gay activists, abortionists, and other sexpert liberationists—is a pathetically self-defeating crusade that has confused liberty with license.

Gardiner Spring, the eloquent pastor-patriot during the early nineteenth century in New York, persuasively argued that the kind of free society America aspired to be was utterly and completely impossible apart from moral integrity:

> Every considerate friend of civil liberty, in order to be consistent with himself must be the friend of the Bible. No tyrant has ever effectually conquered and subjugated a people whose liberties and public virtue were founded upon the Word of God. After all, civil liberty is not freedom from restraint. Men may be wisely and benevolently checked, and yet be free. No man has a right to act as he thinks fit, irrespective of the wishes and interests of others. This would be exemption from all law, and from the wholesome influence of social institutions. Heaven itself would not be free, if this were freedom. No created being holds any such liberty as this, by a divine warrant. The spirit of subordination, so far from being inconsistent with liberty, is inseparable from it.[131]

Similarly, Aleksandr Solzhenitsyn, the exiled Russian novelist, historian, and Nobel laureate, stated:

> Fifty years ago it would have seemed quite impossible in America that an individual be granted boundless freedom with no purpose but simply for the satisfaction of his whims. The defense of individual rights has reached such extremes as to make society as a whole defenseless. It is time to defend, not so much human rights, as human obligations.[132]

The ACLU desires to divorce rights from responsibilities. The danger is that if they ever do entirely succeed, rights will become extinct. "There is a way that seems right to a man, but its end is the way of death" (Proverbs 14:12).

The ACLU desperately wants to legislate morality. Its morality. Or should I say, its immorality. Despite all its high-sounding rhetoric—limiting majorities to protect minorities—it is intent on remaking the American legal system after its own image. It is intent on holding the majority captive to the fancies, follies, and foibles of the minority.

Freedom is a rare and delicate thing—as the last 5,000 years of recorded human history readily attest. It can only survive in an ecology of Christian morality. Our founding fathers knew that only too well.

It was the opinion of one of early America's most distinguished statesmen and jurists, Fisher Ames, that, "No man can be a sound lawyer in this land who is not well read in the ethics of Moses and the virtues of Jesus."[133]

That is as true today as it was then—regardless of what the ACLU may or may not believe.

SIEGE ALERT

AMERICAN CIVIL LIBERTIES UNION

Here is what the new social engineers at the American Civil Liberties Union have in mind for you and your children in the weeks and months ahead:

- They want to redefine liberty and freedom. They want to remake the Constitution in their own image. They want to usher in their notion of a benevolent state-controlled limited pluralism. In order to accomplish such lofty aims they know that their number one priority right now has to be infiltrating the bureaucratic infrastructure of government. They know that they can no longer depend upon a hodge-podge of court cases to reform the legal system, so they are seeking to secure key appointments throughout the governmental apparatus—to run it from the inside rather than try to control it from the outside.

- The plan includes securing political appointments to the Justice Department, the Department of Housing and Urban Development, the Department of Health and Human Services, and even the Defense Department—thus enabling the organization to implement their radical agenda first through administrative directives and then through precedent, to the population at large.

- The end result of such a plan would be federally mandated loosening of restrictions in some areas—such as the distribution of child pornography, the regulation of sexually oriented businesses, and the prosecution of violent crimes against properties and persons—while simultaneously strengthening restrictions in others—such as public expressions of faith, protection of religious convictions in the workplace, or the freedom to participate in alternative pro-life activities such as crisis pregnancy care or counseling.

- In addition, the ACLU will aggressively pursue the implementation and prosecution of "hate crimes" regulation and legislation designed to quaff any attempts to identify aberrant behavior as "sinful" or even "undesirable."

- Watch particularly for administrative or executive orders to implement such goals at both the local and the national levels.

SIX

UNNATURAL AFFECTIONS

ACT UP

Always jackdaw with jackdaw.[1]

—Aristotle

Men of a side like birds of a feather will flock together.[2]

—Thomas Paine

When the members of a small Baptist church in San Francisco gathered for Sunday evening worship recently, they knew it might be an extraordinary service. But no one could have prepared them for just how extraordinary it turned out to be.

A guest speaker had been invited to address the congregation on the subject of homosexuality. Although there had been no public notice of the special event—just a brief mention in the church's regular Sunday bulletin—a local homosexual tabloid announced the meeting with a splashy front-page spread.[3]

According to the pastor, David Innes, that week the church received a number of threatening phone calls. "They demanded that our guest not be allowed to speak—and they said that they intended to stop him if he tried."[4]

Fearful that there might be some kind of an altercation, the pastor placed several calls to the San Francisco police. He was reassured that he and his congregation would be completely safe.

About an hour before the service was scheduled to begin, dozens of belligerent homosexual demonstrators began gathering around the church facilities. They carried signs and banners bearing messages like "We're Here and We're Queer," "Refuse and Resist," "Queens, Queers, and Quays," "Bash Back," "Dykes on Bykes," "Dykes with Tykes," "I'm a Lesbian . . . Get Used to It."[5] Threatening lethal violence, they blocked entryways and crowded onto sidewalks and adjacent properties.

Before long a full-scale riot was underway. The little church building was vandalized. Frightened members of the congregation were surrounded and harassed as they arrived in the parking lot. One woman was accosted and nearly dragged out of the frantic clutches of her family. Rocks and eggs pelted the doors and windows of the sanctuary.

Blocking traffic of two busy thoroughfares, several protesters began to shout obscenities and shriek perverse slogans over megaphones and portable sound systems. Along the side of the church building several more pounded fiercely on the walls, windows, and doors. Others exposed themselves to passersby and simulated sex acts with one another. A fluttering lavender and pink ACT UP flag was run up the flagpole and lurid posters were plastered throughout the property.

Inside the besieged church, children clung to their parents in terror. One elderly blind woman—mistaking the pounding and banging for gunshots—became hysterical. Attempting to maintain some semblance of order, Innes assured the congregation that the police would protect them.

In fact, the police seemed either helpless to come to the aid of the church members, or deliberately chose not to. Although Innes and others repeatedly requested that the officers call for backup, none was forthcoming. And no arrests were made.[6]

When the church members finally decided to try to leave for their homes, the rioters surged toward the building with new fury. In an eerie replay of the scene at Sodom, several began to chant, "We want your children. Give us your children."[7]

Several hours after it had begun the melee slowly dissipated. But before leaving the property the last of the rioters promised, "We will be back. This war is not over. It has just begun."[8]

Quite an Act

"Now the tide has turned," asserts ACT UP spokesman Steve Warren.[9] "We have at last come out," he explains, "and in so doing we have exposed the mean-spirited nature of Judeo-Christian morality. You have been narrow-minded and self-righteous. But with the help of a growing number of your own membership, we are going to force you to recant everything you have believed or said about sexuality."[10]

Writing in *The Advocate*, the nation's most prestigious homosexual magazine, Warren goes on to offer a startling list of ACT UP's nonnegotiable demands:

- "Henceforth, homosexuality will be spoken of in your churches and synagogues as an honorable estate."[11]
- "You can either let us marry people of the same sex, or better yet abolish marriage altogether, since it will give the lie to everything you have said or done about sexuality."[12]
- "You will also instruct your young people in homosexual as well as heterosexual behavior, and you will go out of your way to make certain that homosexual youths are allowed to date, attend religious functions together, openly display affection, and enjoy each other's sexuality without embarrassment or guilt."[13]
- "If any of the older people in your midst object, you will deal with them sternly, making certain they renounce their ugly and ignorant homophobia or suffer public humiliation."[14]
- "You will also make certain that all of the prestige and resources of your institutions are brought to bear on the community, so that laws are passed forbidding discrimination against homosexuals and heavy punishments are assessed."[15]
- "Finally, we will in all likelihood want to expunge a number of passages from your Scriptures and rewrite others, eliminating preferential treatment of marriage and using words that will allow for homosexual interpretations of passages describing biblical lovers."[16]

Warren then concludes with this warning:

> If all these things do not come to pass quickly, we will subject Orthodox Jews and Christians to the most sustained hatred and vilification in recent memory. We have captured the liberal establishment and the press. We have already beaten you on a number of battlefields. And we have the spirit of the age on our side. You have neither the faith nor the strength to fight us, so you might as well surrender now.[17]

This is no bluff.

The justification for such drastic demands is the "ever-escalating" problem of "gay-bashing"—the supposedly commonplace violence committed against homosexuals by heterosexual bigots. The media trumpets such claims—that homosexuals are continually assaulted by "homophobes" who are no doubt inspired by Christian or right-wing prejudices.[18]

While anti-gay "hate crimes" are often highlighted, the media seems to have somehow overlooked any and all acts of violence committed by homosexuals against heterosexuals.

The hundreds of such incidents reported each year cover the gamut from vandalism to rape, from assault to institutional blackmail.[19] And law enforcement officials estimate that straight-bashing incidents may be under-reported by as much as seventy percent.[20]

Threats, intimidation, and violence against the Christian community is a particularly constant phenomenon. When an ordinance was placed on the ballot in Oregon, which would have prohibited any aspect of the government from endorsing or recognizing homosexuality as a legitimate alternate lifestyle, ACT UP flyers appeared on telephone poles "warning" people to vote against it. One showed the Christian icthus fish being roasted on a stick over fire. It read, "YOU BURN US, WE BURN YOU." Another flyer showed the same icthus and warned Christians to vote against the ordinance, "OR WE SHOOT THE FISH." Another said, "CIVIL RIGHTS or CIVIL WAR. Your choice for a limited time only." Finally, another flyer said, with a nary a hint of understatement, that voting against the ordinance "IS A GOOD IDEA." It also clarified what was meant by "civil war," by listing, "QUEER KNIVES, QUEER GUNS, QUEER BULLETS, QUEER MISSILES, QUEER TANKS, QUEER TRENCHES, QUEER FIRE, QUEER WARFARE, QUEER PATRIOTS."[21]

And it is not just Christian politicians or civil activists that the straight-bashers target. Dan Doell of Kansas City spends his time caring for AIDS patients at the Samuel Rodgers Community Health Clinic. Yet, despite his selfless work on behalf of homosexuals, he has been denounced as a traitor and a "missionary of hate" by ACT UP.[22]

Doell's offense is that he has repented of homosexuality. After being seduced as a teenager, Doell spent ten years of his life as a practicing homosexual before leaving the lifestyle. Now, he exposes how arbitrary it is to base one's identity on one's sexual proclivities: "People don't stand on a street corner or wear a T-shirt that says, "I'm greedy," or "I'm a gossiper. I was born that way and I'll never change."[23]

For his apostasy from the homosexual subculture, ACT UP in Kansas City started a letter-writing campaign to get Doell fired from his job helping homosexuals. While they attempt to make sure no one can fire them for their own sexual practices, homosexuals seem all too ready to use intimidation to get others fired.

John Freeman, the executive director of Harvest ministry in Philadelphia, is another repentant former-homosexual. His ministry has had great success in ministering to homosexuals and discipling them into a moral lifestyle. According to *World* magazine: "People who follow the 'once gay always gay' belief usually do not look at the choices in life, Freeman said. People are rarely consciously aware of when they started feeling same-sex attractions, but when actions are traced through the years, small choices began to accumulate."[24]

Claiming that homosexuality involves choice causes fury among homosexual activists. The offices of Harvest have received numerous bomb threats. The staff has also received other hysterically hostile phone calls. In 1992, sixty demonstrators tried to force their way into the building and take over the offices. But for some odd reason, this doesn't count as a hate-crime.[25]

Acting Up

The AIDS Coalition to Unleash Power—known by its popular acronym ACT UP—was founded in 1987 by New York writer Larry Kramer as a direct action campaign to draw attention to the plight of AIDS sufferers.

And draw attention it did—right from the start. "ACT UP was the two-by-four that whacked the American public," says homosexual author Randy Shilts.[26] "And they made a huge difference."[27]

The group gained quick notoriety with high-publicity protests—called "zaps." Its brash style and grass-roots appeal immediately grabbed headlines, dominated newscasts, and struck fear in the hearts of politicians, administrators, and executives throughout the country and around the world.

The organization's arresting slogan, "Silence=Death," underscoring a pink triangle emblazoned on a black T-shirt, became not just an "urban fashion statement" but a trademark for activism and "uncivil disobedience."[28]

According to the *Boston Globe*, "Few activist groups have as quickly become so controversial, so revered, and so despised. And few have achieved such focused, limited goals so quickly."[29] The *New York Post* said, "ACT UP may well be the most potent force in modern grass-roots activism."[30] And the *Los Angeles Times* quipped, "It is a combination of Robin Hood, Geronimo, and El Cid all rolled into one."[31]

The group now has more than a hundred chapters throughout the U.S. and Canada.[32] It has also spawned several splinter groups including Queer Nation, Treatment Action Guerrillas, Women's Action Coalition, and Lesbian Avengers.[33]

Mark Damien argues that, "There is no homosexual group today that has more power, more influence, or more chutzpah than ACT UP."[34] Damien, a social service administrator for an AIDS program in Seattle, says that though there are several "mainstream political organizations with access to the White House, the Department of Health and Human Services or whatever, none of them are able to tap into the energy of the gay community like ACT UP can. In activism, power devolves to those who can make the streets come to life."[35]

If that is true, then a great deal of power must have devolved to ACT UP in the last few years. It has certainly made the streets come to life:

- Five ACT UP pioneers got onto the floor of the New York Stock Exchange where they handcuffed themselves to a balcony railing, blew foghorns, and unfurled a large banner urging traders to sell the stock of drug companies accused of running up the price of AIDS treatments.
- A team of three protesters sneaked onto the set of *The CBS Evening News* and disrupted the broadcast, while over at PBS another team attempted to chain themselves to Robert MacNeil of *The MacNeil/Lehrer News Hour.*
- For several months running, activists stalked New York City

Health Commissioner Stephen Joseph, occupied his office, drowned out his speeches, and sloshed paint on his home.

- Calling New York's Cardinal O'Connor "the city's sickest mass murderer" and his church "a perverse institution with a seventeen-hundred-year-long history of intimidation, torture, and murder," protesters have disrupted worship services at St. Patrick's Cathedral, pelted parishioners with condoms, and splattered the walls with blood, feces, and paint.

- In Los Angeles, activists plastered buildings, phone booths, and bus stops with a poster of former President George Bush with the caption, "Before He Kills You, Kill Him."

- Ray Chalker—owner of a gay bar and publisher of a gay newspaper—was targeted by protesters after he rented his facilities to a film company producing a movie ACT UP decided was demeaning to gays.

- More than ten thousand activists linked arms and clutched a red ribbon stretching a mile around the U.S. Capitol, demanding that Congress spend more federal money on AIDS research.

- Twenty ACT UP protesters were stopped by Washington police before they could throw the embalmed body of AIDS activist Tim Bailey over the White House gates in a lurid protest of U.S. AIDS policy—it was Bailey's final wish.

Author and editor Simon Watney has said that these unorthodox tactics have indeed made ACT UP a force to be reckoned with: "It is no exaggeration to state that ACT UP has become the most significant direct-action campaign in the United States since the anti-Vietnam war movement in the 1960s."[36]

Just as the first law of heraldry is to wear your heart on your sleeve, the first law of activism is to wear out your welcome. It is a paradox that seems to contradict every vestige of sound logic in this poor fallen world—which is precisely why it is so effective.

Not only has ACT UP drawn a significant amount of media attention—thus heightening public awareness of AIDS—but it has also been able to force potential treatments onto the market quicker, tremendously increase the funding base for AIDS research, and strengthen the political and cultural influence of the homosexual movement at large.

As a result, it seems everything has changed.

The Great Action Adventure

"I have a vision and you're part of it."[37]

That pledge, made to homosexual activists at a fund-raiser in Los Angeles, may well prove to be Bill Clinton's best-kept campaign promise. The President's controversial push to open the U.S. military to admitted homosexuals is just the tip of the iceberg in fulfilling that promise.[38]

Even though he quickly reneged on key campaign pledges made to much larger, mainstream constituencies, early on, the President took steps to make good on his commitment to the gay political agenda.

"I have spent the last year of my life telling this community that our agenda will be accomplished through this administration," said gay activist David Mixner, a longtime Clinton friend and advisor who turned down a job in the new administration so that he could lobby the President to fulfill his promises "in a timely manner."[39]

"There's a lot of support from the administration for the efforts of the gay and lesbian community," said Romulo Diaz, the newly appointed deputy chief of staff and counselor to Energy Secretary Hazel O'Leary.[40]

Besides instituting his sweeping "don't ask, don't tell" directive that has effectively lifted the ban on gays in the military, the President has ordered a series of administrative policy changes—unleashing a veritable tidal wave of government-promoted homosexual advocacy.

- The Office of Personnel Management has issued formal recognition to a homosexual employees group within the federal bureaucracy, saying any future questions about homosexuality in background checks of applicants or employees would be prohibited.[41]
- The White House has announced that it had revised its Equal Employment Opportunity Statement and bestowed "protected minority class" status on homosexuals.[42]
- Attorney General Janet Reno has issued an order to all branches of the Justice Department—including the FBI—that forbids discrimination based on sexual orientation, status, or conduct.[43]

In addition the President has made dozens of specific promises to the homosexual movement that are dramatically reshaping federal priorities:

- He said he would issue an order barring "discrimination based on sexual or affectation orientation" in the federal government—effectively giving homosexuals protected "minority" status in the two-million-member federal bureaucracy.[44]
- He said he would support a national "gay rights" bill. In fact, Clinton supports the bill to amend the Civil Rights Act by adding "sexual orientation" to the list of protected classifications. The bill would make homosexuals a protected "minority," akin to racial minorities and the disabled.[45]
- He said he would implement affirmative action policies for homosexuals.[46]
- He said he would support condom distribution programs.[47]
- He said he would increase federal funding on AIDS research as part of a "Manhattan Project" to wage a real "war" on the disease.[48]
- He said he would appoint an "AIDS czar" to implement all the recommendations of the President's National Commission on AIDS.[49]
- He said he would oppose content restrictions for the National Endowment for the Arts, the Public Broadcasting Service, and National Public Radio.[50]
- He said he would demand that the Justice Department crack down on "hate crimes" against gays and lesbians.[51]
- He said he would oppose mandatory HIV testing in *all* circumstances.[52]

Making good on those promises, according to the *Washington Blade*, a homosexual tabloid in the nation's capital, he has appointed more than two dozen homosexuals to high-level positions in the administration and hundreds more throughout the federal bureaucracy.[53]

Roberta Achtenberg, for example, left a "major ideological hole" in Northern California's "progressive coalition" when she accepted Clinton's appointment to an under-secretary post at the Department of Housing and Urban Development.[54] A radical lesbian activist serving on the San Francisco Board of Supervisors, she helped push the city's political agenda to the furthest fringe of American life. Until joining the new administration her most noteworthy accomplishment was leading a national campaign to defund the Boy Scouts of America on the grounds that the organization's leaders were "anti-gay." And in her world view anyone who opposes "gay rights" is a "bigot."[55] As a result of her efforts, the United Way, Bank of America, Levi Strauss, and innumerable other public and private institutions have withdrawn their financial support from scouting.

So much for trustworthy, loyal, helpful, friendly, courteous, kind, obedient, cheerful, thrifty, brave, clean, and reverent. In her new post she will be responsible to enforce the nation's housing anti-discrimination laws and affirmative action requirements.

Kara Lichten, a scouting representative from the San Francisco suburbs, says,

> That a person of the character and demeanor of Roberta Achtenberg is countenanced, much less welcomed, in Washington is a sad commentary on how far down the road toward complete cultural disarray we have gone. When what was sworn at is now sworn by and what was once sworn by is now sworn at, amoral politics has come to dominate our all-in-all.[56]

And Achtenberg is but one of many. "We conquered the world," says ACT UP's founder and leading light, Larry Kramer.[57]

Although that is probably a bit of an exaggeration, clearly, the movement is stronger than ever before, with more influence than ever before, and more opportunities than ever before. Every government agency at every level is now receptive to the demands of homosexual activists, regardless if those demands may compromise the health, security, or welfare of the general population.

"Who would have ever dreamed that we would be in this kind of a position—even just two years ago?" exulted Bryce Tomlinson.[58] "We're basically in the driver's seat politically and culturally. To change the metaphor, the deck is stacked entirely in our favor." Tomlinson, an ACT UP coordinator in Maryland believes that some of this cozy new receptiveness in government is "just sheer luck."[59] But the "great preponderance" of it is "due to the fact that we've put pressure on where that pressure has the best and most effect: the streets."[60] ACT UP has served the movement as the "advance shock troops," he says. "We're the hard core, the cutting edge. We've made the difference. We're here, we're queer, and we're in charge. Get used to it."[61]

The Last Action Hero

For many years Larry Kramer was best known as the Oscar-nominated screen-writer of Ken Russell's *Women in Love* and the author of the best-selling satirical novel *Faggots*. His career achievements in theater, film, and publishing fill a remarkable resume that has been variously described as "brilliant,"[62] "incisive,"[63] and "substantially profound."[64]

But today, all of that fairly fades from memory. Instead, he is best known as either "a desperate and perverse rabble rouser"[65] or "one of America's most valuable troublemakers."[66] For better or for worse, he is almost universally recognized as the world's premier homosexual activist.

It is not a role or a reputation he particularly relishes:

> I've always slightly bristled when I'm described as an activist. It's a word I'm uncomfortable with. I think it's usually meant pejoratively. It's used as a categorizer—to set one apart.[67]

But despite his reticence, there can be no denying, he is, indeed, a man "set apart."

Fresh from Yale and the army, Larry Kramer made his way into the hustle-bustle world of Hollywood full of lofty ambitions and high ideals. Because he was a gifted writer and was unafraid to learn the business side of the entertainment industry, he found quick success. He was an associate producer by the time he was thirty. He was an executive producer at thirty-three.

Though he thought of himself as a homosexual, he cautiously hid his sexual appetites—even going so far as to escort women to various Hollywood parties, screenings, and openings. Because he was first and foremost career-minded, he did not want to publicly flaunt his promiscuous behavior and thus jeopardize his climb up the ladder of success.

Besides, he found the gay social identity uninteresting at best, embarrassing at worst:

> I certainly wasn't interested in gay concerns. Like many others, when Gay Pride marches started down Fifth Avenue at the end of June, I was on Fire Island. Gay politics had an awful image. Loudmouths, the unkempt, the dirty and unwashed, men in leather or dresses, fat women with greasy, slicked-back ducktail hairdos. Another world. Certainly not a world that connected to mine. Nor

did I want it to. On Fire Island, we laughed, in those long-ago days of health, when we watched the evening news on Sunday night flash brief seconds of those straggling, pitiful marches.[68]

But that was before AIDS. When that dreadful disease began to ravage the homosexual community in New York, Kramer became more than a little concerned. So, he began to do a bit of research.

What he discovered shocked him—and changed his once carefree life forever. He found, to his dismay, that even without AIDS, the homosexual community was sick and dying.

The median age of homosexual men dying from AIDS is thirty-nine,[69] of homosexual men dying from all other causes is forty-two,[70] of lesbians at death is forty-five.[71] Compared with the population at large—where age at death for men is seventy-five and for women is seventy-nine—those are sobering figures.[72] Only one percent of homosexuals die of old age.[73] Less than three percent of all homosexuals today are over the age of fifty-five.[74]

Kramer came to the startling realization that the very nature of the homosexual lifestyle is destructive of health and hygiene. No amount of denial would enable him to escape that reality.

Besides the fact that gay socializing revolves around the bar scene—with its incumbent drinking, drugs, and late-night carousing—gay sexuality inevitably involves brutal physical abusiveness and the unnatural imposition of alien substances into internal organs, orally and anally, that inevitably suppresses the immune system and heightens susceptibility to disease.[75] In fact, gay sex is a veritable breeding ground for a panoply of diseases.[76] Among them are colonitis, an excruciating inflammation of the mucus membrane; mucosal ulcers in the rectum; and Kobner's phenomenon, a psoriasis of the rectum and genitals.[77] In addition, a group of rare bowel diseases, previously considered tropical, are now epidemic in urban gay communities. Popularly dubbed "Gay Bowel Syndrome," these afflictions include:

- Amebiasis, a colon disease caused by parasites, causing abscesses, ulcers, and diarrhea;[78]
- Giardiasis, a parasitic bowel disease, again causing diarrhea and sometimes enteritis.[79]
- Shigellosis, a bacterial bowel disease causing severe dysentery;[80]
- Hepatitis A, a viral liver disease, which its victims can spread to

others through handling food, and even through the water splashed on toilet seats.[81]

Even the more conventional sexually transmitted diseases are especially acute among homosexuals. Male homosexuals are actually fourteen times more likely to have syphilis than heterosexuals, eight times more likely to have had hepatitis A or B, and hundreds of times more likely to have had an oral infection by venereal diseases through penile contact.[82] Furthermore, female homosexuals are nineteen times more likely to have had syphilis than their heterosexual counterparts, twice as likely to have had genital warts, four times as likely to have had scabies, seven times more likely to have had infection from vaginal conflict, twenty-nine times more likely to have had oral infection from vaginal contact, and twelve times more likely to have had an oral infection from penile contact than female heterosexuals.[83]

Kramer ran across a disturbing article from a 1976 issue of *The Advocate*, the nation's most prestigious homosexual magazine. There he read that more than half of America's syphilis carriers are gay.[84] That meant that every thirty seconds in America a gay man was contracting a sexually transmitted disease.[85]

And then there is AIDS.

Dr. Luc Montagnier of Paris' Pasteur Institute, who first isolated what is now called the Human Immunodeficiency Virus which is generally supposed to be the retro-viral cause of AIDS, has argued that promiscuity among homosexuals may have created the disease in the first place. *Time* magazine revealed that:

> Montagnier supported a controversial theory that mycoplasma, a bacterium-like organism, is the trigger that turns a slow-growing population of AIDS viruses into mass killers. According to Montagnier, the explosion of sexual activity during the 1970s fostered the spread of a hardy drug-resistant strain of mycoplasma. HIV, meanwhile, lay dormant in Africa. The AIDS epidemic began, Montagnier speculates, when the two microbes got together, perhaps in Haiti.[86]

Despite such overwhelming medical evidence, Kramer discovered that homosexuals, for the most part, still engaged in dangerous behaviors. A study of 655 homosexual men in San Francisco found that while "knowledge of health guidelines was quite high, this knowledge actually had no relation to sexual behavior."[87]

In fact, the idea that homosexuals should limit their promiscuous encounters seemed to be entirely untenable to homosexuals. During the International Conference on AIDS, for instance, researchers concluded that "simply being informed about the AIDS virus does not make people any more likely to practice safe sex."[88]

Amazingly, even the experts themselves were undeterred from practicing promiscuous behavior:

Any residual doubts about the place of sex—hot, sweaty, raunchy sex—in the AIDS-prevention campaign disappeared at the global conference on AIDS in Montreal. For five days the discos were packed with gay doctors, nurses, activists, and researchers shamelessly cruising one another. A nearby bathhouse was doing a land-office business. A jack-off club posted promotional fliers in the conference exhibit hall. And in the middle of the hall a monitor was showing a "safe-sex" video sponsored by a West German health agency. The video was played and replayed all day long for two days, and there seemed never to be fewer than twenty-five or thirty viewers—men, women, straight, gay—gathered about the screen in a fidgety semi-circle. Two men who, except for their blondness, might have been Michelangelo's models were demonstrating a wide array of "safe" erotic possibilities.[89]

Kramer determined that somehow, some way, such suicidal behavior had to stop. He attempted to spread the word about the prevalence of certain diseases—and the necessity to take certain precautions. Without a lot of fanfare he began a modest campaign to educate the homosexual community. He wrote a series of articles about health and hygiene. He gave talks to gay groups. He tried to mobilize public opinion. At the time, he was especially concerned about the prevalence of Kaposi's Sarcoma—the first of the virulent cancers associated with AIDS to spread through the gay population.

He might have expected to have his warnings met with a measure of credulity, apathy, or denial in those early days before celebrity safe-sex campaigns or glitzy condom ads. Instead, though, he was surprised by a rash of outright hostility.

Robert Chesley, for instance, attacked Kramer's efforts in the homosexual tabloid the *New York Native*:

Basically Kramer is telling us that something we gay men are doing—drugs or kinky sex or both—is causing Kaposi's Sarcoma. Being alarmist is dangerous. We've been told by such experts as there are that it's wrong and too soon to make any assumptions about the cause of Kaposi's Sarcoma, but there's another issue here. It is always instructive to look closely at emotionalism, for it so often has a hidden message which is the *real* secret of its appeal. I think the concealed meaning of Kramer's emotionalism is the triumph of guilt: that gay men *deserve* to die for their promiscuity. . . . Read anything by Kramer closely. I think you'll find the subtext is always: the wages of gay sin is death. . . . I am not downplaying the seriousness of Kaposi's Sarcoma. But something else is happening here, which is serious: gay homophobia and antieroticism.[90]

Such criticism was all too common. Kramer's warnings were almost universally scorned—and he was despised and rejected. As one journalist put it:

For trying to get gay men to believe what they preferred doggedly to ignore—that AIDS is, indeed, spread sexually, and that promiscuity had become a guarantee of early death—he was denounced by large numbers of New Yorkers as *alarmist* and *sex-negative*; he was also accused of saying *I told you so*. The fact that he had every right to say it cut no ice.[91]

Amazingly, Kramer began to believe that the AIDS epidemic—and even the criticism he'd received—was all part of a terrible plot to eliminate homosexuals:

Genocide is occurring. We are witnessing—or not witnessing—the systematic, planned annihilation of some by others with the avowed purpose of eradicating an undesirable portion of the population. I know straight Jews, and other heterosexuals, find this comparison of holocausts repugnant. I am not unfamiliar with charges of hysteria and hyperbole. To read Primo Levy is to know that our suffering, as of this moment, is still small in comparison. But Primo Levy also writes that a certain dose of rhetoric is perhaps indispensable for memory to persist. One inadvertent fall-out from the Holocaust is the growing inability to view any other similar tragedies as awful, the insistence on its primogeniture frustrates efforts to arouse equal public concern when the newest children on the block arrive, demanding immediate succor.[92]

He deliberately set out to transform the homosexual community's anger and loss into collective action. He turned out one pot boiler after another. His articles were full of rage and desperation.

He was trying to somehow startle gays with the severity of the crisis at hand:

> If this article doesn't scare . . . you, we're in real trouble. If this article does not rouse you to anger, fury, rage, and action, gay men may have no future on this earth. Our continued existence depends on just how angry you can get.[93]

When at last the epidemic numbers of deaths were too great to ignore any longer, a handful of people began to listen.

Kramer was able to convince some prominent members of the New York homosexual community to join him in establishing a private agency to deal with the crisis no one wanted to face. Thus began the Gay Men's Health Crisis, which is today the largest non-government AIDS service organization in the world.[94]

Focusing on treatment, counseling, education, support, and prevention, the organization quickly carved out a prominent place for itself in the medical and social services communities. It gained a reputation for effective administration, proficient management, and circumspect cooperation—all highly esteemed professional virtues.[95]

But that was not enough for Kramer. He felt that far more needed to be done politically—and the board of the new organization was determined to steer clear of the thorny problems of lobbying and advocacy.

Just as he was beginning to garner a bit of respectability, he openly and vociferously denounced the board's commitment to non-partisanship. A breach became inevitable. "There is nothing in this whole AIDS mess that is not political," complained Kramer. "When are we gonna wake up? When are we gonna muster the courage to do what needs to be done?"[96]

He began to advocate "any and every means" necessary to end what he called "the ongoing gay genocide."[97] He even broached the subject of civil disobedience:

> I hope we don't have to conduct sit-ins or tie up traffic or get arrested. I hope our city and our country will start to do something to help start saving us. But it is time for us to be perceived for what we truly are: an angry community and a strong community, and therefore a threat.[98]

In a boil of querulousness he took on all comers. He criticized the government, the pharmaceutical industry, the religious community, business leaders, the media, and the Hollywood elite. But he saved his fiercest criticism for gay leadership. He was perfectly justified in this he thought: "Go ahead, be offended—I don't know how else to reach you, how to reach everybody."[99]

Before long, his life had collapsed into a pother of brawls. Former friends and lovers anathematized him. His picarous perfidies stigmatized his presence. He was angry and cast about for an outlet for that anger.

Despite this, in the spring of 1987, he was invited to fill in as a substitute speaker for the monthly lecture series at the New York Gay and Lesbian Community Center—the invited speaker had canceled at the last minute.

That spontaneous decision would have profound repercussions.

Kramer was in rare form that night. His speech was a barn-burner of whipsaw yawps and gaudy eviscerations. He quickly roused the political libido of everyone in attendance.

He expressed their greatest fears:

> Two thirds of you—I should say of *us*, because I am in this, too—could be dead within five years.[100]

He expressed their deepest passions:

> Unless we fight for our lives, we shall die. In all the history of homosexuality we have never before been so close to death and extinction.[101]

He expressed their fiercest outrages:

> How long will it take before we get angry and fight back? What does it take for us to take responsibility for our own lives? I sometimes think we have a death wish. I have never been able to understand why we have sat back and let ourselves literally be knocked off man by man—without fighting back.[102]

And he stirred them to action:

> I want to talk to you about power. We are all in awe of power, of those who have it, and we bemoan the fact that we don't have it. Power is little pieces of paper on the floor. No one picks them up. Ten people walk by and no one picks up the paper on the floor. The eleventh person walks by, and is tired of looking at them, and so

he bends down and picks them up. The next day he does the same thing. Soon he's *in charge* of picking up the paper. And he's got a lot of paper that he's picked up. Now think of that paper as standing for responsibility. This man or woman who is picking up paper is, by being responsible, acquiring more and more power. He doesn't necessarily want it, but he's tired of seeing the floor littered. All power is the willingness to accept responsibility. But we live in a city and a country where no one is willing to pick up pieces of paper. Where no one wants any responsibility. Well, until we all bend over and pick up the paper, I don't have to tell you what's going to happen.[103]

A furious discussion followed the speech. Ideas were tossed back and forth with frenetic fury. As the hour grew late the crowd agreed to regroup two days later to map out strategies.

During the follow-up meeting Kramer suggested that a whole new organization be established to work alongside existing institutions like the Gay Men's Health Crisis, the AIDS Action Council, and as a kind of *ad hoc* community protest group. He envisioned it as a street-savvy strike-force in order to put pressure on government agencies, pharmaceutical companies, and health-care providers. The immediate aim was to speed the release of experimental AIDS drugs like AZT. But, of course the long-range agenda was to win a flurry of concessions for the homosexual community.

Thus was the AIDS Coalition to Unleash Power—ACT UP—born. And Kramer was once again in the forefront of the homosexual movement. He led sit-ins. He appeared in the media. He testified before congress. He lobbied and cajoled.

His success was consummate. AIDS became America's number one health priority almost overnight—despite the fact that there are some thirty-four other terminal diseases that afflict more people every year.[104] Major cities like New York, Chicago, and Los Angeles began condom distribution programs, AIDS awareness educational initiatives, and pilot exchange programs.[105]

Even so, there was still no cure in sight. And the homosexual population, despite its political gains, was in danger of extinction.

Now infected with the disease himself, Kramer increased his already frantic pace of activism. In 1990, he published a chronological selection from the steady torrent of articles and speeches he had produced since the beginning of his awareness of the AIDS epidemic. Entitled *Reports from the Holocaust: The Making of an AIDS*

Activist, the book ably explored all the dark alleys of propaganda. The *Washington Post* called it "the manifesto of AIDS activism."[106] The *New York Times* said it was "infuriating, riveting, outrageous, nasty, and finally, impossible to ignore."[107] *New York Newsday* called it "a powerful book," both "eloquent" and "convincing."[108] And Randy Shilts, author of *And the Band Played On*, asserted that Kramer's book was "inarguably one of the most influential works of advocacy journalism of the last decade."[109]

The book was intended to be a brash apologetic for ACT UP. Full of sour impotence and infectious dithyramb, it is a storehouse of cleverly articulated bilious pessimism. Dispensing with the sugarcoated pills of lesser sages, Kramer takes ghastly stabs at all pretense and all convention. In the very raisins of his bill of fare and the texture of his woolen shirt there is some note of impatient revolt. The man is bitter.

At the heart of his bitterness, he says, is "envy."[110] And that is a terribly frightening confession.

Jealousy says: "I want what you have. So, I will take it."[111]

Envy says: "I want what you have, but I know I can't take it. So I will destroy it."[112]

According to Mark Damien, "ACT UP's all-or-nothing attitude doesn't stop with the attainment of equal rights or even a protected legal status. The movement is hell-bent on utter and complete annihilation of society—at least as we know it."[113] Thus, the philosophy of ACT UP necessarily leads to the destruction of our families, our communities, and even our culture.

Legislating Morality

ACT UP apologists have demurred that the only reason they have had to resort to extreme activism is that traditional values not only oppress the homosexual community, they oppress everyone. They argue that to impose "community standards" of ethics and decency is "a violation of the spirit of American democracy" and a "contradiction of our most basic constitutional tenants."[114] Thus any attempt to do so goes beyond "bigotry" or "intolerance" to "despotism" and "tyranny."[115]

You simply "can't legislate morality," they say.

On the contrary, as Dr. D. James Kennedy has so often asserted, "Morality is the only thing you *can* legislate."[116] That's what legislation *is*. It is the codification in law of some particular moral concern—generally so that the immorality of a few is not forcibly inflicted on the rest of us.[117]

Murder is against the law because we recognize that the premeditated killing of another human being is a violation of a very basic and fundamental moral principle that we all hold dear: the sanctity of human life. Theft is against the law because we recognize that taking someone else's belongings without permission is a breach of another one of our basic and fundamental ethical standards: the inviolability of private property. The fact is, all law is some moral or ethical tenant raised up to social enforceability by the civil sphere.

Thus, the question is not "Should we legislate morality?" Rather, it is "Whose morality should we legislate?" And "What moral standard will we use when we legislate?"

There was no ambivalence among founders of this nation on that question. The standard of morality that they unhesitatingly codified into law was the Bible.[118] The *Declaration of Independence* was a document carefully informed by a scriptural notion of life and law.[119] The *Articles of Confederation* were thoroughly entrenched in the biblical world view.[120] The Constitution was undeniably influenced by Christian legal standards.[121] The *Federalist Papers* were birthed of the great verities and profundities of liberty found only in the Bible.[122] The *Bill of Rights* would have been inconceivable apart from the moral standard wrought by God in His Word.[123] Every major document, every major consultation, and every major institution that the founding fathers forged from the fires of freedom to create and guide our remarkable legal system was a conscious affirmation and imitation of biblical ideals, values, standards, ethics, and morals.[124]

Now, to be sure, there were a number of other historical and philosophical influences that helped to shape the course of American law: Justinian's *Roman Civil Law*, Alfred the Great's *English Common Law*, Charlemagne's *Rule of the Franks*, William Blackstone's *Commentaries*, and John Locke's *Second Treatise on Civil Government*. However, each of these in turn were themselves derived, at least in part, from the biblical standard.[125]

Robert Goguet, in his authoritative history of the development of judicial philosophy in this country, argued that the founding fathers' legislation of biblical morality was more than simply a reflection of their personal faith or cultural inheritance, it was a matter of sober-headed practicality:

> The more they meditated on the biblical standards for civil morality, the more they perceived their wisdom and inspiration. Those standards alone have the inestimable advantage never to have undergone any of the revolutions common to all human laws, which have always demanded frequent amendments; sometimes changes, sometimes additions, sometimes the retrenching of superfluities. There has been nothing changed, nothing added, nothing retrenched from biblical morality for over three thousand years.

The framers were heavily influenced by the writings of Thomas Hooker, learned Puritan divine and founder of the city of Hartford in the Connecticut colony; thus they agreed wholeheartedly with his oft-quoted maxim on the wellspring of law and order in society:

> Of law there can be no less acknowledged, than that her seat is in the bosom of God, her voice in the harmony of the world. All things in heaven and on earth do her homage; the very least as doing her care, and the greatest as not exempt from her power. Both angels and men, and creatures of what condition, though each in a different sort of name, yet all with one uniform consent, admire her as the mother of their peace and joy.[126]

John Jay was one of the most influential of the founding fathers and the first Chief Justice of the Supreme Court. He too affirmed the necessity of virtue for the proper maintenance of civil stability and order:

> No human society has ever been able to maintain both order and freedom, both cohesiveness and liberty apart from the moral precepts of the Christian Religion applied and accepted by all the classes. Should our Republic ere forget this fundamental precept of governance, men are certain to shed their responsibilities for licentiousness and this great experiment will then surely be doomed.[127]

James Madison, our fourth President, primary author of the Bill of Rights, and champion of liberty throughout the founding era echoed that sentiment:

We have staked the future of all our political institutions upon the capacity of each and all of us to govern ourselves, to control ourselves, and to sustain ourselves according to the Ten Commandments of God.

Again and again that same refrain was repeated. The men who framed our nation had a particular goal in mind: building a free society of responsible and morally upright men and women. They wanted to build a "city on a hill," a "light to the nations," and a godly legacy. They were willing to give sacrificially—often giving their very lives and livelihoods—to achieve those ends.

As a result, America became a great nation. It became great because its character was rooted in Christian morality. Thus, during his visit to the fledgling American republic in 1832, Alexis de Toqueville observed, "America is great because America is good."[128] But the sage French nobleman went on to warn, "If America ever ceases to be good, it will cease to be great."[129]

In light of all that has transpired since, that is a sobering thought indeed.

SIEGE ALERT

ACT UP

Here is what the new social engineers at ACT UP have in mind for you and your children in the weeks and months ahead:

- They want to reorient America's whole view of sexuality issues. They not only want to end discrimination against aberrant behaviors, they want preferential and protected minority status afforded to those behaviors. In order to accomplish such lofty aims, they know that their number one priority right now has to be a full-scale development plan for AIDS funding and support. Utilizing the full weight of the federal government, they hope to accomplish at the national level what they have been unable to do at the local level: institutionalize homosexual concerns in the health-care and policy-making apparatus.
- The emphasis on health-care reform offers them a prime opportunity to universalize coverage for behavior-related maladies as well as to integrate other homosexually-oriented into the medical mainstream.
- Education will play a key role in the success of their plan—thus, they are emphasizing the necessity to mandate sensitivity training in all schools at all levels to homosexual behaviors, lifestyles, and concerns.
- In addition, they are pushing for an official implementation and prosecution of "hate crimes" as well as an unofficial stigmatization of "insensitive beliefs" or "hate groups" such as churches or private schools.
- Watch particularly for administrative or executive orders in schools and workplaces to "remedially" help students or employees "overcome stereotypical fears" or to "expose" them to "alternative lifestyles."

SEVEN

THE NANNY STATE

CHILDREN'S DEFENSE FUND

*The keep of the nursery chore holds volcanic stock
and so much more.*[1]

—Ben Howth

*The hand that rocks the cradle is the hand
that rules the world.*[2]

—William Ross

Lachelle Washington was just twelve days away from her fifteenth birthday when the test confirmed her suspicions. She was pregnant. And she couldn't have been happier. The way she figured it, her timing was perfect.

Far from being an inconvenience, Lachelle believed that the pregnancy was a ticket to "bigger and better things." Now she would have all the privileges and conveniences that her teenage ghetto boyfriends simply could never have hoped to provide.

At least, that was the theory.

As a welfare mother, Lachelle assumed that she would have a piece of the "good life." She'd be completely out on her own, with no one to answer to and no one to answer for.

It was an opportunity she thought she just couldn't afford to pass up. Like her mother and three older sisters before her, she began to plan her life around her children and the myriad of federal benefits they'd be eligible to accrue.

She knew, for instance, that under the government's carefully fabricated system, welfare mothers and their children could actually receive benefits simultaneously from as many as eighteen different programs—covering a dizzying gamut of family concerns from the basic living expenses of food, shelter, and clothing to health care and child care.

Naturally, she applied for them all.

And perhaps just as naturally, the legion of social workers and bureaucrats assigned to her case summarily approved her for them all:

- The Child Nutrition Program;
- The Food Stamps Program;
- The Special Supplemental Food Program;
- The Special Milk Program;
- The Lower-Income Housing Assistance Program;
- The Rent Supplements Program;
- The Public Health Services Program;
- The Medicaid Program;
- The Public Assistance Grants Program;
- The Work Incentive Program;
- The Employment Services Program;
- The Financial Assistance Program for Elementary and Secondary Education;
- The Public Assistance Services Program;
- The Human Development Services Program;
- The Action Domestic-Care Program;
- The Legal Services Program;
- The Community Services Program;
- The Head Start Program.

Lachelle's situation was hardly unique. Overlap is practically universal among all the hundred-odd welfare assistance programs, since only five of them currently limit eligibility on the basis of participation in other programs.[3] But even then, when overlap is considered, recipients are usually not turned away.[4] In fact, many of the programs, including the basic cash subsidy entitlements like Aid for Families with Dependent Children (AFDC), Supplemental Security Income (SSI), Social Security, and Unemployment Insurance Compensation, actually will encourage applicants to multiply their benefits by applying for any and all overlapping programs.[5]

Lachelle's mother always used to say, "If the government's

gonna be givin' it away, we might as well be in on the gettin'."

Like mother, like daughter.

But, by the time she was twenty-eight, Lachelle had come to the disturbing realization that life on the dole was not all it was cracked up to be. Conditions in the public housing project where she lived were brutally abysmal with persistent violent crime, a rampant drug culture, unsanitary garbage and waste disposal, and hostile neighbors. And despite the fact that all her children had participated in special kindergarten and after-school Head Start programs, she could already see that they were headed down the road to ruin. Her oldest son, Melvin, had acquired a rap sheet longer than his thin, street-toughened arm, and her other three, James, Leslie, and William, were steered in the same direction. None could read or write well enough to fill out even the simplest of forms or applications.

At one point, years ago, she'd tried to work. But her salary jeopardized her welfare income, and since her earning power was no match for her federal benefits, she quit out of sheer economic necessity. Later, when she'd had a bellyful of welfare, not caring if she kept her benefits or not, she found that she couldn't keep a job. Even a minimum wage job. She just couldn't adjust to the working life. Welfare had become a trap for her. A dismal, debilitating, disastrous trap.

According to the Children's Defense Fund—the major proponent for institutional welfare maintenance today—there is "no evidence" that a "welfare culture" exists in our urban centers.[6] Despite overwhelming empirical evidence to the contrary,[7] the organization has unswervingly defended the efficacy of government entitlements. And it has emerged as the nation's premiere advocacy organization for the perpetuation and expansion welfare programs, benefits, and funding—as well as the major obstacle to any form of substantive welfare reform.[8] It persistently argues that the experience of second- and third-generation welfare recipients like Lachelle demonstrates the need for more programs not fewer, for greater spending not less.[9] It steadfastly denies the apparent failure of the vaunted "war on poverty." "This new myth," it argues, "simply does not accord with logic."[10]

"I don't know much about logic," Lachelle retorts, "but when I look around this neighborhood, I see nothing *but* a welfare culture.

It's obvious. It's everywhere. And it's destroying us and what's left of our families. We're enslaved by it—and by the government *massas* that keep propping it up in the name of justice and compassion."

For Lachelle Washington and millions like her, the "war on poverty" has become a veritable "war on the poor."

And for that, she holds the Children's Defense Fund no less culpable than the welfare bureaucrats and the liberal politicians.

The Alms Race

In his State of the Union message of 1964, President Lyndon Johnson declared an "unconditional war on poverty."[11]

Almost immediately, the full energies of the most powerful nation on earth were marshaled against the dark denizens of privation and want. Studies were authorized. Commissions were established. Images of Appalachian shantytowns and ghetto hovels filled the television screen. A helter-skelter of ambitious renewal and rehabilitative programs was launched. Governors and mayors set out on hopeful pilgrimages to Washington to lobby for their "fair share."[12]

And the federal coffers were loosed.

The "war on poverty" was supposed to reform the entire social fabric of our nation. The hungry were to be fed. The naked were to be clothed. The homeless were to be sheltered. The jobless were to be employed. The helpless were to be protected. Racial discrimination was to be dispatched. Women, children, the disabled, and the elderly all were to be brought to full equality. Through legislation and litigation, through education and communication, through taxation and distribution, the disadvantaged were to be unshackled from structural poverty.[13]

But thirty years and untold billions of dollars later, the hungry are hungrier than ever. The poor, the deprived, the weak, and the dispossessed are more vulnerable than ever. Instead of decreasing the incidence of infant mortality, the "war on poverty" only increased it.[14] Instead of decreasing the incidence of illiteracy, the "war on poverty" only increased it.[15] Instead of decreasing the incidence of unemployment, the "war on poverty" only increased it.[16] We have actually lost ground.[17]

Despite its abject failure, the massive welfare apparatus remains fiscally and politically sacrosanct thanks in large part to the diligent efforts of the Children's Defense Fund.

Established in 1968 as a kind of adjunct to the "Poor People's" protest movement, the organization has grown enormously in both size and influence through the years. It is acknowledged by friend and foe alike as one of the most powerful forces in Washington today.

According to journalist Mickey Kaus, it is among "the capital's best-known, best-connected lobbies," and has become its "major liberal statistic factory."[18] Senator Orrin Hatch asserts that it is a "strong, formidable, and forceful" advocate for social change. And it has become, he says, "one of the most effective political organizations in America today."[19] Former White House chief domestic advisor Stuart Eizenstat says, "It is quite simply one of the best lobbies for any cause in the country."[20]

Though originally envisioned by its founder, Marian Wright Edelman, as merely a "litigatory levee" for the civil rights movement, it has expanded the scope of its work to include "demographic research, public education, legislative and administrative advocacy, and publishing."[21] Besides its busy Washington, D.C., headquarters, the nonprofit organization maintains offices in Texas, Ohio, and Minnesota with a staff of more than 120 "experts, researchers, attorneys, and local organizers."[22]

Supported by substantial grants from the likes of the Rockefeller, Ford, Carnegie, Hearst, and Kellogg foundations as well as donations from the Aetna, Dayton Hudson, Time, Coca-Cola, General Mills, AT&T, Exxon, Mobil, American Express, and Warner-Lambert corporate philanthropies, the Children's Defense Fund has utilized its $9 million annual budget to dramatically reshape the nation's domestic policy toward the poor:[23]

- It successfully stymied federal welfare reform efforts during each of the Nixon, Ford, Carter, Reagan, and Bush administrations.[24]
- It secured passage of the Family Leave Act—which massively expanded the reach of the federal government's social welfare regulation of enterprise, business, and industry.[25]
- It won several key court battles including *Mattie v. Halliday, Gary v. Louisiana, Goss v. Lopez,* and *Rose v. Rose*—each dramatically inflating welfare access policies and programs.[26]

- It not only successfully defended the Head Start, WIC, and AFDC entitlements against proposed budget cuts during the Reagan-Bush years, it insured a massive escalation of both their size and their scope—thus effectively blocking any and all attempts to cut the federal budget deficit.[27]
- It secured huge expansions in Medicaid family coverage despite the burgeoning tax-and-spend crisis on Capitol Hill.[28]
- It won concessions in the tax code for lower income brackets on personal exemptions, zero-line deductions, and earned-income tax credits.[29]
- It had a major hand in crafting special welfare-specific provisions in the Tax Reform Act of 1986.[30]
- It secured targeted tax subsidies for county and municipal government day care programs.[31]
- It insured that a myriad of state welfare reform proposals for means testing, voucher programs, work incentives, technical assistance, enterprise zones, decentralization, and privatization were each defeated in turn.[32]
- It exercised its considerable influence in the courts to halt several experimental workfare programs at both the state and the national levels.[33]

Working in cozy concert with Planned Parenthood,[34] the ACLU,[35] Greenpeace,[36] and the Feminist Majority Foundation,[37] the organization has built a well-greased political juggernaut to oppose conservative court appointments, support an ever larger government role in our daily lives, and decrease the autonomy and authority of parents over their families.[38] That and its special proximity and influence in the Clinton regime make the Children's Defense Fund a particularly potent force for contemporary liberalism.

According to international political analyst Jonathan Ridley-Jones:

> The Children's Defense Fund is at the hub of a vast matrix of organizations and movements covering the gamut of liberal concerns. If one were to attempt to comprehend the current centralizing tendencies of government over and against society in the Clinton era, one could do no better than to study the political pronouncements of Marian Wright Edelman and the social engineering priorities in her organization's latest policy manual.[39]

Big Brother's Mother

Heralded as "America's universal mother" by *Harper's Bazaar*,[40] a "master insider" by the *Washington Post*,[41] an "impassioned and relentless champion" by the *New York Times*,[42] and the "101st senator" by Ted Kennedy,[43] Marian Wright Edelman is the epitome of consummate political correctness—the modern equivalent of sainthood.[44] The "founder and spiritual guide" of the Children's Defense Fund thus enjoys praise as gaudy as a sheik's seraglio. To the unscotchable scriveners of our day she has what the *New Republic* calls a "near-unassailable reputation aura" of virtue:[45] She is a valiant and heaven-kissing heroine, a metaphysical Joan of Arc, an economic Carrie Nation, a moral Knight Hospitaller, earnest, lionhearted, and ideologically pure. She is, in a word, none other than Zarathustra reincarnate.

Born the daughter and granddaughter of Baptist preachers on June 6, 1939, in Bennettesville, South Carolina, she grew up in a well-educated and politically active home. Long before civil rights were lauded by the media as national obligations they were modeled as family obligations by her parents. She was expected to serve. She was expected to get involved. She was expected to achieve.

And she did.

After graduating from Spellman College and Yale Law School, she joined the New York office of the NAACP as a staff attorney. A year later, in 1964, she was sent to open the organization's legal office in Mississippi where she took a leading role in the civil rights movement.

Those were halcyon days and Edelman thrived.

Caught up in a whirlwind of street activism and ideological radicalism, she rubbed shoulders with everyone from Martin Luther King and Ralph Abernathy to Malcolm X and Jesse Jackson. She marched. She organized. And she agitated. She led voter registration drives and lunch counter sit-ins. As the first Black woman admitted to the Mississippi bar, she catalyzed a legal revolution.

Her insatiable appetite for social change led her to associate with a number of militant groups as well. For instance, she joined—and for two years lead—the Student Nonviolent Coordinating Committee—which despite its name helped to spawn the violent unrest of the Black Power movement. With the likes of Stokely Carmichael, H. Rap Brown, and Eldridge Cleaver fomenting radicalism from within, the group was nudged into the orbit of various subversive communist-front organizations from the Black Panthers and the Mustafa League to the National Black Liberators and the Trans-Africa Forum. According to an FBI report at the time, the group actually planned political assassinations, guerrilla warfare tactics, and widespread urban terrorism.[46]

Despite her attraction to such extreme leftism, Edelman's temper was restrained by a fierce pragmatism—ingrained by years of Sunday school moralism. So, by 1968, she had the foresight to realize that popular support for radicalism had begun to wane. "The country was tired of the concerns of the sixties," she later observed.[47] "When you talked about poor people or Black people, you faced a shrinking audience."[48]

Although she still believed that revolutionary social change was necessary, she began casting about for a more appropriate and practical means to that end. It was at about that time that she conceived the plan for the Children's Defense Fund. "I got the idea that children might be a very effective way to broaden the base for change," she said.[49]

Robert Louis Stevenson once quipped that:

> The successful social insurgent preys upon popular sentiment as a cover to exploit any existing inconsistencies in the system. He will then exercise those inconsistencies to reveal their most extreme but most natural conclusions—thus achieving the heretofore unachievable.[50]

Edelman understood that principle only too well. Realizing that the needs of children afforded her with the sentimental cover to sway popular opinion and that the welfare system afforded her the existing inconsistencies to effect sweeping political changes, she set out to achieve the unachievable. Her objective was not so much focused on children, or their defense, as on what cultural dividends children's defense might ultimately pay to her espoused movement: liberalism. As conservative family advocate Phyllis Schlafly has observed, the organization's agenda "is not about children; it is about power. It is thus a threat to some of our most precious freedoms, our civil liberties, and our families."[51]

Although she quickly attracted kudos for her new venture from the inveterate reformers and mountebank therapists of the establishment left, Edelman had a difficult time breaking into the good ol' boy network in Washington—where there was a fiercer apartheid than she'd ever encountered in Mississippi. But then, in 1970, she met a bright, young, first-year law student at Yale who would change her fortunes forever.

The student was Hillary Rodham.

For the next quarter century the two women would labor together to make the Children's Defense Fund the bulwark of a rejuvenated liberal assault on family and culture. Serving first as a summer intern, then as a staff attorney, and finally chairman of the governing board, Hillary brought the organization a unique combination of verve, tenacity, and vision. She brought the organization academic credibility, fund-raising savvy, and administrative acumen. And that was just the beginning.

When she married her live-in college boyfriend—and he successively became governor of Arkansas and President of the United States—she brought the organization even more. For instance, she made certain that the Clinton cabinet was literally stacked with Edelman's friends, associates, and board members: Donna Shalala in the Department of Health and Human Services, Henry Cisneros in the Department of Housing and Urban Development, and Janet Reno in the Justice Department.[52] She insured that the Clinton economic plan mirrored Edelman's agenda: reduction of military spending, expansion of welfare entitlements, and consolidation of social service administration.[53] And she insisted that the Clinton legislative strategy follow Edelman's scheme: comprehensive health-care reform, universal coverage of entitlement benefits, and funding for sexuality education and abortion services.[54]

The Clintons' first post-election appearance in Washington was at a Children's Defense Fund banquet. After lauding her mentor, Hillary leaned down and whispered, "I love you very much," in Edelman's ear.[55]

Afterward one top administration official was asked what would be the top priorities for Clinton's domestic agenda. He replied, "Whatever Marian Wright Edelman wants."[56]

Liberalism's Litany

According to her two best-selling books, *Families in Peril* and *The Measure of Our Success*, all Edelman really wants is to "move our nation forward in the quest for fairness and opportunity for every American."[57]

The books are slender volumes filled with the easy pieties and seething fuss of yearbook maxims: "There is no free lunch,"[58] "Don't be afraid of risks or of being criticized,"[59] "Clean up your own mess,"[60] "Help America remember that the fellowship of human beings is more important than the fellowship of race and class and gender in a democratic society,"[61] "Never think life is not worth living,"[62] "Be a can-do, will-try person,"[63] "Try to live in the present,"[64] "Meditate and learn to be alone without being lonely."[65]

That such trivial *ars notaria* pass in our day as a surrogate for sage counsel is tragic. That such saccharined sentimentalities pass as a guise for militant liberalism is worse.

According to reviewer Max Lichten, "Edelman wears a very thin disguise. Under all that grandmotherly sweetness and light of artless truism lies a sinister agenda to usher in a kind of beneficent nanny bureaucracy."[66] Her aim, he says, is to "pablumize the profound—offering an all-encompassing welfare state with all the bustling airs of a schoolmarm or a maiden aunt."[67]

Indeed, intermingled with the cute epigrams and the telling quotations from liberal icons—such as Gandhi,[68] Gorbachev,[69] Tutu,[70] Myrdal,[71] Niebuhr,[72] Tillich,[73] and DuBois[74]—Edelman drops hints at what it is that she *really* wants:

- She wants a vastly expanded "partnership of family and government" in those areas traditionally reserved as parental prerogatives, thus transforming the very nature of both family and government in the process.[75]
- She wants to replace "private charity" with what she calls "public justice."[76]
- She wants to expose what she deems as the "perverse national values, hidden behind pro-family, traditional values rhetoric."[77]
- She wants to implement "comprehensive and convenient services for teenagers, in and out of school settings" to provide a full range of abortion, contraception, and "family life education"[78] services, realizing that "moralizing will not solve the teen-pregnancy problem."[79]

- She wants to greatly diminish the importance of "the greedy military weasel that can never seem to get enough"[80]—thus breaking "with our purchase of Armageddon by reflex."[81]
- She wants to "re-empower the old liberal coalition"—of feminists, street activists, labor unionists, and socialists—with a government-sponsored social agenda to "re-invent society."[82]

According to Max Lichten, "It should come as no big surprise that what Edelman really wants is simply the old liberal agenda of her sixties radical days all prettified for the nineties with cant about children."[83] Her agenda—and thus the agenda of the entire Clinton regime—is, he says, "a clever rehash of the Great Society War on Poverty—only universally applied to everyone, everywhere, whether they like it or not."[84]

Of course, the problem with Edelman's ideal of social engineering is not simply that its coercive redefinition of the family, its abrogation of fundamental values, and its redistribution of wealth are gross violations of the basic principles of free enterprise, private property, and civil liberty. It is that it actually fails to help the poor—much less anyone else.

The War on the Poor

A funny thing happened on the way to the liberal utopia. Before the social welfare "war on poverty" approximately thirteen percent of Americans were poor—using the official definition.[85] The unemployment rate was running at less than four percent.[86] Over the next thirty years, social welfare spending increased more than twenty times and the welfare bureaucracy grew a hundredfold.[87] The result? Approximately eighteen percent of Americans are now poor—again, using the official definition.[88] And the unemployment rate continually fluctuates between five percent and eleven percent.[89]

Something has gone wrong—terribly wrong.

The welfare system has spawned a number of unintended side effects, second- and third-order consequences. Unintended. Unanticipated. But inevitable.

First, the implementation of liberal welfare programs and policies has actually halted in its tracks the ongoing improvement in the lot of America's poor. Writers and social scientists as diverse as

Charles Murray, George Gilder, Thomas Sowell, Walter Williams, Stuart Butler, Marvin Olasky, Henry Hazlitt, Calvin Biesner, Clarence Carson, Richard John Neuhaus, Hilaire Belloc, Robert Nisbett, Allan Carlson, and Murray Rothbard have shown conclusively that instead of enabling the infirm and the elderly to lead full and productive lives, and instead of empowering the poor to control their lives and rise from poverty, social welfare programs have rendered them impotent, dependent, and helpless.[90] The sheer numbers ought to be enough to convince anyone. After billions upon billions of dollars spent, after a monumental effort that mobilized the ablest minds and the finest machinery, there are more poor than ever before. There are more homeless than ever before. There are more hungry than ever before. Something has gone wrong.

Second, the implementation of liberal welfare programs and policies has actually contributed to the disintegration of poor families.[91] The welfare system subsidizes idleness, provides institutional disincentives to family life, and reduces faith to a blind trust in the paternalism of the state.[92] Fatherless homes are rewarded with extra benefits and welfare perks, while intact homes are penalized and impoverished. Illegitimate pregnancies are generously gratiated while moral purity is snubbed. Something has gone wrong.

Third, the implementation of liberal welfare programs and policies has actually provided incentives to avoid work.[93] Each increase in welfare benefits over the past twenty years has resulted in a huge shift from the payrolls to the welfare rolls. When entitlement programs become competitive with the salaries of lower—or even middle—income families, it is only sensible to expect that many, especially the poorly trained and poorly educated, will choose the path of least resistance. In New York State, for example, one-and-a-half times the minimum wage would have to be earned in order to equal the welfare benefits available.[94] What inner-city teen is going to work at McDonald's flipping hamburgers for minimum wage when they can "earn" nearly twice that on welfare? Something has gone wrong.

Fourth, the implementation of liberal welfare programs and policies has actually contributed to the already enormous problem of governmental waste. Instead of helping to reduce waste by returning more and more citizens to productivity, welfare has proven to be the most inefficient slice of the budgetary pie. Only thirty cents of each anti-poverty dollar actually goes to actual programs to empower the poor or alleviate their plight. And of that thirty cents, only about half ever makes it outside the Washington Beltway.[95] Shocking, but true. All the rest is gobbled up by overhead and administration. So, during the supposedly "lean and efficient" Reagan years, for example, an average of one hundred twenty-four billion dollars was spent annually to reduce poverty, yet those expenditures reduced poverty by less than thirty-seven billion dollars: not a terribly impressive return on the taxpayers' investment.[96] In theory, the one hundred twenty-four billion dollars should have been enough, not only to bring poor households up to the sustenance level but also to bring these and all other households up to twenty-five percent above the sustenance level and still have forty-eight billion dollars left over for other purposes, such as reducing the deficit.[97] Something has gone wrong.

Fifth, the implementation of liberal welfare programs and policies has actually reduced the opportunities of the poor in the open marketplace. Walter Williams, in his brilliant book *The State Against Blacks,* and Thomas Sowell, in his equally insightful book *Civil Rights: Rhetoric or Reality?* have shown beyond any reasonable doubt that most liberal welfare measures decrease work benefits through higher taxes, decrease job creation especially at the lower levels, and decrease entrepreneurial activity due to increased risk.[98] Such measures as the minimum wage, occupational licensing, union supports, and the regulation of the taxi and trucking trades, instead of protecting the unskilled poor, only eliminate them from the marketplace.[99] Upward mobility becomes impossible because the unskilled poor never get to square one. Not only that, everyone else in the economy is harmed as well by the attendant shrinking of venture capital reserves. Something has gone wrong.

Sixth, the implementation of liberal welfare programs and policies has actually contributed to the demise of American industry. Massive governmental interference in the marketplace has artificially sustained a whole host of antiquated businesses.[100] Instead of launching workers into new fields, new technologies, and new opportunities, welfare's union guarantees federal bailouts, and job placement programs have encouraged them to remain with stagnating industries, to be content with outdated skills, and to be fearful of innovation. Something has gone wrong.

The "war on poverty" has become, in fact, a "war on the poor." Welfare has become a trap, victimizing its supposed beneficiaries.

Nevertheless, Marian Wright Edelman and her Children's Defense Fund are committed to dramatically escalating that war in every way, shape, and form:

- It has called for increasing the spending levels for Head Start by $200 million every year "for the next several years."[101]
- It supports a "comprehensive health-care initiative" to essentially expand Medicare to "universal coverage."[102]
- It has called for a "massive upgrade of the minimum wage" with "built-in provisions to keep pace with inflation and the cost of living."[103]
- It wants to set "national minimum benefits standards" requiring that "the combined value of AFDC and food stamp entitlements equal at least seventy-five percent of the federal poverty level."[104]
- It advocates passage of the United Nations Convention on the Rights of the Child, which would give sweeping new powers to government while originating all rights with central governing authorities.[105]
- It even has suggested that welfare be universally expanded to provide a "guaranteed wage" to every citizen.[106]

Edelman dismisses with a flurry of disgust anyone who might have the temerity to oppose such an agenda. They are "greedy," she says.[107] They "don't care about the plight of children," she says.[108] They are more concerned about "three-martini corporate lunches, golf outings, sports tickets, and barber shops for defense contractors" than about "poor working mothers."[109]

According to Max Lichten, "Anyone who disagrees with even the minutest detail of the Children's Defense Fund vision for a smothering welfare society is deemed an ogre who is bent on oppressing the poor and denying justice to the needy. Hundreds of years of private initiative charity notwithstanding, Edelman equates compassion with government action—and only with government action."[110]

A Compassion Consensus

Of course, concern for the poor did not begin with Lyndon Johnson and his liberal economic strategists in the sixties. In fact, the idea of universal social welfare put asunder a long-standing consensus about the role and purpose of government-sponsored relief. It was a consensus that had remained virtually unchanged throughout the history of our nation, and, in fact, reached as far back as England's enactment of the Reformation era Poor Laws.[111]

It was a consensus that operated on the basic admission that civilized societies do not let their constituents starve in the streets. Instead, they attempt to make some sort of decent provision for those who would otherwise languish helplessly in utter destitution. But, that decent provision was by no means promiscuously unqualified. It was, in fact, hedged round about with limitations, prerequisites, and stipulations. Our forebears were unashamedly wary. Though perhaps necessary to the maintenance of civilized societies, government-sponsored emergency relief was still looked upon as a hazard of compassion at best, a sentimental vice at worst.

Why a hazard and a vice?

Because, they believed that the responsibility for charity lay with the family, the church, and private institutions—not with the government. Real social security could only be had through the agencies of faith, family, and work.[112] Thus, welfare was allowed only as a temporary, emergency measure when every other support apparatus failed during times of grave disaster—and that was all.

For centuries this was the unquestioned consensus view of compassion—even among the so-called "ultra-liberals."

Franklin Roosevelt and his New Deal legislative railroad, for instance, may have radically altered the distribution of welfare with the introduction of Social Security, AFDC, Workman's Compensation, and Unemployment Insurance, but the purposes for social welfare remained unchanged. The consensus remained unchallenged. The concerns of character continued to hold sway over the uneasy conscience of compassion. In 1935, he told Congress, "The federal government must, and shall, quit this business of relief. To dole out relief is to administer a narcotic, a subtle destroyer of the human spirit."[113]

John Kennedy also held to this view of welfare. In 1962, he launched a poverty assistance offensive with the slogan, "Give a hand, not a handout." The program was based solidly on that old time-tested consensus that no lasting solution to the problem of poverty can be bought with a welfare check. He understood that the best welfare policy is the one that allows the poor to overcome poverty by the only means that have ever proven effectual: by conscientious faith, by a cohesive family, and by disciplined work.

The original Poor Laws, enacted in 1589, sought to "reinforce righteousness," to "strengthen the family bond," to "set the poor to work," and turn the country into "a hive of industry." Although far from ideal, the laws accomplished just that, and became the model for centuries of unprecedented liberty and prosperity. If welfare was to be a compromise, it was to be a carefully conditioned compromise. Workhouses and labor yards were established so that those willing to work could "pull themselves up by their own bootstraps" while maintaining family integrity. Cottage apprenticeships were initiated so that the youth would "be accustomed and brought up in labor, work, thrift, and purposefulness." Disincentives were deliberately incorporated so that unfaithfulness, irresponsibility, sloth, and graft could be kept to a minimum. From all but the disabled, industry was required.

This legacy of conditioning government welfare on faith, family, and work was carried across the sea by the early American settlers. Knowing that the Poor Laws were based on the fundamental scriptural balance between discipline and responsibility, the colonists maintained the old consensus. As a result, the poor could expect justice and compassion even along the rough-hewn edges of the new frontier. But it was a justice and compassion that demanded responsibility, effort, and diligence of its beneficiaries. It was a justice and compassion rooted in the biblical family and work ethic. It was a justice and compassion that was administered, not by an army of benevolent bureaucrats, but by a gracious citizenry. It was a justice and compassion that created opportunities, not entitlements.

Alexander Hamilton wrote, "Americans hold their greatest liberty in this, our poor arise from their plight of their own accord, in cooperation with, but not dependent upon, Christian generosities." Thomas MacKay wrote, "American welfare consists in a recreation and development of the arts of independence and industry." And Benjamin Franklin was fond of paraphrasing the old Talmudic proverb, asserting that American charity "is the noblest charity, preventing a man from accepting charity, and the best alms, enabling men to dispense with alms." So America came to be known the world over as the home of the free and the brave, the land of opportunity. The old consensus remained an unchallenged bastion in the determination of domestic social policy.

That old consensus died in 1964. It was the first casualty in the "war on poverty."

The members of President Lyndon Johnson's task force on poverty—including Michael Harrington, author of the influential book, *The Other America*, Bill Moyers, the high-profile tele-journalist, Sargent Shriver, pioneer of the Peace Corps, and Joseph Califano, later a chief aide to President Jimmy Carter—forged a new and invincible consensus.

This new consensus decried the old consensus as "harsh," "unrealistic," "insensitive," and "discriminatory." Rejecting the notion that poverty was in any way connected with individual or familial irresponsibility, the new consensus adamantly asserted that poverty was the fault of the system. Environment was the problem. Oppression, discrimination, materialism, and injustice were the *prima facie* causes. And society was to blame.[114]

Thus, society would have to be made to do penance.[115]

One day, Califano called a group of reporters, social workers, and activists—including the young Marian Wright Edelman—into his office at the White House to explain the President's legislative initiative, increasing social welfare spending. He told them that a government analysis had shown that only fifty thousand people, or about one percent of the eight million people on permanent welfare, were capable of being given skills and training to make them self-sufficient. Of the other twelve million people on temporary welfare programs, only about half were trainable, he said.[116]

In other words, the welfare system had created for itself a permanent underclass. A modern form of serfdom had been created—all in the name of compassion. The American Dream had been transformed into the Servile State.

True Compassion

What then should the Children's Defense Fund actually be advocating? What can the government do to reverse its dismal welfare track record? What can the government do to *really* help the poor?

According to economist Murray Rothbard, the only correct answer is, "Get out of the way." Thus he says:

> Let the government get out of the way of the productive energies of all groups in the population—rich, middle-class, and poor alike—and the result will be an enormous increase in the welfare and the standard of living of everyone, and most particularly of the poor, who are the ones supposedly helped by the miscalled welfare state.[117]

Similarly, in his book, *Welfare Without the Welfare State*, Yale Brozen points out:

> With less attempt to use state power to compress the inequality in the distribution of income, inequality would diminish more rapidly. Low wage rates would rise more rapidly with a higher rate of saving and capital formation, and inequality would diminish with the rise in income of wage-earners.[118]

If the government were to reduce the level of taxation, remove industrial restraints, eliminate wage controls, and abolish subsidies, tariffs, and other constraints on free enterprise, the poor would be helped in a way that AFDC, Social Security, and Unemployment Insurance could never match. Jobs would be created, investment would be stimulated, productivity would soar, and technology would advance. If that were to happen, says Rothbard, "the lower income groups would benefit *more* than anyone else."[119]

The "war on the poor" can be turned around. It can be as it was intended to be from the start: a "war on poverty." But only if the government leaves the "war" machinery substantially alone—that is, leaves the "war" machinery to *us*.[120]

Like honoring our parents, caring for the poor is a command with a promise. The Bible tells us that if we would uphold the mandate to be generous to the poor, we would ourselves be happy (Proverbs 14:21); God would preserve us (Psalm 41:1-2); we would prosper and be satisfied (Proverbs 11:25); and we would be raised up from beds of affliction (Psalm 41:3). Care for the needy is at the heart of true faith.[121] Thus it has always been the aspiration of faithful churches to be "zealous of good works" (Titus 2:14).

According to the *Westminster Confession of Faith*, a venerable expression of Reformation thought crafted in 1649:

> Good works, done in obedience to God's Commandments, are

the fruits and evidences of a true and lively faith: and by them believers manifest their thankfulness, strengthen their assurance, edify their brethren, adorn the profession of the Gospel, stop the mouths of the adversaries, and glorify God, whose workmanship they are, created in Christ Jesus thereunto; that, having their fruit unto holiness, they may have at the end eternal life.[122]

At a time when any and all other Christian virtues seem to have been utterly abandoned, this one—caring for the needy through good deeds—still remains. We are all agreed that charity is a good thing. Unfortunately though, because charity remains in isolation, its good-intentioned naiveté has caused more harm than good. As a good out of its place, it has at times ceased to be good.

Charles Haddon Spurgeon, the great Victorian pulpiteer, said:

They say you may praise a fool till you make him useful: I don't know much about that, but I do know that if I get a bad knife I generally cut my finger, and a blunt axe is far more trouble than profit. A handsaw is a good thing—but not to shave with. A pig's tail will never make a good arrow; nor will his ear make a silk purse. You can't catch rabbits with drums or pigeons with plums. A good thing is not good out of its place.[123]

The problem with the Children's Defense Fund agenda is not that Marian Wright Edelman and her legion of welfare activists want to do a good thing. It is that a good thing is not good out of its place. As Wall Street journalist Gerald Wisz has argued, "Government cannot do what the church must."[124]

SIEGE ALERT

CHILDREN'S DEFENSE FUND

Here is what the new social engineers at the Children's Defense Fund have in mind for you and your children in the weeks and months ahead:

- They want to create a comprehensive paternalistic state. They want to remake government into a primary care giver for all Americans, thus extending various aspects of social welfare programs to everyone. In order to accomplish such lofty aims, they know that their number one priority right now has to be the reshaping of welfare reform so that it actually increases not decreases the variety and duration of benefits and entitlements.

- The plan primarily involves lobbying—particularly at the executive and administrative levels where the budgets and programs are actually crafted. This is obviously more than just a pocketbook issue—although there is no doubt that a massive increase in taxes to fund such reforms would be debilitating to most families—it is a moral issue that involves crime, violence, the decay of the social infrastructure, the decline of family integrity and autonomy, as well as incentive and motivation in the workplace.

- Nationally standardized education standards are crucial to the plan to remake America's social welfare system—kids must be uniformly prepared to accept the role and authority of the state, not only in the regulation of markets, industries, economies, and social benefits, but in the regulation of family behaviors and the exercise of rights and liberties.

- In addition, universal access to the myriad of social welfare services provided by such groups as Planned Parenthood is essential to the plan. Therefore, the Children's Defense Fund is already lending support to various aspects of health-care reform and educational reform.

- Watch particularly for "social values" curricula in schools and in community or recreational facilities that undermine parental authority or traditional morals and ethics—thus riding on the heels of national and even international legislation limiting the prerogatives of parents.

EIGHT

MEDICINE SHOW

WORLD HEALTH ORGANIZATION

*What good comes by their physic the sun sees; but in their art, if
they have bad success, that the earth covers.*[1]

—Thomas Heywood

He's a fool that makes his doctor his heir.[2]

—Benjamin Franklin

When Jane Hummert arrived at the health-care forum she was
handed a thick packet of brochures, pamphlets, charts, graphs,
and worksheets. Sponsored by the local chapter of the United Way
and coordinated jointly by the federal Department of Health and
Human Services and the World Health Organization, she had assumed that the meeting would be uniquely informative. She was
right.

Not surprisingly, the auditorium was already abuzz with expec-
tation—each participant had been selected either because of prior
medical difficulties or an inability to secure adequate insurance. If
they were anything like Jane, they were hoping to have a lot of their
questions answered and their anxieties alleviated concerning the
government's most recent health-care reform plan.

Jane's husband had been sick for twelve years before finally
succumbing to cancer in 1982. A year later Jane was involved in a
serious automobile accident and was forced to endure several
rounds of orthopedic surgery. Then in 1986 her youngest son was
stricken with Osteomylitis. Her family long ago had been deemed

199

uninsurable by most of the standard—or affordable—insurance policies.

Looking around her now, she assumed that most of the people in the room had similar stories to tell.

Before the meeting started, she glanced through the packet of materials she'd received. It contained a statistical and demographic profile of the current "health-care crisis" in America. Prepared by researchers at the World Health Organization, the profile painted a rather dismal picture:

- Nearly a quarter of all Americans are uninsured.[3]
- Half of those uninsured live below the poverty line.[4]
- About one-fifth of them are impoverished children.[5]
- Another one-fourth are elderly—living on less than adequate fixed incomes.[6]
- Infant mortality rates are rising dramatically—especially among the disadvantaged.[7]
- A quarter of the unborn are "substance exposed."[8]
- As many as one-eighth of all school children are not immunized.[9]
- Nearly one-fifth of all factory workers remain uninsured.[10]

Although unsubstantiated, Jane had no reason to doubt the figures—though they did seem to portray a crisis of far greater proportions than even she could have imagined.

After a brief greeting and a few introductory remarks, the participants were led in an "awareness exercise." Ten medical case studies were presented to illustrate the gravity of the "health-care crisis" and the need for immediate "reform":

- "Betty is a 35-year-old mother with bad teeth. She is a waitress, but without dentures she can't find a job. Dentures cost around $800, and Medicaid won't pay."[11]
- "Jimmy is a baby with breathing problems. An operation could help, but there is a 50% chance that Jimmy will be mentally impaired if he lives. The operation would cost about $85,000."[12]
- "Mabel is 62 years old, has heart trouble, and needs a pacemaker. The medication she needs without a pacemaker costs $200 a month. A pacemaker operation would cost $22,000. It would not significantly improve the condition of her heart, but it would make day-to-day life easier."[13]
- "Curtis is homeless and has no job. He is also mentally ill. Reg-

ular psychiatric treatment would cost between $10,000 and $15,000 a year."[14]

- "Mary is 30 years old and has brain disease. She cannot remember things. A blocked intestine makes her cough up blood. Surgery would cost $31,000, but it might not actually fix her intestinal problem."[15]
- "Barbara is a 40-year-old mother with three children. She has never had a mammogram, and breast cancer runs in her family. Regular mammograms would cost about $5,800."[16]
- "Katie is a five-year-old with bad kidneys. Her parents often miss work to care for her. A kidney transplant would help Katie live a normal life. It would cost about $40,000."[17]
- "Frank is a 32-year-old father of two preschool children. He drinks too much and is always depressed. He thinks about suicide. Treatment would cost between $10,000 and $20,000 a year."[18]

Participants were then asked to "prioritize" the cases. Although Jane was a bit uncomfortable with the idea that she could make that kind of value judgment with such scanty information, she went along with the exercise.

After a few moments, participants were asked to break up into small groups where they were to "discuss their prioritized lists" and then "come to a group consensus."

It was beginning to dawn on Jane just where this exercise was headed.

Once each of the groups had arrived at a consensus, they were told that they were to act as a "health-care alliance resource delegation committee." They were given a hypothetical budget of $100,000. They were to "delegate" treatment to those patients "with the most compelling needs" while "remaining within their budgets."

When Jane objected to the "group facilitator" that the exercise was little more than "situational ethics" and "values clarification," she was asked either to cooperate or leave the meeting altogether.

"I was outraged," Jane later said. "It was evident that the organizers of the forum had no intention whatsoever of answering our questions or dealing with our concerns. They were there to reshape our thinking. They were there to condition us with the idea that some kind of health-care rationing was not only necessary, it was morally commendable."

Although she had long struggled with sickness, inadequate insurance, and debilitating medical bills, Jane's experience at the forum that day convinced her that the government-sponsored reform plan might not be all it was cracked up to be:

> I began to wonder just what the government—or the World Health Organization, for that matter—had to gain by selecting who would be treated and who wouldn't, who would receive delegated care and who wouldn't, would live and who wouldn't. I came away from the meeting thinking that maybe—just maybe—all the politics surrounding health-care reform was more about politics than it was about health care.

Redefining Health

At the end of the Second World War, the newly convened United Nations approved a joint proposal from Brazil and China that an international health organization should be established. According to Brock Chisholm—a delegate from Canada who would eventually become the director of the new organization—that decision was truly momentous:

> History is studded with critical dates—wars, invasions, revolutions, discoveries, peace treaties—that are firmly implanted in our minds. But the establishment of the World Health Organization may well go down in history as one of the most far-reaching of all international agreements. It will surely be a positive force with broad objectives, reaching forward to embrace nearly all levels of human activity.[19]

Chisholm's almost messianic expectations were apparently shared by the other delegates and thus were reflected in the new organization's charter—it opened with a commitment to nine principles that all the participating nations agreed were "basic to the happiness, harmonious relations, and security of all peoples."[20] Those principles were stated in broad terms and open language:

- "Health is a state of complete physical, mental, and social well-being and not merely the absence of disease or infirmity."[21]
- "The enjoyment of the highest attainable standard of health is

one of the fundamental rights of every human being without distinction of race, religion, political belief, economic or social condition."[22]

- "The health of all peoples is fundamental to the attainment of peace and security and is dependent upon the fullest cooperation of individuals and states."[23]
- "The achievement of any State in the promotion and protection of health is of value to all."
- "Unequal development in different countries in the promotion of health and control of disease, especially communicable disease, is a common danger."[24]
- "Healthy development of the child is of basic importance; the ability to live harmoniously in a changing total environment is essential to such development."[25]
- "The extension to all peoples of the benefits of medical, psychological, and related knowledge is essential to the fullest attainment of health."[26]
- "Informed opinion and active cooperation on the part of the public are of the utmost importance in the improvement of the health of the people."[27]
- "Governments have a responsibility for the health of their peoples, which can be fulfilled only by the provision of adequate health and social measures."[28]

Early critics claimed that such a charter was:

> A magna charta for unrestricted and global meddling; a limitless grant of power to investigate and legislate on almost anything and everything imaginable.[29]

Even its supporters admitted that the new organization had been given extraordinary ambiguous powers. Indeed, Charles A. Winslow of Yale University said, "It would be difficult to imagine a broader charter."[30]

By defining health as "a state of complete physical, mental, and social well-being, and not merely the absence of disease or infirmity" and as a "fundamental right,"[31] the framers had not only placed conventional medical concerns under the organization's purview but also such things as housing standards, nutritional balance, economic status, labor relations, environmental concerns, mental and emotional fulfillment, and any and all social, religious, administrative, or political conditions that might be construed to affect public health in some way, shape, or form.[32] In fact, it would be difficult to imagine any area of human thought or activity—private or public, individual or collective, local or international—not covered by the juridical authority of the World Health Organization.

Amazingly, the participating nations also pledged to yield the power of enforcement to the new organization as well. The charter brashly asserts absolute sovereignty in this regard:

> The Health Assembly shall have authority to adopt conventions or agreements with respect to any matter within the competence of the organization.[33]

And since there is virtually no matter which is not within its competence, the organization has a virtual blank check for dictatorial discretion:

> Each member State undertakes that it will, within eighteen months after the adoption by the Health Assembly of a convention or agreement, take action relative to the acceptance of such convention or agreement. Each member shall notify the director-general of the action taken.[34]

Establishing its international headquarters in Geneva, with six regional offices spread out around the globe—in Washington, Manila, New Delhi, Copenhagen, Alexandria, and Brazzaville—the organization quickly fulfilled its founders' expectations and grew to become one of the largest and richest cultural forces the world has ever known.[35] And, today, with an annual budget of more than one and a half billion dollars a year[36] and activities in some one hundred sixty-six nations,[37] the organization enjoys more prestige and power than ever before.[38]

Though its activities through the years have included a variety of legitimate health-care concerns ranging from securing pure water supplies and adequate modern sanitation facilities to containing malarial infection and AIDS transmission, senior World Health Organization staffers have always placed a heavy emphasis on socio-behavioral issues. Accordingly, a special objective of the agency has always been to provoke changes in traditional family values. Thus, according to Chisholm:

> The basic psychological distortion capable of producing ill-

health, in every civilization of which we know anything, is morality—the concept of good and evil with which to keep children under control, with which to prevent free-thinking, and with which to impose loyalties.[39]

Later, he would comment:

I think that there is no doubt that the idea of sin creates much havoc in our relationships with other cultures. We must remember that it is only in some cultures that sin exists. For instance, the Eskimos didn't have this concept until quite recently. Now they have; they caught it from us. They were formerly in a state of innocence, but they had to be made to feel sinful so they could be controlled.[40]

The mission of the World Health Organization would be to remove "such debilitating obstacles" to "mental health" from the face of the earth.[41] And such unambiguous animosity toward traditional values has indeed been systematized through the years in innumerable programs and projects. For example:

- In Communist China, the organization was instrumental in launching a brutal, no-holds-barred, one-child-per-couple government policy.[42]
- Nearly one hundred million forced abortions, mandatory sterilizations, and coercive infanticides later,[43] the organization continues to maintain that the totalitarian government's genocidal approach to population control is a "model of efficiency."[44]
- It has fought to maintain independent international funding of the Chinese operation,[45] and has continued to increase its own funding and program support involvement[46] despite widespread reports of human rights atrocities.[47]
- Similar draconian measures targeting the integrity of families and the sanctity of life have been implemented at the organization's behest in Bangladesh, Zaire, Sierra Leone, Ethiopia, India, Pakistan, and Indonesia.[48]
- Providing each of these countries with detailed restraints and quotas, suggested compulsory incentives and disincentives, and assistance in circumventing public opinion and moral opposition, the organization has taken the lead in the international campaign to crush the rights and authority of parents, local communities, and religious or ethnic institutions.[49]
- It has been at the forefront of the drive to bring "AIDS educa-

tion" to the popular mass media—going so far as to help the Centers for Disease Control and the Department of Health and Human Services design a series of soft pornographic condom ads for prime-time television in the U.S. and Canada.[50]

- It has pushed for ratification of the United Nations Convention on the Rights of the Child, which would strip away parental rights, authorize vast new coercive government education powers, and create a new international bureaucracy to enforce its globalist aims.[51]

The pinnacle of this assault on the integrity of the family has been the organization's rabid commitment to RU–486 and other abortifacient drugs.[52] From the beginning, it was the World Health Organization that provided the funding,[53] the research facilities,[54] the political pull,[55] and the public relations expertise[56] necessary to insure the drug's positive medical reception.[57]

According to the organization's Division of Public Information, "The acceptance of RU–486 is a major objective of the World Health Organization. We are prepared to spare no expense to insure its deployment."[58]

Why such an all-out commitment to a pharmaceutical treatment that has yet to prove itself safe in clinical tests,[59] that represents no major technological advance over existing techniques,[60] and that is more painful,[61] more costly,[62] and more time-consuming[63] than standard procedures?

According to Dr. Calvin Cuthbert, a medical researcher for the National Institutes of Health, the answer is simply that, "The World Health Organization is not nearly as interested in good medicine as it is in social control and social transformation. For the bureaucrats and cultural visionaries in the organization, health is just politics by another means. They are social engineers in search of an ideological utopia, not physicians in search of a medical cure."[64]

In this regard, the organization is not at all unlike the institution from which it had its genesis: the United Nations.

Progeny Prodigy

The United Nations was founded in 1945 as "man's last, best hope for peace."[65] And by all outward appearances the task of keeping the global peace has been its primary objective ever since—

sending blue-helmeted troops to the world's hot spots to render humanitarian aid, to arbitrate cease fires, and to enforce detente and accord.

But appearances can be deceiving. Of the $7.8 billion spent by the labyrinthine organization in 1992, a mere 10 percent went to peace-keeping and political affairs, while nearly 90 percent went to the organization's sundry social programs.[66] Of the 10,000 employees at the vast international headquarters complex in New York, only 25 now work in the peace-keeping division.[67]

Far from devoting themselves to security issues, the denizens of the behemoth secretariat are consumed with—among other things—the various committees and commissions on apartheid (16 at last count—even though apartheid no longer exists).[68] They serve on decolonization conferences and platforms (42 at last count—more than the number of remaining colonial regions in the world today).[69] They constitute and convene discussions on population problems (32 separate conventions in 1992), on environmental problems (18 separate conventions in addition to the vast Rio Earth Summit confab), and on the peculiar problems of international feminism (11 separate conventions).[70] They also work on economic commissions for Europe, Africa, Asia, and Latin America—each with its trade and technology division, its natural resource division, and its human impact division, and with offices in places like Luxembourg, Vienna, Brussels, Singapore, and Addis Ababa—where they continue to commission studies, conduct research, assemble concords, and issue manifestos.[71]

On those few occasions when the United Nations actually does what it was chartered to do—attempt to keep the peace—it almost invariably botches the effort with all the clumsiness of the lumbering bureaucracy that it is. Witness its recent efforts in such far-flung realms as Somalia, Bosnia, and Kashmir—or before that in Biafra, Bangladesh, Angola, Nambia, Uganda, Kampuchea, Afghanistan, and Korea. Historian Paul Johnson has said, "The United Nations has become a corrupt and demoralized body, and its ill-considered interventions are more inclined to promote violence than to prevent it."[72]

One could hardly expect its subsidiaries to be any better. And they're not. As Michael Barnet, a Wall Street investor and financial commentator, has said:

The entire system is afflicted with the same malignantly bureaucratic contagion. From the World Bank to UNICEF, from the Population Fund to the World Health Organization, the whole globalist lot is a riot of second-bests full of the dotage and dust of failed socialist and universalist ideals.[73]

Thus, according to international health correspondent Anne Arnot:

The fact that the World Health Organization spends most of its time, energy, and resources on things other than health is understandable—given the environment from which the organization has grown. Just as the United Nations focuses on anything and everything but uniting the world's nations, so the World Health Organization focuses on anything and everything but the health of the world's peoples. In both instances, the aim is to obtain power—to centralize control of the social apparatus in the hands of their technical experts and bureaucratic administrators.[74]

In fact, Arnot says, that is the only way that the organization's most recent pet project—universal access health-care reform—can be adequately explained:[75]

The push for international health-care reform has little to do with access to or improvement of medical services. It is simply a convenient means to the overall end of social consolidation and collectivization.[76]

Indeed, the organization's enthusiasm for such health-care proposals as the Clinton administration's plan is not based on the objective criteria of need, efficiency, or cost effectiveness. The fact is, every nationalized health system it has ever helped to devise has failed miserably—in Britain,[77] in Sweden,[78] in Germany,[79] in Holland,[80] and most notably, in Canada.[81] According to virtually every empirical study published over the last decade, each of those systems has faced the inevitable problems of chronic shortages, lower standards of care, and rationing of medical services and supplies—the natural accoutrements of all socialistic enterprises.[82]

A Poison Pill

According to World Health Organization literature, "It is essential that governments attempt to control rising health-care costs in order to effect universal coverage and to insure comprehensive care to all the citizens of the world."[83] The fact that the American system is by far the best the world has to offer,[84] that it is the envy of physicians and technicians everywhere,[85] and that it affords almost universal access and care,[86] doesn't seem to matter. The organization made health-care reform a major priority—with the U.S. its particular target—devoting billions of dollars and untold millions of man hours devising programs, policies, and prototypes for governments worldwide:

- It has sponsored national and international conferences stressing the social and political importance of health-care reform—often in exotic locales so that VIPs can be effectively wined and dined and lobbied.[87]
- It has held innumerable "citizen forums"—like the one Jane Hummert attended in South Carolina—to introduce people to the basic philosophies and principles of reform.[88]
- It has assembled a consulting team of health-care professionals, insurance brokers, and administrative experts to conduct informational workshops for political and business leaders worldwide.[89]
- It has forged a symbiotic relationship with several relief and development agencies, human rights groups, and environmentalist organizations in an effort to piggy-back health-care reform with other forms of political and economic reform.[90]
- It lent its full resources to Hillary Clinton's secretive task force to draft the initial health-care reform package for the U.S.[91]

The trouble is, whenever governments have attempted to follow its blueprints for reform and have actually intervened in the medical industry, the resulting avalanche of regulation has only made services more expensive and remote.[92]

According to Anne Arnot, America's only "health-care crisis" is the existence of bureaucratic intrusions—and the threat of more to come:

> Most doctors will tell you their biggest headache is paperwork. Most nurses complain more about compliance with the huge number of regulations imposed on them than anything else. Medicine has become a legal nightmare because of existing government intrusion—and now it wants more. Just look at the record thus far.[93]

Indeed, the past record of government-imposed reforms does not bode particularly well for the future.

For instance, Health Maintenance Organizations—or HMOs as they're more commonly called—are often thought of as a creation of the free-market insurance and medical-service delivery systems. In fact, they were created and promoted by the World Health Organization and implemented in this country by Congress in 1973 as a "solution" to rising health-care costs.[94] Largely because of huge government grants and subsidies, these franchise-like group programs grew from 26 plans and 3 million subscribers that year to 556 plans with 38 million enrollees by 1992.[95] Despite their rapid proliferation they have not worked out as well as had been expected. Not only has the quality of care deteriorated often with long waits, hasty diagnosis, and impersonal treatment—but medical costs have risen even faster than before.[96]

In an attempt to control Medicare costs, the government replaced the old cost-plus system of hospital reimbursement in 1983 with something called the Prospective Payment System.[97] According to this World Health Organization-devised plan, Medicare established fixed fees in all participating hospitals for the treatment of each of 475 different "diagnostic related groups of illnesses."[98] If the actual cost to the hospitals was less than the fee, they kept the difference; if it was more, they had to absorb the loss. The objective was to somehow encourage price consciousness within the industry and to promote competition among the participating hospitals.[99]

Unfortunately, the Prospective Payment System caused the same shortages and misallocations that price controls have always caused in other industries.[100] It shifted excess costs to services and procedures not covered by the controls, forcing non-Medicare patients to make up the difference between the controlled price and the actual cost.[101] Not only did this pricing ploy actually raise the cost of health care in the aggregate, it even failed to hold down Medicare costs. From 1983 to 1988, the average annual rate of growth in Medicare spending was 6.5 percent for the Hospital Insurance program and 13.8 percent for the Supplemental Medical Insurance program—much higher in both cases than the overall rate of inflation.[102]

Another reform idea the World Health Organization introduced was the "mandated benefit." According to this prescription, insurance companies were required by law to pay for specific medical services while others remain optional. In 1970 there were about a dozen state-mandated benefit laws nationwide; today there are over a thousand.[103] In practice mandated benefit regulations create a two-tier delivery system: The specified procedures are essentially made generic while all other services are effectively made elective. The inevitable result has been an over-supply of some services and a scarcity of others. That too has increased cost and decreased quality.[104]

Interestingly, mandated benefits are also a major reason why many people lack health insurance: Increased costs simply price marginal buyers out of the insurance market. According to the National Center for Policy Analysis, as many as one out of every four uninsured persons lacks health insurance because state regulations have made coverage too expensive.[105] Health analyst Terree Wasley concludes that "as many as 9.3 million people lack insurance because of government intervention in the medical market."[106]

New government red tape involving the approval and distribution of pharmaceuticals and medical devices by the Food and Drug Administration have likewise contributed to the dramatic increase in health-care costs. In 1962, the World Health Organization recommended amendments to the Food, Drug, and Cosmetic Act. The revised code mandated that new medications had to pass a whole new battery of clinical and market tests before physicians could prescribe them for treatment. Since then, the process by which a new drug receives approval has become increasingly complicated, lengthy, and costly. In 1965 it took approximately two years for approval at a cost of about $4 million; by 1989 the time had increased to three years and the cost had skyrocketed to $231 million.[107]

In 1992, the experts at the World Health Organization struck again. At their recommendation, something called the Resource Based Relative Value Scale replaced the system of reimbursement used by Medicare since 1965.[108] The new scale was to be based on the time and effort doctors supposedly devoted to each medical procedure.[109] The new payment schedule meant higher fees for doctors in such specialties as family practice, internal medicine, and obstetrics, and lower fees for surgeons and radiologists.[110] The scale imposed a complicated formula for calculating how much fees can rise each year. In addition, legislation carefully regulated the possibility of "balance billing"—the amount doctors are allowed to charge patients above what Medicare guidelines recommend for a procedure or office visit.[111]

The result has been the suppression of certain essential medical services and the subsidizing of others—regardless of the pressures of supply or demand in the medical market.[112] Thus again, prices have risen inordinately and the quality of care has declined.[113]

At every turn the World Health Organization's recommended health-care reforms have resulted in diminished efficiency, limited access, and increased costs—the very opposite of their stated objectives. And with new reforms looming large on the horizon, it appears that the worst is yet to come.

According to Charles Gowen, an insurance remarketer for a major hospital consortium in Europe:

> From a medical perspective none of the reforms that the organization has proposed, and certainly none of the reforms that have actually been implemented, make much sense—if any. But when you realize that the World Health Organization is primarily concerned with political control and with social transformation, they make perfect sense. In fact, from that perspective, they are downright ingenious.[114]

Ultimately, that is the real problem with the organization's agenda. Of all the deleterious consequences of the socializing of medicine, the most tragic has nothing to do with rising prices or bureaucratic obfuscation. Instead, it is the progressive subversion of the high call of healing to mere politics. It is reducing the caring art of medicine to the banal business of social control.

Malpractice

The advancement of medicine over the past one hundred years represents one of the greatest episodes of human endeavor. The list of its achievements is startlingly impressive.[115]

Thanks to antibiotics like penicillin, many infectious diseases such as scarlet fever, rheumatic fever, gonorrhea, and meningitis can now be almost entirely controlled. Vaccines have saved the lives of millions of children and made such scourges as polio, diphtheria, and smallpox nearly extinct. Diabetes, gout, arthritis, high blood pressure, emphysema, and other chronic illnesses have become more and more manageable with the help of innumerable innovative treatments. Countless lifesaving surgical procedures have followed on the heels of the development of sophisticated antiseptics and anesthesias. In the battle against cancer and heart disease, a phenomenal arsenal of high-tech weaponry has been marshaled: radiation therapy, laser surgery, elemental bombardment, organ transplants, orthoscopic incising, particle transfusions, mechanical prostheses, gene replication, and receptor articulation.

Virtually every malady and condition known to man has faced an unrelenting barrage of new drugs or techniques or operations or therapies or treatments or formulas or procedures. Manned space flights to the moon almost pale in comparison to the flights of fancy that have actually been realized by doctors in search of the sure cure.

Not surprisingly, along with the development of this remarkable technological boom has come a financial boom as well. Medicine is a major growth industry all around the globe. More than a trillion and a half dollars are dedicated to it every year—providing hospitals, pharmaceutical companies, research institutes, and alternative clinics with a lion's share of the world's fiscal resources.[116] In the United States, health care dominates one seventh of the entire economy.[117]

While it is generally recognized that medical care probably costs too much—inflation-adjusted expenses have risen more than five hundred percent during the last ten years—the common consensus is that, despite that solitary drawback, health-care institutions do a pretty good job at what they do.[118] With nary an exception, people accept as a matter of demonstrable fact that great advances in the medical technology and health-care industries have greatly improved our health and well-being. They simply take it for granted that medicine has extended the average life expectancy. They believe with a special ardency that discovering the cures for most diseases is just a matter of time. It is a foregone conclusion for them that prescribed drugs can alleviate the ills of almost any abnormal condition—and that whatever our medical institutions sell us, can and should be taken in good faith.

But none of this is entirely true.

While medicine has been turned into a standardized commod-

ity, a staple, an essential element of modern life, it has simultaneously become a central concern to politicians, social planners, and
business interests. And as a result, the human elements of the
healing arts have been progressively minimized. Medicine in all too
many instances has become an impersonal dispensary of technological gadgets and nostrums.

And without the human touch—the personal, individual, and
compassionate hand of the committed care giver—health care
ceases to be the wonder of the modern world. Medicine is most successful as a relationship between physician and patient.[119] It is
least successful as a technological physic.[120]

The fact is, the greatest advances in health care over the past
hundred years have been the result of sanitation, hygiene, and nutrition—not technology or pharmacology.[121] Simple things like a
pure water supply, a decent sewage system, and a healthy diet have
saved far more lives than open-heart surgery or chemotherapy.[122]
Brushing teeth, washing hands, and shampooing scalps have affected the well-being of millions more than immunology or neuro-
surgery.[123]

There is very little empirical evidence to support the notion that
the health status of modern man has significantly improved merely
as a result of the proliferation of technological medicine.[124] In fact,
in many places the average life expectancy has actually begun to
decline.[125] Epidemics still rage uncontrolled.[126] And human misery
remains a mysterious unchecked scourge. While medicine has undoubtedly tasted some real success in a number of areas, it has
hardly lived up to either the claims or the expectations that have
been universally attached to it by the political prognosticators. On
the contrary, as the respected medical ethicist Ivan Illich has revealed, sometimes modern technological medicine may actually do
more harm than good. "The medical establishment has in some
cases become a major threat to health," he says. In fact:

> A vast amount of contemporary clinical care is incidental to the
> curing of disease, but the damage done by medicine to the health
> of individuals and populations is very significant. These facts are
> obvious, well documented, and well repressed.[127]

Illich goes on to assert that:

> It is doctors and nurses and technicians that have made mod-

ern medicine the success that it is. Sadly, the more politics, paper-work, and pundits interfere with the great human endeavor of health care, the more disastrous the technologies of modern med-icine will appear.[128]

Amazingly, one of the most common maladies today is iatro-genic—in other words, medically caused sicknesses or complica-tions.[129] The plethora of therapeutic side effects and pathogens caused by modern medical technology has actually reached pan-demic proportions.

Horror stories abound of unnecessary surgeries, operating room mix-ups, and procedural errors.[130] Professional callousness, imper-sonal negligence, and sheer incompetence often seem to dominate the highly bureaucratized clinical environment these days.[131] Worse, bizarre practices reminiscent of Nazi-era medicine—like fe-tal harvesting, genetic engineering, virtual reality, cryogenics, dae-liaforcation, cybernetics, euthanasia, cell reailination, and infanti-cide—have come back into vogue and almost become commonplace.[132] But the most troubling aspect of the kind of im-personal technological medicine the World Health Organization promotes is its promiscuous reliance on chemical treatments.

Pharmaceuticals have always been potentially poisonous, but their risks have only increased with their potency and widespread use.[133] Every day between fifty and eighty percent of adults in the industrialized West swallow a medically prescribed drug.[134] Some take the wrong drug—either because the doctor wrongly diagnosed the problem, or the pharmacist made a mistake, or the patient picked up the wrong bottle out of the medicine cabinet. Some get an old or contaminated batch of the drug. Some take an inferior coun-terfeit or generic version. And some take several drugs in danger-ous combinations.

There are a number of drugs on the market that are addictive, others mutilating, and others mutagenic—particularly in combi-nation with food coloring or insecticides. Many of them have very little therapeutic value or are entirely unproven but are prescribed nonetheless because of convenience or especially effective market-ing by pharmaceutical companies in the medical community.[135]

But even proven yeoman drugs can cause grave harm. In some patients, for instance, antibiotics can alter the normal bacterial flora and induce a superinfection, permitting more resistant organisms to proliferate and invade the host.[136] Other drugs contribute to the breeding of drug-resistant strains of bacteria.[137] Subtle new forms of poisoning have thus spread even faster than the bewildering variety and ubiquity of nostrums. Every year, more than seven percent of all non-ambulatory hospital admissions are due to adverse reactions to prescribed drugs.[138]

Pharmaceutical malpractice is especially acute in gynecological medicine—reflecting an overall trend toward the political and economic feminization of medicine.[139] In a fevered rush to get various contraceptive and abortifacient drugs to market, women have suffered under the strain of almost unending complications and side effects.[140] In essence, women using birth control have served the industry as guinea pigs—unwitting subjects in prolonged and deathly dangerous experiments.[141] Today, seven of ten most frequently prescribed drugs in the West are gynecologically related—which is especially frightening in light of the fact that three of the four most frequently performed surgical procedures are also exclusively gynecological—thus making the womb a literal war zone for the practitioners of modern medicine.[142]

Frederick Robbins, a noted figure in pharmacological research and a delegate to the World Health Organization, justified the use of unsafe gynecological drugs saying:

> The dangers of overpopulation are so great that we may have to use certain techniques of contraception that may entail considerable risk to the individual woman.[143]

Thus, when all is said and done, a woman's health considerations and personal choices take a backseat to the economic, political, and social agenda of the new techno-medical industrial complex.

Not surprisingly, in the face of the depersonalization of health care the number of medical malpractice suits has soared over the last two decades. It is now estimated that the average doctor will face at least three major lawsuits sometime during his career.[144] But the average gynecologist can expect at least twelve.[145]

Often feeling as victimized as their patients by the sudden sea changes in medicine, doctors—often the best doctors—are actually leaving the profession in droves.[146] Dr. Matthew Carmichael comments:

A revolution has swept through medicine leaving many of us to wonder if all the years of training and sacrifice is worth it anymore. I got into medicine because I wanted to help people—hurting people. In a large institutional setting I found myself dealing with the management side of things—the business side of medicine—far more than I was seeing patients. So I opened a small practice. There I was forced to spend so much time adhering to regulations—be they IRS standards or OSHA standards or whatever—that again, I was away from the thing that I got into medicine for in the first place. I don't want to be a businessman or an administrator or a fund-raiser or a bureaucrat. I want to be a doctor. But I'm afraid that may be a dying profession.[147]

Francisco Goya, in *Los Caprichos*—a series of etchings the artist executed in 1786—shows a man asleep at his laboratory desk with his head on his crossed arms while monsters surround him. The inscription on the desk reads: *"El sueño de la razón produce monstruos"*—literally, "the dreams of reason produce monsters."

Goya knew that medicine, like art, when not in the service of heaven is most likely in the service of hell.

It appears that the politicization and depersonalization of the health-care industry has engineered the dreams of reason. And the result is monstrously hellish.

Maltheory

It may well be that the usurpation of medicine by business, politics, and the business of politics is much more a maltheory than a malpractice. In other words, the problem with the World Health Organization's approach to modern medicine is not so much bad technologies in the hands of men as bad philosophies in the heads of men. And those philosophies may arise not so much out of malice and malignancy as out of directionlessness.

According to C. Everett Koop, the former Surgeon General of the United States:

I don't think a medical student is ever told what his mission in life is. Certainly no one ever told me what was expected of me as a lifetime goal in assuming the role of a physician.[148]

Similarly, Sami Ladourvec has said:

With the subtle secularization and industrialization of medicine, has come a rootlessness, a lack of cohesiveness, and a latitudinarianism. There is no longer a philosophical definition to our profession. The tragic result is that young doctors have no real sense of calling, and they either have to find meaning and purpose in raw financial gain or in some ideological pursuit. What we are seeing then is the inevitable fragmentation of medicine into a thousand cults and sects.[149]

"When you don't have any clear purpose or direction," says entrepreneurial business consultant Charles Handy, "whether it is in a company, a government, a family, or a profession, anything can and will happen—usually it is bad."[150] Indeed, the proliferation of everything from homeopathy and iridology to applied kinesiology and acupuncture under the rubric of modern health care, demonstrates that the splintering of medical philosophies has indeed resulted in a splintering of medical practices.[151]

According to Ladourvec that kind of professional anarchy has very serious consequences for us all:

> In an atmosphere like that, the tools of technology can be very destructive—it is perhaps no less dangerous than if we were to allow every petty Third World tyrant to have access to nuclear weapons.[152]

Of course, the present intellectual schizophrenia is a fairly recent development. Up until this century, medicine had a consistent and cohesive philosophical foundation.

The earliest medical guild appeared on the Aegean island of Cos, just off the coast of Asia Minor. Around the time Nehemiah was organizing the post-exilic Jews in Jerusalem to rebuild that city's walls, Aesculapius was organizing the post-exilic Jews there on Cos into adept medical specialists—for the first time in history, moving medical healing beyond folk remedies and Pagan rituals. It was not long before this elite guild had earned renown throughout the Mediterranean world under the leadership of Hippocrates, son of Panacea, son of Hygeia, son of Aesculapius, son of Hashabia the Hebrew, an exile of fallen Jerusalem.[153]

Thus, the great Greek school of healing that laid the foundations of modern medicine—that gave us the Hippocratic Oath and the scientific standards for hygiene, diagnosis, and systematic treatment that form the basis for comprehensive health maintenance—wasn't actually Greek at all. It was Hebrew—the fruit of biblical faith.[154]

In the centuries that followed, wherever and whenever biblical faith flourished, so did medicine. The fact is, medicine has always been a special legacy of believers—provoked by biblical compassion, fueled by biblical conviction, and guided by biblical ethics. When plague and pestilence convulsed the peoples of the past, it was merciful Christians who stood steadfast amidst the terrors establishing hostels, clinics, and ultimately hospitals. Even a cursory survey demonstrates that, throughout history, Christian nations have always been havens of medical proficiency and personalism—carefully guarding the sanctity of life. Whereas in pagan nations, medical technology invariably degenerated into crude superstition and mechanical detachment—just one more bludgeon to exploit the weak, the poor, and the helpless.

It takes more imagination to dismiss the civilization that gave us Stephansdomplatz, Chartres, and Westminster than to accept them. But of course, the modern social engineers of the World Health Organization's ilk are terribly imaginative.

And so today, on the one hand there are doctors who no longer make house calls or sit on the edge of beds because their science has become so institutional, on the other hand there are doctors who perform occult and cabalistic rites because their science has become so mystical. On the one hand medicine is transformed into a vast bureaucracy-laden industry, on the other hand it harbors distopic visions for the transformation of society into an ideological *impresse*. Either way, their respective practices have ceased to be entirely human—one is black impudence. The other is black nonsense. Both are black magic—an utterly alien rite to the world-view application that lent the profession its earlier greatness.

According to Illich:

> Medical procedures turn into black magic when, instead of mobilizing and enlisting responsible participation in the healing process, they transform the sick man into a limp and mystified voyeur of his own treatment. Medical procedures turn into bad philosophy—even bad religion—when they are performed as rituals that focus the entire expectation of the sick on scientific or mystical mechanisms.[155]

The World Health Organization has, from its earliest days,

maintained a commitment to that kind of radical departure from the original vision of the healing arts—which ultimately accounts for its fervid desire for health-care reform.

Sadly, the end result of that departure is some form of inhuman tyranny—running roughshod over the very people doctors were supposed to save.

Perhaps T. S. Elliot had this awful paradox in mind when he lamented:

> Where is the life we have lost in living?
> Where is the wisdom we have lost in knowing?
> The cycles of heaven in twenty centuries,
> Bring us farther from God and nearer to dust.[156]

SIEGE ALERT

WORLD HEALTH ORGANIZATION

Here is what the new social engineers at the World Health Organization have in mind for you and your children in the weeks and months ahead:

- They want to universalize the notion of health. They want to bring all human concerns under the rubric of health care. They are social visionaries who want to use medicine as a means to reshape society itself. In order to accomplish such lofty aims, they know that their number one priority right now has to be the passage and implementation of a comprehensive health-care plan for universal coverage.

- Integration of social, educational, and political concerns under the auspices of government is a crucial aim for this overall plan—giving control over the most intimate and personal aspects of people's lives to regulators and bureaucrats.

- The full weight of their international organization—with its incumbent political, economic, and ideological clout—will be directed at mandating not only universal coverage but universal participation. Medical care would then be governed by the dictates of current politically correct standards without the possibility of alternative care—thus effectively marginalizing large families, at-risk pregnancies, "extraordinary" perpetual care for non-ambulatory or elderly patients, or other unacceptable behaviors.

- In addition, employment standards in business and industry would have to be more severely regulated than ever before simply because the high cost of health care will create a black market for products and services— a prospect entirely unacceptable to a universal coverage plan.

- Watch particularly for compromise pressures in schools and in the workplace in an effort to make the reforms more palatable—again emphasizing the irresponsibility of families and the private sector to provide "essential care" to all.

NINE

OLD NEW AGE

TIKKUN

Hell is fully lined with good desires.[1]
—Bernard of Clairveaux

The road to hell is paved with good intentions.[2]
—James Boswell

The air was pure and cold, as befitted Martinmas. The far reaches of the horizon had level lines of light above them, deeply colored, full of intrigue and quest. There was a little mist above where I supposed the river lay, and a white line of it in the growing dimness under the shadowy watch of downtown. It was not yet quite dark, but the first stars had come into the sky, and the pleasant scent of cafes and bistros was already strong upon the evening air when I found myself on the crest of a hill facing a panoply of Moorish towers, tiled Spanish arches, pale Italianate brickworks, and rich Mediterranean marbled glass. The vista lent me a happy panorama of busy shoppers and loitering commuters taking in, just as I was, the aura of the twilight.

Much the most strikingly original quality of the Plaza is, I think, its integrity. I use the word not—at least not exclusively—in its secondary sense, of having the character of uncorrupted virtue, but in its primary one, defined in the dictionary as "the condition of having no part or element wanting; an unbroken state; a material wholeness, a completeness and entirety." It has what William Faulkner called "an indelible sense of place."[3]

Unlike so many of America's most exclusive shopping areas—Las Olas in Fort Lauderdale, Rodeo in Los Angeles, or Fifth Avenue in New York—the Plaza seems to be fully part of the warp and woof of the wider community. Built in 1922 as America's very first shopping center, the landmark development lies along the old Santa Fe Trail just east of the Missouri River near downtown Kansas City. Boasting more fountains than any other city in the world except Rome (more than 200) and more boulevard miles than any other city except Paris (more than 155), Kansas City is a beautiful town of rolling hills, snug neighborhoods, and innumerable cultural attractions. But even against this backdrop, the Plaza still dominates the life of the city. Its outdoor murals, tree-lined walks, striking statuary, and varied shops have made it far more than just a commercial attraction. It has become, through the years, the gathering place for men, women, and children from every strata and segment of society.

On this night it reflected that broad diversity with a gleeful energy. As shopkeepers began to prepare for the hectic season just ahead, families clustered in front of dazzling window displays composing wish-lists and sharing dreams. One elderly couple quietly reminisced of holidays past as they strolled up and down the sidewalk. A mom pushing a tot in an umbrella stroller glowed with obvious anticipation—it would be her child's first Christmas. A dad, accompanied by four rambunctious boys, emerged from a sporting goods store laughing and giggling—about what, I don't know. All around me was displayed the wild and varied spectacle of simple joys.

At a community information booth just off 47th Street, I shuffled through coupons, advertisements, and store promotions as well as a wide assortment of left-wing pleas to save the planet, to recycle trash, and to stop sundry social ills—from racism and homophobia to fur coats and aerosol deodorant. After a few bemused moments, I found what I was looking for: a flier advertising a local Tikkun salon that was to meet later on that evening.

I walked slowly back into the blithe crowd of humanity. A father just ahead of me was trying to help his young son negotiate a giant double-decker ice cream cone. It looked like more ice cream was getting on the boy than in him. Across the street a young couple, arm in arm, gazed longingly at the display case in a jewelry store. A gaggle of teens nearby jostled and jabbed one another with carefree abandon. The streets actually teemed with a vibrant extraordinary ordinariness—of the sort that is never discovered because it is always obvious.

The meeting had already begun when I walked into the boxy unadorned synagogue a few blocks from the river. I checked my watch; I double-checked the flier; I wasn't late—in fact, I was ten minutes early. But obviously things were in full swing. Twenty or so yuppyish men and women—all apparently outfitted rather uniformly by Banana Republic and L. L. Bean—were chanting the words to a contemporary Hebrew folk song. Although the lyrics were difficult for me to entirely make out, apparently they involved somehow the ideas of justice, diversity, and responsibility.

The sing-song chant ended rather abruptly and a grim young man wearing a splendid blue, beaded yarmulke stepped forward to lead the group in a kind of responsive *Al Cheyt* prayer—a modern variation of the traditional antiphons for Jewish high holy days:

> *Ve-al kulam, Eloha selichot, selach lanu, mechal lanu, kaper lanu.* For all our sins, may The Force that makes forgiveness possible forgive us, pardon us, and make atonement possible.

Awkwardly, I tried to make my way into the meetingroom toward an empty seat. The group solemnly intoned:

> For the sins we have committed before you and in our communities by being so preoccupied with ourselves that we ignore the larger problems of the world in which we live; For the sins of accepting the current distribution of wealth and power; And for the sins of giving up on social change and focusing on personal advancement and success; For these sins we ask God and each other to give us the strength to forgive ourselves and each other.

I looked around the room; no heads were bowed; no eyes were closed. Though the antiphon seemed to take the outward form of *Rosh Hashanah* prayer, it was oddly couched more as a political manifesto than as a confession of iniquity or a declaration of repentance:

> For the sins of participating in a racist society and not dedicating more energy to fighting racism; For the sins of not doing enough to save the environment; For the sins of not doing enough

to challenge sexist institutions and practices; For the sins of turning our backs on—or participating in—the oppression of gays and lesbians; For these sins we ask God and each other to give us the strength to forgive ourselves and each other.

A young woman near the front of the room was angrily shaking her fist, as if to heaven. Another was growling out each line of the supplication like a heckler at a protest. This *Al Cheyt* almost seemed to be a despised discipline or an unwanted therapy:

> For the sins we have committed by not forgiving our parents for the wrongs committed by our parents when we were children; For the sins of not seeing the spark of divinity within each person we encounter, or within ourselves; For the sins of doubting our ability to love and to get love; For the sins of not recognizing the beauty within ourselves; For these sins we ask God and each other to give us the strength to forgive ourselves and each other.

The leader took a deep breath, and then after a long pause repeated:

> *Ve-al kulam, Eloha selichot, selach lanu, mechal lanu, kaper lanu.* For all our sins, may The Force that makes forgiveness possible forgive us, pardon us, and make atonement possible.

At that point he suggested that the people divide into small groups of four or five to discuss what particular aspects of the "prayer" made most sense to them, what they intended to do differently in the coming year, and what support they felt they might need from others in order to make the necessary changes in their lives and their world. I thought this might be a good time to take a rest room break. I tried to slip out unobtrusively.

A long table in the hallway was crowded with books written by Michael Lerner. There were cassette messages by Michael Lerner. There were video tapes featuring Michael Lerner. There were pamphlets and *pronunciamentoes, philippics* and *pasquinades* by Michael Lerner. And, not surprisingly, there were several back issues of Michael Lerner's *Tikkun* magazine. No diversity here.

I came back into the room just as the group exercise was concluding—perfect timing. The leader was making a few announcements: There would be a vegetarian potluck supper following the meeting; the next week salon members were to gather at the State Health Department building downtown for an AIDS protest; a solidarity meeting with several other "social action organizations," including Greenpeace, ACT UP, and Planned Parenthood, would be held at an area Baptist graduate school; a seminar on "para-spiritual meditation as a catalyst for social activism" would be held at the nearby Unity Church; and finally, there were several personal matters involving Michael Lerner's recent move from California to New York that still demanded resolution.

The leader then launched into the evening's lecture—which consisted primarily of long block quotes from the works of, you guessed it, Michael Lerner: With a fog of fatalism sterner than any supralapsarianism he condemned "the individualism and me-firstism of the competitive market." He bemoaned the fact that most Americans were suffering "a kind of insidious hidden pain—a pain related to the breakdown of values, a crisis in relationships, an escalating divorce rate, and a growing frustration with the ongoing alienation of the workplace." He spoke of the "shameless victimization of the American working class and the vile subjugation of the proletariat."

He used a flurry of the buzz words of nineties sensitivity: diversity, communitarianism, multi-culturalism, understanding, tolerance, and, of course, love. "The reason America is so sorely lacking in these attributes," he said, "is because of the political skullduggery of an evil conspiracy of industrialists, imperialists, militarists, and right-wing fundamentalists."

After nearly an hour of such maudlin hooey and politically correct bibble-babble, the meeting came to a close.

I stood around for a few moments while several young women opened Tupperware bowls of bland-looking tofu salads and pallid sprout casseroles. Everyone looked rather sad and serious and the thought passed through my mind that such a funk was understandable considering the menu. But after the homily on love, community, and harmony I'd expected a bit more joviality.

I mentioned my concern to a painfully withdrawn fellow standing beside me. As if with a shock of recognition, he whispered conspiratorially in my ear, "We love mankind—it's people we can't stand." He chuckled ever so slightly. Then with averted eyes he said, "Seriously, according to Michael Lerner it is only when we have that kind of unsentimental approach to life that we can have any hope of instituting real love, real community, and real diversity in this corrupt society. Weighty matters tend to make us somber."

He looked my way once more and then quickly walked away to his curds and whey.

No one else spoke to me after that so, after a few moments, I left. So much for communitarian love.

As I walked back toward the Plaza a bracing breeze blew. Though it was getting late, the streets were still crowded with happy shoppers. Carefree laughter filled the air. The family behind me chattered excitedly in Spanish. A little boy and a little girl—one white and one black—toddled ahead of me, hand in hand while their parents pointed and smiled knowingly. A small crowd gathered cooing and goo-gooing around a newborn in a carriage. Amidst this riotous community of vicissitude I couldn't help but observe that truly weighty matters tend to make us anything but somber.

Though I knew that all was not well with the world—far from it— I had the distinct impression that as admirable as diversity is in orderly social theory, it is far more admirable in disorderly social practice and thus as necessary as American reform may be, the reform of American reformers is more necessary still.

With a newfound determination to corroborate such profundities, I made my way into a little sidewalk bistro; I ate a steak.

Transforming the World

Tikkun began as little more than "Michael Lerner's one man cottage industry."[4] But it is an industry that has somehow spawned "a remarkably influential movement of para-spiritual Jewish leftism."[5] Legally incorporated as the Institute for Labor and Mental Health in 1986, the organization does little more than publish Lerner's books and booklets, distribute his bi-monthly magazine, reproduce his cassette messages, and host his salons—much like the one I attended in Kansas City. It is thus difficult to differentiate between the man and his fledgling movement; they seem to be natural extensions of each other.

Throughout his career Lerner has labored in relative obscurity—and thus to describe Tikkun as a "movement" would have been, until very recently, hyperbole at best. His bizarre views of everything from the nature of spirituality to the essence of social justice and from the significance of marriage to the meaning of politics have made him *persona non grata* among the increasingly conservative American Jewish middle class. Even so, he has enjoyed a tiny but loyal following amidst the radical left fringe of Jewish community life. According to the *New York Times,* "Though his intellectual foes virtually ignore him, among his followers he has an almost messianic image."[6]

Marked by his quirky opinions, his voluminous output, and his unique knack for transforming drama into melodrama, Lerner has been variously described as "a disheveled, chubby man of fifty, brimming with nervous Jewish charm,"[7] "a dynamo of inchoate ideas and passions,"[8] and "a cultish tyrant who walks with a heavy-footed clumsiness and waxes inelegantly on every subject imaginable."[9] Likewise, his movement inspires starkly contrasting observations: from "an eccentric cult, a Jewish heresy no less, that mixes the Old Testament with a dash of medieval cabala mysticism, and a good deal of 1960s campus Marxism"[10] to "a herald of a spiritual renaissance luring countless alienated Jews back into the fold."[11]

The primary conduit for the work of this "bristly, iconoclastic intellectual" and his movement is the magazine.[12] Dubbed a "bimonthly Jewish critique of politics, culture, and society," the journal looks to be modeled after its chief competitor for the hearts and minds of American Jewry, *Commentary.* Like that venerable old mainstay of neo-conservatism, Lerner's publication is a provocatively dense, polemical, and varied forum for social controversy. It counts among its contributors some of America's most respected Jewish thinkers and rabbis as well as a distinguished assortment of feminists, social activists, civil rights advocates, homosexual theorists, and left-wing intellectuals. Taking its name from the Hebrew word meaning "to heal or repair," the magazine was originally conceived in order to combat what Lerner believed was the "malevolent influence of *Commentary.*"[13]

"Like its editor," says media critic Thomas Fields-Meyer, "*Tikkun* is unpolished, overflowing with fervor and conviction, with a tendency toward verbosity. It is not so much a Jewish magazine as an opinion journal with a Jewish point of view."[14] He says it "has the look of a slightly souped-up academic journal. Its cover art is staid—often an abstract oil painting—and the pages are dense with prose, broken up only here and there with a line drawing."[15] In addition, there are few advertisements and the writing is "occasionally sloppy and often self-consciously cerebral."[16] According to

Fields-Meyer, its obsessions are obvious: "the Democratic party, relations between Jews and Blacks, feminism, the American role in world affairs, and the politics of the 1960s."[17] With its odd mixture of long ideological diatribes, prissy free-verse poetry, and intellectual inglenooks, it is vociferously strident, unashamedly biased, and spiritually obtuse. It is difficult to classify and even more difficult to read.

That is hardly a typical recipe for publishing success.

But after less than a decade of publication, *Tikkun* now boasts a circulation of some 40,000 copies, thus reaching nearly as many readers as its bitter rival—a remarkable feat by any standard.[18] "Obviously," says the *New York Times*, "Lerner has touched a nerve."[19]

Indeed he has. According to Leonard Fein, a regular columnist on American Judaism in the *Jewish Forward*, Lerner's magazine has "reached out to a constituency that nobody else was reaching in quite the same way, or at all. Its success therefore needs to be taken quite seriously."[20]

But the newsstand success of Lerner's magazine is hardly the most compelling reason to take him seriously. Rather, it is his remarkable influence over the affairs of state.

White House Guru

One week after the devastating electoral loss of Michael Dukakis and Lloyd Bentsen in 1988, Michael Lerner published a nine-page summary of his political philosophy. It was an eclectic critique arguing that the Democrats had lost their way because they had long ignored what he called "the crisis of meaning in life."[21]

Shortly thereafter Lerner says he received a letter "out of the blue" from "the first Democratic politician who really seemed to get it."[22]

The politician was Bill Clinton.

"You have helped me clarify my own thinking," wrote the rather obscure Arkansas Governor, "and to feel a little more convinced to say what I feel."[23]

To hear Lerner tell it, four years later Clinton was able to dumbfound the experts and recapture the White House for the Democrats "precisely because" he adopted the "cultish psycho-social approach to the world" that Lerner calls "the politics of meaning."[24] In addition, Clinton has continued to buck the odds, winning key legislative victories for his budget, trade, and health deals because he has "explicitly and consciously" embraced Lerner's New Age "ethos of caring and connectedness."[25]

Regardless of whether Lerner's ideas have indeed helped to spawn the string of Clinton's surprising comebacks or have rather contributed to his epochal public unpopularity, there is no doubt that they have been—and remain—a dominant influence. According to a whole host of Washington insiders, Lerner continues to provide the administration with "its moral compass."[26] He infuses "heart and soul into virtually every policy decision" and lends "a para-spiritual motivation to its decision-making process."[27] He has thus become, for all intents and purposes, "the guru to the White House."[28]

When Hillary Clinton gave what the *New York Times* called a "passionate, at times slightly incoherent, call for national spiritual renewal"[29] and a revival of "a politics of meaning,"[30] she was borrowing heavily from the ideas of Tikkun and Lerner.[31]

"What do our governmental institutions mean? What do our lives in today's world mean?" Mrs. Clinton asked. "What does it mean in today's world to pursue not only vocations, to be part of institutions, but to be human?"[32]

In order to divine the answer to such deep and metaphysical questions she suggested a radical transformation of both society and self. "Let us be willing to remold society," she said, "by redefining what it means to be a human being in the twentieth century, moving into a new millennium."[33]

Shortly after the speech, Lerner was invited to the White House. Mrs. Clinton gushed to him that it was "amazing how much we seem to be on the same wavelength." Lerner agreed and offered to be available to regularly consult the administration on "how to take the politics of meaning into a policy direction."[34]

"The following Monday," he recalled later, "I was in her office in Washington for half an hour. The conversation was actually quite amazing."[35]

Mrs. Clinton was reportedly as amazed by their harmonic convergence as was Lerner. "What am I?" she gasped. "Your mouthpiece?"[36]

As Lerner described it, the entire meeting was punctuated by fits of recognition. "It was almost like half sentences, because she had read everything I had written on the politics of meaning. She had understood everything."[37]

And even as Lerner must know, that really is a daring feat. Virtually no one else quite understands either him or his Tikkun movement. "The politics of what?" asked *Time* magazine.[38] Similarly, the *New Republic* sagely observed, "It's good to know that the First Lady is pro-meaning. But before signing on, one question: What on earth are these people talking about?"[39]

Some have asserted that there is actually little to understand. The *Wall Street Journal* simply dismissed Lerner as an "aging sixties radical."[40] According to *Human Events* his vaunted "politics of meaning" is little more than "silly socialism" or political "goo-gooism."[41] And Charles Krauthammer, writing in the *Washington Post*, characterized Tikkun as a predictably immature idealism. "Most Americans," he said, "come to these thundering truisms early in life."[42] He went on to worry that the White House had been turned over to college kids or their intellectual equivalents, asking, "Aren't there any proctors in this dorm?"[43]

In an attempt to answer the dismissive cynicism of the media, Lerner has made the rounds of the talk-show circuit and written a steady stream of editorials for the nation's most influential newspapers, journals, and digests. The inveterate self-promoter seems to be utterly tireless. His enormous energies seem to know no bounds.

But despite his omnipresence on the national stage, Lerner has generated far more questions than answers.

Marx and Moses

Michael Lerner was born in 1943 in Newark, New Jersey. His parents were political activists and Zionists—part of the early American contingent pushing for a national homeland for the Jewish people in Palestine. Joseph Lerner, the son of an ultra-orthodox rabbi, found success as a municipal court judge. His wife, Beatrice, was a prominent Democratic Party organizer and an aide to New Jersey senator Harrison Williams.

Thus, his youth was a heady mix of politics and Judaism. No

wonder that from his earliest days he was torn between the aspiration to become a rabbi or a congressman. As a youngster he read the daily *Congressional Record* and he simultaneously steeped himself in the writing of esoteric theologians like Abraham Joshua Herschel.

In remembering those days, Lerner recounts several arguments he had with prominent political leaders—most notably a nasty tiff with Adlai Stevenson. Asked how a child could muster the gumption to challenge such a figure, Lerner simply says it was "no big deal." The politicians were, after all, "just people hanging out in my house. They didn't seem to me to be anything special."[44]

Following high school Lerner continued the double-track of politics and Judaism entering both Columbia University and the Jewish Theological Seminary. Gradually though, he grew disillusioned with the narrow pedestrianism of the seminary. He decided to turn down his admission to rabbinical school and instead began to pursue a degree in philosophy. When he moved to Berkeley shortly thereafter in 1964, he hardly seemed a likely candidate to become a campus radical. He wore conservative jackets and ties and paid for his tuition by teaching Hebrew school and supervising a synagogue youth group.

But the inexorable tug of social radicalism drew him into the ranks of the free-love, anti-war, hippie movement. "I didn't like it," he later said, "but I was forced by the logic of the arguments. The morality of the situation pushed me further and further into radical politics."[45]

He joined the exclusive nine-man committee of the Free Speech Movement and led the local chapter of the Students for a Democratic Society—a Communist Party youth front notorious for violent campus takeovers and riotous protests. He roomed with Jerry Rubin—the outspoken Marxist student leader and founder of the Yippies—and became a part of an increasingly disruptive network of activists that included Tom Hayden, Douglas Wachter, Bettina Aptheker, and Bernadine Dohrn. He helped to organize teach-ins, sit-ins, and marches. He led the Berkeley campus denunciations of the "oppressors," "exploiters," and "Al Capones who run this country."[46] And he even vented his anger on his Judaic roots saying, "The Jewish community is racist, internally corrupt, and an apologist for the worst aspects of American capitalism and imperialism."[47]

As the student movement gradually shifted from protests to resistance to outright acts of terrorism it was not long before Lerner ran afoul of the law. He was in and out of jail several times for obstruction of justice, criminal mischief, and disturbing the peace.

In 1968 while serving as a teaching assistant at the university, he had a "love child" with one of his students to whom he says he ultimately "married religiously but not legally." At their cohabitation ceremony, a wedding cake was decorated with the words "Smash Monogamy."[48] True to form, he left both mother and child shortly thereafter in order to "actively organize sedition" and "build a guerrilla force" on college campuses and in inner-city communities throughout the western U.S.[49]

Inevitably, one of his war protests turned violent. In 1970, he and six other insurgents were indicted as the "Seattle Seven." When the FBI dubbed Lerner "one of the most dangerous criminals in America" his trial became a national cause célèbre.[50] Though he did time in a federal penitentiary, the charges were ultimately dropped and his record was cleared.

Martin Van Buren once observed that, "Most men are not scolded out of their opinions."[51] Certainly that is true of Lerner. His trial exposed the revolutionary intentions of the student movement for all to see. The tide of opinion, once moderately sympathetic, had now turned against the radicals and they were held up to public scorn. But Lerner didn't seem to notice. He tried to pick right up where he'd left off: attempting to mobilize the masses for one final grand assault on the establishment.

In 1973, he wrote what he hoped would be a manifesto for the movement, entitled *The New Socialist Revolution.* It was volatile and untempered in its call for a radical overthrow of the system. He wrote:

- "The only changes that make sense in America are those that will move this country to socialism."[52]
- "Socialism cannot be achieved by relying on the political system to move slowly in the direction of socialism but can be realized in this country only through revolutionary struggle."[53]
- "Can the American Revolution occur without violence? This is a crucial question, which worries most Socialists. . . . But when

the question of violence is addressed to the Left, it is only to distort reality. The real question must be asked of the rulers of this country: will they allow their system of unequal power and wealth to be overthrown without violence?"[54]

- "The question of violence is being answered for us every day by the ruling class. Will they allow us to revolutionize the world nonviolently? Absolutely not. On the contrary, they will fight to the last drop of our blood and the blood of every mercenary they can buy or coerce."[55]
- "Revolutionary violence must be understood in this context."[56]
- "Both our humanity and our reason demand that we engage ourselves in the struggle for Socialist revolution."[57]

By the time the book came out, though, the halcyon days of radicalism had already passed. The movement had succumbed to both entropy and atrophy. It was not long before his entire organization evaporated altogether. At a loss to know just what to do with himself, Lerner did what so many former radicals did: He went back to school. He eventually earned two doctorates—one in clinical psychology and another in philosophy. He then reluctantly put his hand to the plow: He got a job as a psychologist in the blue-collar bedroom communities of California's bay area. Even so, it appears, he was forever looking back wistfully at the world of political activism.

The Repairman

The failure of the radical student movement in the sixties taught Michael Lerner a bitter lesson: Regardless of how well organized the Left might be, regardless of how correct its cause might be, regardless of how brilliant its strategists might be, without money sweeping social change was simply a pipe dream. The revolution needed money. Lots of money.

Marxism is the most materialistic of all social theories. It sees history through the lens of money. It organizes its methodology, stirs its passions, mobilizes its concerns, and structures its strategies all in terms of money. Its enmity with capitalism is based solely on the notion that capitalists have the capital.

Eventually, Lerner set out to try and change that.

Admittedly, working as a clinical psychologist among the lower middle-class working communities of northern California does not at first glance seem to be the best career path for a gold digger. But like so many of the social visionaries of the past, Lerner knew he had to have a niche. In order to attract big dollars he needed more than a vague conception of the ills of modern American life and a passion for revolution—he needed a marketing angle.

Thus he set up a string of nonprofit community organizations, foundations, and associations around his counseling practice—including the Institute for Labor and Mental Health, and the Committee for Judaism and Social Justice. He worked as a therapist for several labor unions and activist groups. And he bided his time.

Eventually he caught the eye of Nan Fink. However much his apparent aversion to monogamy clouded his judgment, he still knew a good thing when he saw it: Fink was a millionaire drugstore heiress with a penchant for radicalism. In 1986, after a brief romance, the two were married—in a relatively conventional ceremony this time.

It was later that year that they decided to launch the work of Tikkun with a massive infusion of Fink's fortune. The magazine alone consumed somewhere in the neighborhood of a million dollars.[58]

They chose the Hebrew word *tikkun* because they had both recently become fascinated by an odd kind of cabalistic spirituality. The notion of "healing, mending, or repairing" is "the central focus" of a late medieval manuscript entitled *Zohar*.[59] For centuries, the manuscript has inspired "various occultic Jewish sects and splinter groups to posit the primordial perfection of the human soul."[60] It also inspired them to "strive for the inner healing of psychic reconciliation" as the only means to "restore the therapeutic societal values of respect, tolerance, and justice."[61] Indulging in what today we loosely dub "New Age" spirituality, those sects have always been regarded as heretical by mainstream Judaism. In fact, according to Rabbi Abel Rothmann, "It would be difficult to characterize these cult-like groups as Jewish in any other way than in origin."[62]

Although the bizarre mix of meditation, psycho-therapy, and occultism of *Zohar* spirituality was able to help repair Lerner's flagging efforts to usher in sweeping social change, it did little to repair his life or relationships. Within three years, his marriage had failed and he had divorced Fink.

Again though, Lerner showed little patience for self-examination or reevaluation. He was a man on a mission to bring peace and harmony to the world—even if he could not bring peace and harmony to his own home. In an unintended self-parody of modern liberalism, he blamed society for his profound personal failures:

> The breakdown of families—the deep trouble people are having in finding and sustaining relationships—is rooted in the psychodynamics of the capitalist marketplace.[63]

Again, he wrote:

> Most Americans are experiencing . . . a pain related to the breakdown of values, a crisis in relationships, an escalating divorce rate, a growing frustration with the alienation people experience in the world of work.[64]

And the only solution to this crisis of angst, this rank victimization of the proletariat is, of course, revolutionary social change—what Lerner calls "the politics of meaning."[65]

The Politics of Meaning

Senator Ted Kennedy asserted that, "The ballot box is the place where change begins in America."[66] Although he has been fiercely and vehemently wrong in the past, Kennedy has never been more wrong than this. As George Will has argued:

> There is hardly a page of American history that does not refute that insistence, so characteristic of the political class, on the primacy of politics in the making of history or meaning.[67]

In fact, he says, "In a good society, politics is peripheral to much of the pulsing life of society." Similarly, columnist Paul Gigot has wisely observed that, "Americans seek meaning through their families, their churches, and their daily lives, not the good intentions of the state."[68] That is why most of us are far more concerned with what happens in the little white house in our own hometown than we are with the what happens in the big White House in Washington. We know that politics is important, but it is not all-important—and it certainly is not going to solve our everyday problems or bring meaning and satisfaction to our lives. The vast majority of Americans consider themselves conservatives.[69] And the essence of conservatism is a healthy skepticism of politics.[70]

But according to Michael Lerner any such skepticism about the transformational power of politics is not just wrong-headed, it is downright "pathological."[71] In fact, he says, conservatism is itself an indication of the deep psychosis of the American soul:

> People attracted to conservative politics . . . are often people in a great deal of pain, and their attraction to right-wing ideas is often a response to that pain.[72]

Again, he says:

> Many of the people who are sometimes attracted to right-wing perspectives are basically decent people whose perceptions are distorted by emotional trauma.

Thus, arguments against the politics of meaning only emphasize its crucial importance all the more:

> It seems quite plausible that there is a hard core of as much as twenty percent of the American population whose racism, sexism, homophobia, or anti-Semitism is so deeply ingrained, and their fears of softness and caring so great, that nothing could possibly get through to them. Yet there is another thirty to forty percent of the population who sometimes swing toward voting for reactionary candidates, but who often do not, and whose pathologies around caring, nurturance, and softness can be addressed and alleviated. . . . The pain and frustration that leads people to the Right can be overcome and it must be overcome.[73]

Not surprisingly, Lerner is full of specific policy ideas about how to overcome the conservative pathology. Besides recommending the usual litany of socialistic entitlements, amoral empowerments, and confiscatory taxation he suggests:

- "Every workplace should be mandated to create a mission statement explaining its function and what conception of the common good it is serving and how it is doing so."[74]
- "Management should produce such a statement, but there should be a totally separate process, fully protected by legal strictures of confidentiality, by which workers can gather and discuss these issues and report on what they believe their workplace is actually doing and how it is doing it—as well as

what kind of changes would be necessary if the workplace were to serve the common good and were to provide meaningful work."[75]

- "To ensure that time is allocated for this purpose, the government should mandate a series of two-hour segments on succeeding weeks in which workers are given paid time to meet together and develop their own positions."[76]
- "The Department of Labor should organize this process and publish the results."[77]
- "The Department of Labor should initiate an annual national Occupational Stress Day dedicated to educating the public and the government about the stress people face at work, the way stress gets brought home into family life, and how this stress might be buffered or reduced."[78]
- "The Department of Labor should mandate that all workplaces offer Occupational Stress Groups (OSGs) in which workers can learn how to recognize stress more fully at the workplace."[79]
- "Every workplace should provide paid leave for a worker to attend twelve two-hour sessions on stress, and providers of these OSGs should be compensated by a fund paid for jointly by the government and the employer."[80]
- "To be effective, OSGs should have no management personnel, and facilitators should be chosen by workers from a list provided by the government."[81]
- "The Department of Labor should mandate that every employer allow workers to elect an Occupational Safety and Health Committee empowered to require changes in the organization of work to increase workers' safety and health, including mental health, and to increase workers' opportunity to actualize their skills and talents."[82]
- "Unemployment insurance must be raised to a level that would make it possible for all employees unable to find work to continue to live at a level of income equal to the amount they were making at the time of their employment or equal to the median income in the society, whichever is less. . . . Such insurance should be available for the first half-year as a right."[83]
- "Federal legislation should be passed to prevent any company from moving or closing its plants in a given area without first

making a social-environmental impact report on the human consequences."[84]

• "Companies would be fined, up to confiscatory levels, for those moves that negatively affect the health of the community, unless they can show that they have done everything economically feasible to convert the facility to worker-controlled enterprises, producing goods that might sustain future employment for those they previously employed."[85]

G. K. Chesterton once said, "The greatest political storm flutters only a fringe of humanity."[86] But if "the politics of meaning" were ever implemented—even partially—the effects would be substantially more than a flutter. Indeed, if "the politics of meaning" were implemented society as we know it would completely vanish.

Which is, of course, just what Michael Lerner has in mind.

Statecraft as Witchcraft

John Quincy Adams once asserted that, "The most healing of medicines, unduly administered, becomes the most deadly of poisons."[87] Or as Tristan Gylberd put it, "Do-gooders are the world's most notorious do-badders."[88]

Clearly, Michael Lerner and his followers in the Tikkun movement cannot be faulted for their concern for the deeper spiritual needs of American families and workers. Where they have gone astray is in taking matters into their own hands, seeking out their own new and novel nostrums. Instead of adhering to the wise and inerrant counsel of the Bible—walking along the well-trod path of Christendom's long experience—they have done "what was right in their own eyes" (Judges 21:25). Like the Pharisees and the Sadducees before them, they do not believe either Moses or Christ and as a consequence have utterly violated God's ultimate plan for true *tikkun*—true healing (John 5:39–47).

Instead, they have turned to the old heresies of gnostic mysticism—the doctrines of the so-called New Age movement—which makes their heresies especially *nouveau*. Author and theologian Peter Jones thus asks:

> Why is homosexuality on the rise? Why is it endorsed by *Time* magazine, promoted on publicly funded radio, and featured in

children's comic strips—with great moral fervor in the name of democracy? Why is feminism such a powerful force today? Why is the movement developing its own goddess spirituality? Why is witchcraft taught in certain California school districts? Why is feminist spirituality making enormous inroads into Christianity? Why is abortion a vitally important part of the feminist manifesto? Is ecology just a neutral concern about the survival of the planet, or does it too have a religious agenda? Why is American Indian nature religion being actively promoted? Why is the work ethic no longer working? Why is multiculturalism and political correctness so important on many college campuses?[89]

Jones concludes this querying litany of woes asking: "Are all these seemingly disconnected issues related in any way?"[90]

His answer is an unequivocal "yes."

He says that despite the great social, cultural, and economic attainments of Christendom around the globe—to say nothing of its spiritual enfranchisement—ancient paganism is now resurgent. The old "gnostic empire," he says, has "returned with a vengeance."[91]

Ultimately Tikkun must be evaluated on that basis. It is not so much that its view of economics, or psychology, or politics is flawed. It is that its view of reality is flawed.

Thus, Tikkun's system cannot work because its reliance on the old New Age ignores the very essence of reality—as does all pagan thought (Ephesians 5:6). It is fraught with fantasy (Colossians 2:8). Only the Bible can tell us of things as they really are (Psalm 19:7–11). Only the Bible faces reality squarely, practically, completely, and honestly (Deuteronomy 30:11–14). Thus, only the Bible can provide genuine solutions to the problems that plague mankind (Psalm 119:105).

We don't need flow-charts and five-year economic projections to see that. It is written on the fleshly tablet of every man's heart:

> All His precepts are sure. They are upheld forever and ever; they [alone] are performed in truth and uprightness. (Psalm 111:7b–8, NAS)

SIEGE ALERT

TIKKUN

Here is what the new social engineers at Tikkun have in mind for you and your children in the weeks and months ahead:

- They want to infuse "meaning" and "psychic fulfillment" into every workplace in the country. They want to turn America into a socialist "workers' paradise." In order to accomplish such lofty aims, they know that their number one priority right now has to be the development of a comprehensive federally mandated therapeutic labor management policy.
- The plan would include government-run workers' advocacy groups—traditionally the domain of labor unions—designed not only to represent labor demands to management but to position government as the purveyor of all primary social needs.
- Vocational training, a crucial element of the plan, would provide necessary job skills complimented with a variety of New Age stress-management "skills" and a host of social expectations government can and will exact from employers.
- In addition, meditation, Eastern mysticism, Kabala occultism, and other forms of pagan spirituality would be introduced to children in the schools as a necessary component part of their educational preparation for the job market.
- Watch particularly for Tikkun or Labor Department seminars in factories and office complexes designed to teach New Age principles in the workplace, undermining traditional authority structures, and demanding greater federal regulation of small businesses and family enterprises.

TEN

US, THEM, AND HIM

'Tis sad, but some always ride before the horse's head.[1]
—Washington Irving

The teacher that setteth the cart before the horse is he that prefereth imitation before precepts.[2]
—Richard Whitinton

Genuine solutions to these many cultural woes are possible. To give in to despair would mean that we believe we see the outcome of our present evil circumstances beyond all doubt—and that we do not. In fact, the solution begins when we step through all of our emotional responses to our circumstances and begin to move forward, following Christ in obedience to truth. Emotions come and go, and they will never drive us through to completing our spiritual race, our calling in Christ.

This is another of those lessons from history that we would be well advised to act upon. And I can think of no greater example from our own history, of a man who knew the living truth of obedience to Christ, than Henry Laurens—one of those American heroes who was also a hero of the Faith and who has generally remained unknown. As we consider what we must do now, in light of all that we have learned about our present-day opposition and tyranny they would impose upon us, we would do well to learn from a man like Laurens.

Where Must We Begin?

He was a prize catch.

Henry Laurens was just off the coast of Newfoundland when the

British cruiser *Vestal* chased and intercepted his lone rebel *packet*, the *Mercury*. Fearing the worst, he emptied all the diplomatic papers from his trunk, stuffed them into a leather bag weighted with shot, and threw the heavy bundle overboard. Unfortunately, he failed to deflate the air within the bag—so it floated, was sighted by an alert sailor on the *Vestal*, and subsequently was hooked on board.

On thus discovering both the identity of the *Mercury's* prominent passenger and his intended mission, the commander of the *Vestal* had the small *packet* boarded and Laurens was arrested.

It was September 3, 1780. The rebellion of England's American colonies was now in its fourth year. And the war was not going particularly well for the mother country. Although the rebels could boast precious few actual field victories, they were a stubborn and elusive lot. They were poorly equipped, under-financed, and lacked even a modicum of formal military training, yet they continued to harass supply lines, out-maneuver troop placements, and evade naval blockades.

The morale of His Majesty's troops was at an all-time low. The distance from home combined with the constant frustration at arms had taken a bitter toll. The war, never particularly popular before, was now stirring a near mutinous restlessness among the conscripts.

The commander of the *Vestal* was hopeful that the capture of Laurens might actually afford the royal cause the advantage it now so sorely needed. He was, after all, one of the most important leaders of the revolution and its fledgling government.

A wealthy merchant from South Carolina, he was a member of the first provincial convention in Charleston in 1775. The next year he was elected vice-president of the sovereign state under its new constitution and was chosen to serve as a representative in the Continental Congress in Philadelphia. He was so highly regarded by his fellow delegates there that when John Hancock resigned his position as president, they unanimously elected Laurens to succeed him on November 1, 1777.

His tenure as the fourth president of the newly independent United States was predictably tumultuous. Besides all the difficulties of trying to mobilize the tiny confederated nation for war against impossible odds, supply the widely dispersed Continental

army, hold together the fractious congress, and secure international recognition for the rebel cause, he also had to deal with the
acrimonious conflict between his Commander in Chief, George
Washington, and the temperamental General Thomas Conway. But
somehow he was able to do it all—with amazing success. Furiously
outspoken, unflaggingly ambitious, and decisively brilliant, his obvious leadership abilities won him the admiration of the American
patriots—and the enmity of the court at Westminster.

At the end of his distinguished term he was appointed to super-
vene John Adams as the legate to the Dutch government at the
Hague. And it was to that assignment that he was traveling when
he was captured.

The commander of the *Vestal* delivered Laurens to his superiors
at home amidst a flurry of publicity and fanfare. The London papers
trumpeted the news with all the gaudy gossip of a palace coup.
They displayed the worst qualities of journalism: all its paralysis of
thought, all its monotony of chatter, all its sham culture and
shoddy jingoism, all its perpetual readiness to cover any vulgarity
of the present with any sentimentalism of the past. One of the papers declared that the rebel cause had at last been "dealt its death
blow."[3] Another predicted that American resistance would likely
"collapse within the month."[4] More prudent press observers, while
admitting the vital significance of the former president to the colonial cause, cautioned that his captivity might only serve to "stiffen
their resistance."[5]

Whatever the American reaction might prove to be, it was clear
that the English reaction was profound. Though he has been
"thoughtfully neglected" in our own day—as the esteemed southern
man-of-letters M. E. Bradford was wont to say—his greatness was
certainly recognized in his own day.[6]

Laurens was imprisoned in the Tower of London. Steeped in English history and in the blood of many of its leading participants,
the infamous fortress on the Thames had dominated the London
skyline ever since William the Conqueror built it to repress his un-
willing Saxon subjects. It had thus served for centuries as the
scene of state and private violence, of torture, murder, and execution.

Although he had been a lifelong churchman, Laurens was not
particularly known for his piety—quite unlike his close friends Pat-

rick Henry and Samuel Adams. But cut off from the noisy forgetful-ness of public life, he resolved his faith into what he called a "God-fearing, Bible-reading, hymn-singing passion for permanent things."[7] Each day he was allowed to attend private services in the St. Peter-ad-Vincula chapel. Within the precincts of the vast Tower compound, to the northwest, the little sanctuary was built by Henry VIII on the site of a previous chapel in 1519. In it were buried his second wife, Anne Boleyn, and his fifth, Catherine Howard—both of whom he had beheaded on the Tower Green a few yards away. Also killed there, and buried ignominiously below the chapel floor paving, were the old Countess of Salisbury, Lady Jane Grey, the Elizabethan Earl of Essex, the rebel Duke of Monmouth, and a host of others. The associations of the place make it rather oppres-sive, even today; old terrors and miseries seem to hang in the air. But Laurens found "an unspeakable comfort" there.[8] Although he would be released at the end of the war—exchanged for Lord Corn-wallis, following the surrender at Yorktown as a part of the negoti-ated cease-fire arrangement—he maintained to the end of his life that it was in that "dismal, haunting chapel" that he found "genu-ine release."[9]

The experience of prison often changes the outlook of men. Ac-cording to the Greek author and journalist Taki, it "strips away all the inconsequential peripherals of daily life and hones close to the bone of what matters most: faith and family, principle and prior-ity."[10] It is, he says, "a fundamental reordering" of what is and is not really important:[11]

> Imprisonment throws a searchlight of brilliant clarity on all that we are and all that we do. Every sham pretense, every false motive, every empty ideal, every corrupt ambition, and every shal-low desire is exposed for what it is. Thus prison either drives men to greater sagacity and keenness or to deeper vapidity and tedium. It either breaks men or makes men.[12]

It *made* Laurens.

Though he was no less irascible in his resistance to English rule, no less belligerent in his revolutionary insurgency, and no less antithetic in his sedition against tyranny, he was far more pen-sive, far more judicious, and far more principled. Years later he would summarize his new "Christian vision" for "social involvement" as the "natural outworking of a threefold covenantal responsibility."[13] He wrote:

> At a time when liberty is under attack, decency is under assault, the family is under siege, and life itself is threatened, the good will arise in truth; they will arise in truth with the very essence and substance of their lives; they will arise in truth though they face opposition by fierce subverters; they will arise in truth never shying from the Standard of truth, never shirking from the Author of truth.[14]

Laurens asserted that this threefold perspective in dealing with the enemies of freedom—focusing as he said, "first on us, then on them, and then ultimately on Him"—was attainable "only by one means: that being the means of grace."[15] He had come to understand that "the crucial question" in squaring off against any political or ideological juggernaut is "not so much: *How have they violated truth?* but *how have we, in word and deed, told it?*"[16]

The Response of the Good

Henry Laurens believed that the proper response to wrongdoing is essentially a matter of *character* apart from merely external, mechanical, legal, or political stratagem. *Knowing* what is right and what is wrong is not nearly so difficult as *doing* what is right and *not doing* what is wrong. Orthodoxy is a far simpler matter than orthopraxy.

Thus, Laurens asserted that the solution to grave societal problems, the antidote to endemic cultural pathogens, and the counterweight to brazen political tyrannies, is to be found first and foremost in the hearts and minds of men, not in the promises and plans of programs.

In stark contrast to that distinctly Christian conviction, many politically charged men and women today—both conservative and liberal—believe that by skillfully combining incentives and disincentives, or by artfully devising advantageous circumstances, or by fabricating a compelling matrix of socio-political programs, all our problems can be solved and all our woes can be ameliorated. This, they believe, can be achieved by enacting the right bills, electing the right politicians, reclaiming the right legacies, initiating the right reforms, recalling the right precedents, or restoring the right priorities.

Laurens understood only too well that security for the family, freedom for the citizenry, and hope for the downtrodden will not—indeed, cannot—spring from these things; true solutions to our problems do not find their genesis in either an accumulation of iconic and sentimental antiquities or a stockpiling of nostalgic documents, precedents, constitutions, and juridications.

Genuine cultural solutions can only emerge from an ethos suffused in godly character: moral righteousness, spiritual goodness, and societal selflessness.

> Righteousness exalts a nation, but sin is a disgrace to any people. (Proverbs 14:34, NIV)

> A throne is established through righteousness. (Proverbs 16:12, NIV)

> In righteousness you will be established; you will be far from oppression. (Isaiah 54:14, NAS)

The history of Israel provides a vivid illustration of that truth. There is no doubt that the tiny sliver of a nation along the eastern shore of the Mediterranean had a remarkable heritage. She was the apple of God's eye (Zechariah 2:8). She had carefully institutionalized right worship, right judicial structures, right civil structures, and right economic structures (Isaiah 58:2). God had revealed His law to her as He had to no other nation or people; He dwelt among them in His holy Temple; He came near to them and established a priesthood to minister in their midst; He instituted a sacrificial system to show them how they might be reconciled to Him; and He warned them about their uncleanness and sin (Deuteronomy 28:1–14).

The Lord's own Anointed ruled over the Israelites. According to every conceivable external measure, constitutional and institutional, Israel was a great nation with every conceivable opportunity and advantage. Yet, God judged her with woe after woe (Acts 7:2–53).

God looked upon the nation and found her sorely lacking (Isaiah 1:11–15). He looked and found her national character riddled with transgression and iniquity (Amos 2:6–8). He found wickedness and corruption, *despite* her apparent external adherence to the letter of the Law (Isaiah 58:1–2). Her people had become weighed down with iniquity; they had abandoned the Lord (Zephaniah 3:1–7). The whole head was sick, and the whole heart faint (Ezekiel 11:5–14). The land had been burned and laid waste by marauding invaders (Micah 3:1–12). Israel had become like Sodom and Gomorrah (Isaiah 1:10).

The Israelites continued to offer sacrifices, but their sacrifices had become meaningless. The priests continued to burn incense, but the incense had become an abomination. They continued to assemble for feasts and new moons, but the Lord had grown to hate them. They continued to lift up their hands in prayer, but their hands were covered with blood (Isaiah 1:4–15).

Is it any wonder the Lord turned against Israel and rejected the offerings He himself had commanded and the festivals He had called? He turned from His people and declared they were not His people. Isaiah gives pointed answers for restoration:

> Wash yourselves, make yourselves clean; remove the evil of your deeds from My sight. Cease to do evil, learn to do good; seek justice, reprove the ruthless, defend the orphan, plead for the widow. (Isaiah 1:16–17, NAS)

But what caused the nation of Israel to fall into such a state? Very simply, they had reduced their faith to a series of formulas. They had forsaken the weightier matters of the Law and had emptied it of its spirit and had left only the shell. They had put their trust in slogans and symbols, chanting, "The Temple of the Lord, the Temple of the Lord, the Temple of the Lord," like a mantra (Jeremiah 7:4). They believed that as long as they had a Temple and the priesthood, they would be pleasing to God. The Pharisees and Galatian Christians would later make the same mistake: believing that certain man-made works, laws, structures, and systems can give rise to national and cultural greatness.

Legalism

The essential difference between Christianity and all other faith systems is that biblical faith is a holistic response to truth, whereas man-centered faith is a formulaic attempt to manipulate truth to man's advantage. Biblical faith is orthodoxy *and* orthopraxy while paganism gravitates toward either one or the other. Thus, biblical faith aims at God's satisfaction; the man-centered faith aims at self-satisfaction.

This difference is seen most obviously in worship. Biblical worship is a kind of holy dialogue with God. Christians worship by listening to God's commands and promises, and then responding with contrition, commitment, and thanksgiving. When God rebukes His people, we are to humbly confess our sins. When He calls us to repent and obey, we are to yield ourselves entirely to Him. When He invites us to His table, we are to give thanks and rejoice at His bounty. Biblical worship is always a response to truth.

All forms of pagan "worship," however, involve the ritual reenactment of some myth or series of myths. In many "primitive" societies, young men must undergo elaborate rites to be initiated into the tribe. They might be enclosed in a pit for several days while the blood of animals is poured over them through an opening above. In some cases they are ritually cut and scarred. In others they must undergo some perilous ordeal. On occasion, the idea is for the young person to experience a kind of ritual "death and resurrection." Though there are a myriad of different customs, there is an underlying unity in the belief that man can be reconciled to the gods by formulaic ritual reenactment.

At first glance these cultic rites and practices may seem a far cry from the ideological humanism of modern ideologues and social engineers. The tribesman believes he is manipulating the gods, while the modern humanist believes he is operating according to mechanical natural laws. The tribesman believes in a mythical past; the modern humanist purports to reject all superstition. The tribesman believes in the primacy of nature; the modern humanist believes in the primacy of natural science. But despite their differences, both the tribesman and the technocrat believe that strict adherence to certain *rules* and *regulations*—either mystical or mechanical—can somehow enable societies and individuals to achieve health, life, and abundance.

Biblical faith is more concerned with character, content, and substance, while man-centered faith is only concerned with physical, material, and external appearances. To be sure, external acts, discipline, and ritual have their place in biblical faith. Man is a spiritual physical being and, throughout the Bible, God commands that faith be expressed through particular external acts: The Israelites were to worship God in sacrifice; Christians are to worship God in song, prayer, preaching, and a common meal. These are external, public acts and are important aspects of true worship.

In orthodox Christianity, however, these external acts are not capable in and of themselves of making us pleasing to God. Singing psalms, in itself, does not satisfy God; psalms must be sung by *clean* lips. Lifting hands, in itself, does not please God; we must lift *holy* hands. Listening to the Word does not make us acceptable to God, unless we are also *doers* of the Word. Eating the common meal can be a means of judgment. The God of the Bible will not and cannot be manipulated. He is a Person. To please God, we must love and trust Him. In orthodox Christianity, no matter how careful we are in external compliance, "without faith it is impossible to please God" (Hebrews 11:6).

The mechanistic and legalistic religion of structuralism is far different—either cultic supernaturalist or modern humanist. Throughout the ages, men like Cain have *used* structuralism to get what they want (Genesis 4:3–8; Hebrews 11:4; 1 John 3:12). Men like Balaam have *used* structuralism to control their circumstances (Numbers 31:16; 2 Peter 2:15; Revelation 2:14). Men like Korah have *used* structuralism to enhance their own position (Numbers 16:1–3; 31–35).

Cain, Balaam, and Korah all believed in the universal power of legal and structural formulas and that they could manipulate both human society and natural elements with law. They also believed that even God would be forced to conform to the desires and demands of men who acted in terms of law: If men would say certain things, do certain things, believe certain things, or enact certain things, then God would *have to* respond. In a very real sense, they believed *man* controlled his own destiny by using rituals and formulas, like *magic*, to save mankind, shape history, govern society, and control God.

That kind of rank heathenism has always been condemned in the Bible. Salvation by works, salvation through law, salvation by legislation, salvation by education, or salvation by constitution are all utterly heretical—by both Old and New Testament standards. It was repudiated by Abraham, Moses, and Isaiah, no less vehemently than by Paul, John, and Peter (Romans 4:3; Galatians 3:6; Deuteronomy 27:26; Isaiah 1:10–18; Romans 9:32; John 5:25; 2 Peter 1:3–4).

Structural legalism is heresy—plain and simple. It abolishes the significance of the Cross (Galatians 5:11), makes light of Christ's sacrifice (Galatians 2:21), nullifies the work of the Holy Spirit (Galatians 3:3–5), and abrogates the necessity of grace (Romans 4:4). "Faith is made void and the promise made of no effect" (Romans 4:14), because it makes man and man's ability the measure of all things (Matthew 15:6–9). Thus, structural legalism is often nothing more than paganism in disguise.

It is always the inclination of sinful men to reject God's grace, going the way of Cain, rushing headlong into the error of Balaam, and perishing in the rebellion of Korah (Jude 11). That is why *statism* is so predominant among rebellious men and nations. After all, if structural legalism *can* save mankind, shape history, govern society, and control God, then obviously men should work to institute a total Law-Order. If the rituals and formulas of socio-political reforms are indeed like magic, then men must erect a comprehensive state structure to govern men comprehensively. If national greatness can be concocted out of an artful development of laws, constitutions, traditions, systems, social programs, structures, and precedents, then men must create and exalt, or restore and extol, those mechanical devices.

Modern liberalism is just such a saving Law-Order. It attempts to rule every aspect of life and solve every problem through the agency of an omnipotent, omnipresent structural state system. It aims to establish a perfect "social and cultural security system." It attempts to create a top-down formalized government, manufacturing goodness and grace by legislation. Whenever any problem arises, instead of relying upon Almighty God and His guidance in the Word, advocates of the liberal state rush to the bar with a whole series of new rules, regulations, and laws.

But modern conservatism can also be a saving Law-Order. Like modern liberals, many conservatives focus on external devices, mechanical systems, and structural solutions to society's problems. Liberals may see salvation in a *new* constitutional system, where conservatives see salvation in an *old* constitutional system. But it is clear enough that both are looking to some *document* or *system* for the ultimate hope. Liberals and conservatives are only divided on the incidentals; on the essentials—their humanism—they are united.

The only real alternative to either of these insidious and tyrannical Law-Order systems is a biblical ethos marked by true spirituality and righteousness—a community-wide character shaped by biblical character traits. Christians must not assume that if we are able to help pass a few good laws, or elect a few good legislators, or appoint a few good judges, or bring back a few good traditions, that we will ensure the integrity of the family or establish the foundations of freedom.

America's *character* must change, not just her laws, not just her judges, her schools, her media, her legislation, or her priorities. And in order for *America's* character to change, the character *of America's Christians* must change.

Only then will we be able to effectively rebuff the mad machinations of modern social engineers from the Children's Defense Fund, Planned Parenthood, Greenpeace, the National Education Association, the American Civil Liberties Union, ACT UP, the World Health Organization, and Tikkun. Only then will we be able to turn back the current siege on the family, and begin to solve the many problems that plague our cities and communities. Repentance, revival, and righteousness among God's own precedes social renewal. It always has. It always will:

> If my people who are called by my name humble themselves, and pray and seek my face, and turn from their wicked ways, then I will hear from heaven, and will forgive their sin and heal their land. (2 Chronicles 7:14, RSV)

Henry Laurens came to understand that the best response to the enemies of family, freedom, and fidelity was the development of community virtue. National character begins with Christian character.

Biblical Character

In writing to the Christians in Corinth, who were sorely divided over structural and legal questions, the apostle Paul provided a succinct definition of righteousness. Though not exhaustive, Paul's definition does afford believers a panoramic perspective of essential biblical character traits:

> Watch, stand fast in the faith, be brave, be strong. Let all that you do be done with love. (1 Corinthians 16:13-14, NKJV)

If Christians are going to help stem the tide of licentiousness in our day, we must begin to exemplify this kind of Christian character and model it for the society at large. We must reject humanism's myth of political, ideological, and structural messianism and begin to demonstrate alertness, steadfastness, bravery, strength, and tenderheartedness.

First, Christians must be sober, watchful, and alert. All Christians are called to watch over themselves (Deuteronomy 4:15, 23; Revelation 3:2-3). We are to watch over our relationships (Exodus 34:12), our hearts (Proverbs 4:23), our lips (Psalm 141:3), the paths of our feet (Proverbs 4:26), and our moral conduct (Revelation 16:15). We are to be alert to the call of Christ (Ephesians 5:14), the judgment of Christ (Micah 7:7), and the coming of Christ (Matthew 24:42-43). We are to be alert in spiritual warfare (Ephesians 6:18), in prayer (Colossians 4:2), and to the snares of our enemies so that we don't fall into temptation (1 Peter 5:8).

> Therefore let us not sleep, as others do, but let us watch and be sober. (1 Thessalonians 5:6, NKJV)

> Awake, awake! put on strength, O arm of the Lord! Awake as in the ancient days, in the generations of old. Are you not the arm that cut Rahab apart, and wounded the serpent? (Isaiah 51:9, NKJV)

Second, Christians must be faithful, steadfast, and unwavering. All Christians are called to stand firm in the faith (2 Thessalonians 2:15). We are to be steadfast in the midst of suffering (1 Peter 5:9), in the face of strange teaching (Hebrews 13:9), and in times of trying circumstances (James 1:12). We are to be steadfast in good works (Galatians 6:9), in enduring love (Hosea 6:4), in conduct (Philippians 1:27), in decision-making (1 Kings 18:21), and in absolute loyalty to the Lord (Proverbs 24:21).

> Therefore, my beloved brethren, be steadfast, immovable, al-

ways abounding in the work of the Lord, knowing that your labor is not in vain in the Lord. (1 Corinthians 15:58, NKJV)

Yet the righteous will hold to his way, and he who has clean hands will be stronger and stronger. (Job 17:9, NKJV)

Third, Christians must be valiant, courageous, and brave. All Christians are called to be fearless in the Lord (Isaiah 12:2). We can face adversity with great courage because of God's omnipotence (2 Chronicles 32:7), His omniscience (Psalm 139:13-19), and His omnipresence (Psalm 118:6). We are to be brave in the face of our enemies (Deuteronomy 31:6), and brave in the midst of chastisement (Job 5:17-24). We are to show valor in obedience to the Word of God (Joshua 23:6), for the sake of His people (2 Samuel 10:12), and in all their service (1 Chronicles 28:20). The cowardly will be thrown into the lake of fire, along with the unbelieving, murderers, sexual perverts, sorcerers, idolaters, and liars (Revelation 21:8).

For God has not given us a spirit of fear, but of power and of love and of a sound mind. (2 Timothy 1:7, NKJV)

The wicked flee when no one pursues, but the righteous are bold as a lion. (Proverbs 28:1, NKJV)

Fourth, Christians must be mighty, stalwart, dynamic, and strong. All Christians are called to be strong in Christ (2 Corinthians 10:3-6). God has not given us a spirit of weakness, but of power (2 Timothy 1:7). The Gospel comes in power (1 Thessalonians 1:5), the Kingdom comes in power (1 Corinthians 4:19-20), and salvation comes in power (Romans 1:16). This is a power that the wicked can never know (Matthew 22:29), but every believer is already anointed with it (Luke 24:49). We have been endowed with the strength to witness (Acts 1:8), to labor (Colossians 1:29), and to do every good thing (Philippians 4:13). Christ has given Christians the strength of His might (Ephesians 1:19), and the strength of His grace (2 Timothy 2:1).

He gives power to the weak, and to those who have no might He increases strength. Even the youths shall faint and be weary, and the young men shall utterly fall, but those who wait on the LORD shall renew their strength; they shall mount up with wings like eagles, they shall run and not be weary, they shall walk and not faint. (Isaiah 40:29–31, NKJV)

Finally, Christians must be respectful, affectionate, and tender-hearted. All Christians are called to be long-suffering in love and tenderness. We are to show love to strangers (Deuteronomy 10:19) as well as neighbors (Leviticus 19:18), to enemies (Matthew 5:44) as well as brethren (1 Peter 3:8). In all things, at all times, we are to be examples of love (1 Timothy 4:12), abounding in love (Philippians 1:9), and walking in love (Ephesians 5:2). We are to comfort one another in love (Colossians 2:2), greet one another in love (Titus 3:15), and labor with one another in love (1 Thessalonians 1:3). For love is the royal law (James 2:8).

> Though I speak with the tongues of men and of angels, but have not love, I have become as sounding brass or a clanging cymbal. And though I have the gift of prophecy, and understand all mysteries and all knowledge, and though I have all faith, so that *I* could remove mountains, but have not love, I am nothing. And though I bestow all my goods to feed the poor, and though I give my body to be burned, but have not love, it profits me nothing. (1 Corinthians 13:1–3, NKJV)

Grace and Character

There is one catch: Genuine godly character is not a human creation. No effort at "moral education," however well-funded, can produce it. No New Age mind-control techniques, however sincerely believed, can duplicate it. No output of sheer will, however powerful, can even imitate it.

Only God can produce Christian character. It takes divine power to make us godly (2 Peter 1:3). As Laurens said, it is attainable "only by one means: that being the means of grace."[17]

In ourselves we are drowsy, wishy-washy, cowardly, weak, and hardhearted. It is only by God's grace that we are awakened from sleep (1 Thessalonians 5:1–6). It is only in God's power that we are made faithful (Philippians 2:12–13). It is because God is a great God that we can be bold (Psalm 33:16–17; Jeremiah 9:23–24). It is when we are weak that the Lord's strength works in us (2 Corinthians 12:9–10). It is God who takes out our heart of stone and puts in us a heart of flesh (Ezekiel 36:26).

This is why biblical character must be built on a foundation of humility. Humiliation before the Lord, penitence for sin, and contrite hearts are all prerequisites for the inculcation of alertness, steadfastness, courage, strength, and love. It might seem odd that national goodness should be founded on national humiliation, but this is indeed the biblical and historical pattern. God promised to heal the land of Israel if her people would repent. Throughout early American history, Christians regularly participated in days of repentance and fasting. Only when we have recognized our failings and sins can we begin to develop Christian character. Only when we acknowledge we have no good in ourselves, can we begin to be instruments of God's righteous rule. Only when we humble ourselves will we be exalted.

Perhaps more importantly, humility also means that we realize we cannot develop biblical character traits in isolation from other Christians. Humility means we submit ourselves to other believers, and we cherish the church.

Character in Context

There is strength in numbers. That is a well-worn cliché, but it is also a biblical principle:

"After God created Adam, He said it was not good for him to be alone." (Genesis 2:18)

"When God made His covenant with Abram, He promised to make him a *nation*." (Genesis 12:2)

God did not deliver a few individuals from their captivity in Egypt—He delivered the whole people of Israel.

- During the exile of the Israelites in Babylon, God promised to reunite the nation in the land (Ezekiel 37:15–23).
- Jesus said He had come to build His Church (Matthew 16:18).

God always forms His people into a community, because it is not good for us to be alone. Not surprisingly then, biblical character is not the result of either individual discipline or isolated humility before God. There have always been Christians who retreated to the desert to work out their own salvation in terrible isolation. But this is not the biblical model. In the biblical model, Christian character is formed in the community of believers.

And not just *any* community of believers will do. Only the church is equipped to form Christian character. It is the church that has the keys of the Kingdom (Matthew 16:19). It is the church that has the power to bind and to loose (Matthew 18:18). It is the church that shall prevail over the gates of hell (Matthew 16:18). It is the church—not para-church groups, evangelistic associations, political action committees, special interest groups, or ecumenical rallies, but the church—that can catalyze the kind of social transformation necessary to protect our families and restore our freedoms.

Biblical character is developed within the body of Christ—the Church.

First, Christians must watch over one another. Christian character requires *mutual watchfulness.*

All Christians are responsible for the welfare of their brothers and sisters. The brethren are to watch over one another (Hebrews 3:12–13). If a brother sins, the Christian is first to rebuke him in private (Matthew 18:15). Even if he is presenting an offering to the Lord, he must leave the offering and first be reconciled to his brother (Matthew 5:23–24).

Church leaders have a special duty to watch over the members of the church. They are called shepherds because it is their duty to guard the "sheep" (1 Peter 5:2) and watch over the souls in their congregation (Hebrews 13:17), for they will one day have to give an account of their care for the flock (Hebrews 13:17).

> Therefore take heed to yourselves and to all the flock, among which the Holy Spirit has made you overseers, to shepherd the church of God which He purchased with His own blood. For I know this, that after my departure savage wolves will come in among you, not sparing the flock. Also from among yourselves men will rise up, speaking perverse things, to draw away the disciples after themselves. Therefore watch, and remember that for three years I did not cease to warn everyone night and day with tears. (Acts 20:28–31, NKJV)

Second, Christians must encourage one another to faithfulness. We all need encouragement from others to be faithful. Christian character requires *mutual encouragement.*

God instructed Moses to encourage Joshua (Deuteronomy 1:38; 3:28). All Christians are to encourage and build up one another in faithfulness (1 Thessalonians 5:11). Those who are fainthearted are especially to be encouraged (1 Thessalonians 5:14). Those whose faith in God's promises is diminished must be encouraged (Isaiah 35:3–4).

Again, church leaders have a special duty to encourage Christians to faithfulness. Barnabas was called to Antioch to encourage those Christians to remain true to the Lord (Acts 11:22–23). Even after being stoned for preaching Christ, Paul accompanied Barnabas through Lystra, Iconium, and Antioch to encourage the saints to persevere in the midst of persecution (Acts 14:19–22). Paul sent Tychicus to the Colossians to encourage their hearts (Colossians 4:7–8), just as he sent Timothy to the Thessalonians (1 Thessalonians 3:2).

> Beware, brethren, lest there be in any of you an evil heart of unbelief in departing from the living God; but exhort one another daily, while it is called "Today," lest any of you be hardened through the deceitfulness of sin. (Hebrews 3:12–13, NKJV)

Third, Christians must pray for courage for one another. We need the prayers of others. Christian character requires *mutual intercession.*

Jesus often went away to pray in the mountains; and as He approached the Cross, He prayed intensely for His Father's aid (Matthew 14:23; Mark 6:46; Matthew 26:39–46). When the Jews began to persecute the early Christians, they gathered together to pray for confidence to proclaim the Gospel (Acts 4:23–31). In Iconium, Paul and Barnabas spoke boldly with reliance upon the Lord (Acts 14:3). From prison, Paul wrote that the prayers of the Philippians would fulfill his hope that he would exalt Christ boldly (Philippians 1:19–20). The prayers of the Corinthians were instrumental in Paul's ministry (2 Corinthians 1:11).

Once we have put on the full armor of God, we are to pray and petition for all the saints so that the Gospel might be preached boldly (Ephesians 6:18–20). By praying without ceasing for one another (1 Thessalonians 5:17), by praying at all times in the Spirit (Ephesians 6:18), we provoke one another to boldness.

> And when the servant of the man of God arose early and went

out, there was an army, surrounding the city with horses and chariots. And [Elisha's] servant said to him, "Alas, my master! What shall we do?" So he answered, "Do not fear, for those who are with us are more than those who are with them." And Elisha prayed, and said, "LORD, I pray, open his eyes that he may see." Then the LORD opened the eyes of the young man, and he saw. And behold, the mountain was full of horses and chariots of fire all around Elisha. (2 Kings 6:15–17, NKJV)

Fourth, Christians must disciple one another. Christian character requires *mutual discipline.*

The Lord trains and tests His people to make them stronger. He puts obstacles in their way. Jacob wrestled with Esau and Laban, and finally with the Lord himself (Genesis 32:22–32). It was the Lord who trained David's hands to be strong for battle (2 Samuel 22:35; Psalm 18:34). The Lord trained and strengthened the arms of the Israelites (Hosea 7:15). Like a father, the Lord disciplines His children (Hebrews 12:1–11). Christians are also to train one another. The weak are to be strengthened (1 Thessalonians 5:14). Parents are to train a child to be strong in the Lord (Proverbs 22:6). Christians are to sharpen one another as iron sharpens iron (Proverbs 27:17). Christians are to hold each other accountable to God's commands.

> Therefore strengthen the hands which hang down, and the feeble knees, and make straight paths for your feet, so that what is lame may not be dislocated, but rather be healed. (Hebrews 12:12–13, NKJV)

Finally, Christians must learn to love one another. Most of us are selfish by ourselves and need to be prodded to love. Christian character requires mutual service.

The church is supposed to model love as a kind of final apologetic (John 13:35). The Spirit who dwells among the church is not a spirit of timidity, but a spirit of power and love (2 Timothy 1:7). Love is evidence of the growing fruit of the Spirit (Galatians 5:22). Thus, Christians are to serve all men, but especially those who are of the household of faith (Galatians 6:10). We are to consider how to spur one another to love and good deeds (Hebrews 10:24). Love for the brethren is a sure sign of one's salvation (1 John 3:10).

Once again, church leaders have a special duty to exhort the people to love and good works. Paul instructed Timothy to encourage the wealthy to be generous and ready to share (1 Timothy 6:17–18). God gave leaders to His church in order to equip the saints for the work of service to one another, the building up of the body of Christ (Ephesians 4:11–12).

> Let nothing be done through selfish ambition or conceit, but in lowliness of mind let each esteem others better than himself. Let each of you look out not only for his own interests, but also for the interests of others. (Philippians 2:3–4, NKJV)

> But Jesus called His disciples to Himself and said, "You know that the rulers of the Gentiles lord it over them, and those who are great exercise authority over them. Yet it shall not be so among you; but whoever desires to become great among you, let him be your servant. And whoever desires to be first among you, let him be your slave." (Matthew 20:25–27, NKJV)

Body Life

Clearly, Christian character is formed, first and foremost, in the church. And the tools Christ uses to form Christian character within the church are the Word, the Sacraments, and the exercise of church discipline.

The *Word* rebukes, refreshes, and keeps us alert (2 Timothy 3:16–17). The Word encourages us to faithfulness (Revelation 3:10) and gives us courage because it reminds us of the greatness of our God (Romans 8:31–38). The Word is our powerful weapon (Hebrews 4:12–13). The Word made Flesh is the supreme example of self-sacrificing love (Philippians 2:5–9). The Word is our food (Matthew 4:4; Deuteronomy 8:3) and drink (1 Peter 2:2).

The *Sacraments* train us in Christian character. The Lord's Supper is a remembrance of Christ's courageous death for us (Luke 22:19). It is a feast of love (1 Corinthians 10:17) wherein we renew our vows of faithfulness. Christ's body is bread indeed, and His blood is drink indeed (John 5:52–59). We prepare for the Lord's Supper by examining ourselves, alert to our sins (1 Corinthians 11:27–32). Baptism is the sign and seal of our enlistment in the army of Christ, and assures us of God's grace, making us strong in faith (Romans 6:1–7).

Discipline is the last of Christ's tools for forming Christian character. Elders watch over us so we do not fall into sin (Hebrews 13:17) and exhort us to faithfulness. They rebuke us for our sins (2 Timothy 4:2) and pray for us to be courageous (Acts 6:4). Elders strengthen us by their example and by training us in God's commands (1 Timothy 3:1–7). Elders lead us to love and good works (Hebrews 10:24–25).

Christian character is formed in the church, and the church is a worshiping assembly. In worship:

- We are taught the wisdom of God that makes us discerning and alert.
- We recommit ourselves to faithfulness, and are trained ritually to respond readily to the command of God.
- We pray for one another to be courageous.
- We receive the signs of the body and the blood of Christ that give us eternal life.
- We express our love for God and for one another.

When God's people assemble, we are to lie down in green pastures beside still waters (Psalm 23:2). As we gather around the throne of grace, we are to take refuge and find sanctuary (Psalm 61:1–4). We are to find rest (Hebrews 4:1–13), restoration (Psalm 19:7), reconciliation (Psalm 32:3–6), and recompense (Psalm 73:15–24) when we worship.

Yes, church membership involves duty, responsibility, commitment, service, obedience, deference, and sacrifice. Yes, Christians should go to church to learn, to share, to serve, to give, and to work. But first and foremost, we are to relax in the joy of the Lord as we collectively recall and reiterate the divine order of redemption.

Christian character is the Christian's reflection of God's character. Christians are called to be perfect, just as their Father in heaven is perfect (Matthew 5:48). The more we know God the more we shall be like Him. The church is God's Temple (1 Corinthians 3:16–17), where Christians assemble to meet with Him in His Word, His Sacraments, and the leaders He has appointed. In the church, we are transformed into His image from glory to glory (2 Corinthians 3:18).

Then and only then can the society at large begin to reflect goodly transformation as well.

Hearing and Heeding

When Alexis de Tocqueville chronicled his visit to the United States in 1834, he emphasized the contribution Christian character had made in the development of this nation's greatness. The rapidly expanding American "experiment" was the marvel and fascination of the entire Western world. Industry was flourishing, cities were growing, farms were prospering, and the arts were proliferating.

According to the visiting French nobleman, the Christian faith, which was setting pulpits aflame and communities apace, had given rise to their vibrant democracy. It had harvested alertness, steadfastness, bravery, strength, and tenderheartedness from the harsh realities of pioneer settlements and had served to provoke true spirituality. "America is great," he said, "because America is good. And if she ever ceases to be good, she will cease to be great as well."[18]

Two centuries before de Tocqueville's visit to America, most of the settlers were committed Christians, steeped in the doctrines of the Reformation. Even at the time of the Revolutionary War in 1776, about seventy-five percent had been exposed to some kind of Reformed church. These churches laid the foundation of the American character; in them, Christian character was molded by the preaching of the Word of God and the functioning of the body of Christ.

In those early days, literally everyone in New England's Puritan colonies attended worship services, where they heard powerful sermons from preachers steeped in both Testaments of the Bible. They regularly heard the Word of God applied to their everyday affairs and common life together—from the proper ordering of the home and the duties of the parents to the proper ordering of the community and the duties of the magistrates.

Preaching dominated Puritan worship, but the early American pioneers also sang psalms and took the Lord's Supper very seriously, like their fathers and forefathers in the preceding centuries. Worship was the fount from which the life of the whole community flowed.

America's early churches were also known for their rigorous discipline. The church had no power to levy fines or to inflict corporal punishment, but, following the model of biblical orthodoxy and the pattern of the church through the ages, they instituted elders along with their pastors and teachers. The elders admonished members who fell into scandalous and persistent sin. If the backslidden member refused to repent, he was disciplined—or in extreme cases, even excommunicated. Regular oversight and discipline helped to shape the Christian character of the people of America.

And that character laid the foundations upon which all our manifold achievements since have been built.

Quite obviously, modern America is the special beneficiary of a marvelous legal, political, and economic heritage. But neither the traditions of freedom, the precedents of bounteous markets, nor the constitutional framework have, in and of themselves, the makings of a great culture.

National greatness *produces* such things; greatness is not derived from them. National greatness is a function of character. When a nation becomes righteous, she becomes great. When a nation begins to display biblical character traits, she begins to achieve greatness—but *only* then.

Four Alternative Movements

The question of course is, can such an ideal still *work*? Can an emphasis on godly character substantially shape our advanced and cosmopolitan culture? What evidence do we have that such ideals may have an effect on the destiny of men and nations in these modern times?

In the good providence of God, the twentieth century has seen four movements within the broad sweep of Christendom tackle the difficulties of legalistic structural modernity and challenge its emerging neo-orthodoxy of ideology. Though they seemed to come from the four ends of the earth temperamentally, philosophically, ecclesiastically, and geographically, they were all spawned in a single year, 1891, and with a single purpose: to demonstrate genuine Christian compassion, justice, and mercy to all men everywhere; to model godly character to all the world.

In 1891, the versatile and prolific Abraham Kuyper—known to all the world as a preacher-turned-journalist-turned-politician in the Netherlands—delivered a sterling address to the first Christian

Social Congress entitled *The Social Problem and the Christian Religion.* Though it spawned decades of healthy debate and constructive activity, its greatest contribution was to ignite the worldwide political phenomenon of the *Christian Democrat Movement.*

In 1891, the brilliant and pious Vincenzo Gioacchino Pecci—known to all the world as Leo XIII—issued the papal encyclical *Rerum Novarum.* It too spawned a decades-long resurgence of dynamic Catholic social policy. But like Kuyper's speech, the encyclical's greatest contribution was to give impetus to the international and ecumenical *Distributist Movement.*

In 1891, the energetic and irascible Alexander Lyle Stuart—known to all the world as a southern Confederate partisan-turned-gentleman book binder—reprinted the works of the great statesman and political theorist John C. Calhoun with a brilliant and stirring introduction that called for a return to the underlying precepts of southern culture. Rallying around his ideas of property, family, and community, a whole new generation of southern intellectuals regenerated the old notions of political decentralization and overlapping spheres of social authority—and thus gave rise to the *Southern Agrarian Movement.*

In 1891, the tireless and articulate Henry Cabot Lodge—known to all the world as an esteemed senator from the state of Massachusetts and a popular historical revisionist—delivered his most famous oration, entitled *Justice as the Fruit of Christian Diligence.* Delivered in Boston before luminaries assembled in celebration of the centennial of the Bill of Rights, the speech had an immediate short-term impact, but its long-term effect was to spawn the *American Progressive Movement.*

In 1891, a Dutch Calvinist, an Italian Catholic, a Southern Confederate, and a New England Caliban suddenly united—albeit unknowingly—to stand against the rising tide of ideology, to posit an all-encompassing world-view alternative, and to affirm with one voice the essential dynamic of the unencumbered Christian social ethic—the only substantial hopes for the disenfranchised and dispossessed in this poor, fallen world. Distinctly anti-revolutionary, they stood on the firm foundation of old truths, long confirmed in the experience of men and the revelation of God.

Thus, as amazing as it may seem at first glance, each of the four great men—and each of the popular Christian resistance movements that they conceived—shared five essential presuppositions. Their astounding unanimity is nothing short of a brash witness to the superintending grace of a sovereign God. Whether Christian Democrat, Distributist, Southern Agrarian, or Progressive, these five principles remained fundamental to them all.

First, they shared a profound distrust of central governments to solve the grave problems that afflicted society. Each believed in a strong and active civil authority—but only in its proper place. Thus, every brand of statist ideology was abhorred by them. Kuyper warned against the danger of "reducing the society to the state or the state to society."[19] Pope Leo argued, "The contention that the civil government should at its option intrude into and exercise control over the family and the household is a great and pernicious error."[20] While Lodge insisted:

> Government is but a tool. If ever we come to the place where our tools determine what jobs we can or cannot do, and by what means, then nary a fortnight shall pass in which new freedoms shall be wrested from us straightway. Societal problems are solved by families and communities as they carefully and discriminately use a variety of tools.[21]

They believed social reform—like so much else in culture—should be designed to avoid what Leo called the "interference of the state beyond its competence."[22] C. S. Lewis, who was apparently influenced by at least three of these alternative movements, wrote:

> Of all the tyrannies, a tyranny sincerely expressed for the good of its victims may be the most oppressive. It may be better to live under robber barons than under omnipotent ideological busybodies.[23]

Nowhere is the omnipotence of ideological busybodies more evident than in the social programs of the therapeutic and messianic state.

The *second* principle that the four movements all shared was a deep and abiding commitment to widespread private property ownership. Each believed that if everyone within the society—rich and poor—were to be equipped and enabled over the long haul, they must be afforded the opportunity to own their own homes, tend their own gardens, and pass on an inheritance to their own children. This precluded all forms of egalitarianism, socialism, and welfarism—as well as the smothering tax structures necessary to support them. As Pope Leo said:

> If one would undertake to alleviate the condition of the poor masses, the centrality and inviolability of private property must be established and protected.[24]

Similarly, Stuart asserted that:

> Ownership of the means of production cannot be entrusted to socialistic bureaucrats any more than to monopolistic plutocrats. Three acres and a cow may seem hopelessly out of date as an answer to the cries of the needy—especially in light of the burden of taxation and regulation heaped upon the freeholds of our day. But the great lesson of history is clear enough: when men are left free to faithfully work at home, they are happiest and society is securest.[25]

True social security, they believed, was what Kuyper called the "broadest distribution of property through legitimate work as is humanly possible."[26]

The *third* principle that the four movements all shared was a healthy understanding of human anthropology. They took into account the Fall. Thus, unlike the prevailing ideologies of the twentieth century, they expected no utopia, no quick fix, no magic wand, no ultimate solutions to the problems of social justice this side of eternity. They recognized the sway that greed, avarice, prejudice, and envy held in human affairs and thus acceded the need for private associations—guilds, unions, community organizations, fellowships, and fraternities—to maintain an appropriately decentralized checks and balances. According to Lodge:

> Multiple jurisdictions and free associations are hedges against both tyranny and anarchy, against both cultural hegemony and civil disintegration. The medieval guilds were not collectivist, but through communal means they enforced the necessity of upholding interpersonal responsibility and accountability—a profound Christian necessity in light of the deleterious effects of sin on men and man.[27]

Stuart concurred saying:

> There is a spiritual cancer at work in the world. The piracy of man's fallen nature invariably mitigates against freedom and jus-

tice. Therefore voluntary associations must needs balance us—
without force of state but nonetheless with force of community—
and hold us to accounts.[28]

Any successful program of social reform, they believed, would
require what Pope Leo called the "cooperation of many and diverse
elements within the community."[29]

The *fourth* principle that the four movements all shared was an
unwavering commitment to the family. Though they believed that
private property was the best means for the poor to obtain a vehicle
for change, and that voluntary associations girded that vehicle
about with protection and integrity, the vehicle itself, they asserted,
was the family.

Kuyper said:

> According to the Word of God, the family is portrayed as the
> wonderful creation through which the rich fabric of our organic
> human life must spin itself out.[30]

Again he said, "The tasks of family in society lie outside government's jurisdiction. With those it is not to meddle."[31] Pope Leo
called the family "the true society."[32] Lodge called it "the primary
building block of our culture. Nay, it is itself our culture."[33] And
Stuart called it "the only means by which real and substantial
change for good might truly be effected."[34] They believed that culture must be family centered if it is to be the least bit effective.

The *fifth* principle that the Christian Democrat, Distributist,
Southern Agrarian, and Progressive movements all shared was the
certainty that the church was central to any and all efforts to mete
out mercy, justice, and truth. They believed that while the family
was the vehicle for substantive change, it was the church that
drove that vehicle.

According to Kuyper:

> Jesus set apart and sent out His church among the nations to
> influence society in three ways. The first and most important influ-
> ence was through the ministry of the Word. . . . The church's sec-
> ond influence was through an organized ministry of charity. . . .
> Third, the church influenced society by instituting the equality of
> brotherhood—in contrast to differences in rank and station. . . .
> Indeed, as a direct consequence of Christ's appearing and the ex-
> tension of His church among the nations, society has been re-
> markably changed.[35]

Pope Leo said, "No practical solutions to our problems will be found apart from the intervention of religion and of the church."[36] And again, "All the striving of men will be in vain if they leave out the church."[37]

Lodge concurred saying:

> Of all the institutions ordained of God upon this earth, this one has the force of integration: the church. We cannot hope to help the helpless apart from the church's ministrations of grace which transform the giver, the receiver, and even the gift itself.[38]

They believed that social reform should be, as Stuart said, "guided, defined, managed, and provoked—in, through, and by the church."[39]

Of all the precepts espoused by the Christian Democrat, Distributist, Southern Agrarian, and Progressive movements, it was this last one that most rankled the ire of twentieth-century ideologues. During the first half of this century, the church had already become the spurned and neglected stepchild of the modern era. It was perceived as being moss-backed and archaic. Or awkward and irrelevant.

And the church's reputation has only diminished with time. Today, it is regarded as little more than a waterboy to the game of life. Sad, but all too true.

Part of the reason for this horribly low estimation of the church is due to the fact that the church has always *limped* through history. Men look at the all too evident, all too apparent, sometimes even glaring, weaknesses of Christ's Bride and just assume that its lame and crippled state is ample justification for dismissing its importance.

The fact is, though, the church's limp is actually a *confirmation* of its power, relevance, and significance.

After the Fall, God told Satan that the Righteous Deliverer, Jesus Christ, would crush his head. But God also said that, in the process, the heel of the Lord would be bruised (Genesis 3:15). The limp, then, that Christ's Body displays is actually a sign of great victory, not a sign of defeat or incompetence. It is an emblem of triumph.

This reality is portrayed throughout the Bible.

For instance, when Jacob, the father of Israel's twelve tribes, wrestled through the night at Peniel, he limped ever afterward as a sign that he had actually prevailed (Genesis 32:31).

The apostle Paul, father of the Gentile church, was given a thorn in the flesh. Since thorns grow along the ground, Paul was pricked—at least symbolically—in the foot. It kept him limping in the eyes of men (2 Corinthians 12:7). Even so, it was in this weakness that Christ's power was affirmed and perfected (2 Corinthians 12:9).

Thus, when the church limps through history, as believers we need not be frustrated or discouraged. On the contrary, we should be encouraged that God's Word is sure and true. For victory has, indeed, already been won.

The reality is that whatever the church does—or doesn't do—directly affects the course of civilization. It determines the flow of historical events (Revelation 5–6).

The church has the keys to the Kingdom (Matthew 16:19). It has the power to bind and loose (Matthew 18:18). It has the authority to prevail over the very gates of hell (Matthew 16:18). It is, thus, the church—not governments or ideologies or systems or causes—that will determine our destiny and the destiny of our world.

The reason for this is threefold:

First, it is the church that offers us the source of life. It offers the Waters of Life (Revelation 22:17), the Bread of Life (John 6:31; 1 Corinthians 11:24), and the Word of Life (1 John 1:1). The sacramental ministry of the church is our *only* source for these grace provisions. There is nowhere else that we can turn for these "medicines of immortality." They effect a tangible offering to God, a consecration *before* God, a communion *with* God, and a transformation *in* God. Thus, they actually readjust us to the ultimate reality.

Second, the church offers us accountability and discipline. Sin cripples any work. Whenever sin is casually tolerated, all our efforts are defiled (1 Corinthians 5:6–13), evangelism is stifled (1 Corinthians 5:1–5), and victory is denied (Joshua 7:1–15). Only the church has the authority to discipline heinous sin (Matthew 18:15–20). The purpose of this kind of accountability is, of course, protective and restorative, not defensive or punitive. It is to erect a hedge of responsibility and respectability around our efforts to confront evil in this poor, fallen world.

Third, the church offers us a place of rest. When, as God's people, we assemble ourselves together, we are at last able to lie down in green pastures, beside still waters (Psalm 23:2). As we gather around the throne of grace, we are at last able to take refuge and find sanctuary (Psalm 61:1–4). We are able to enter His gates with thanksgiving and His courts with praise (Psalm 100:4).

Without the context of the church, even the most dynamic Christian character is exposed to atrophy and entropy. But, within that context, our witness becomes our most powerful weapon in the preordained spiritual warfare of our day—even as we limp along the battlefield of this culture.

A lack of confidence in the state, a reliance on private property, a realistic anthropology, a reliance upon the family, and a subsuming trust in the church: these five principles drove—and to whatever degree they still exist, still drive—the Christian Democrat, Distributist, Southern Agrarian, and Progressive movements.

In fact, they represent the only serious dissent from the failed ideologies of the twentieth century. Together they comprise an altogether alternate sociology—one that was repudiated by the powers and principalities but not by providence. Together they are, "a perpetually defeated thing which survives all its conquerors."[40] So said the great Distributist writer, G. K. Chesterton.

In the end, we must say along with Titus and the apostle Paul, "These things are good and profitable for all men" (Titus 3:8). If we are to build models of Christian character to resist the machinations of Planned Parenthood, Greenpeace, the National Education Association, the Children's Defense Fund, the American Civil Liberties Union, ACT UP, the World Health Organization, and Tikkun, it will not be sufficient to merely accommodate mercy to acceptable notions of politics—the ideological structures of our time. We must offer a sociology of resistance like unto those birthed a century ago—a sociology rooted in the character of the faith which was "once for all delivered unto the saints."

Henry Laurens—like the Christian Democrats, the Distributists, the Agrarians, the Progressives, and so many who have trod the pathway of faithfulness before us—understood all that. He comprehended the notion that the best response we can make to the subverters of the family and the perverters of freedom is the inculcation of godly virtue, of moral ethics, of Christian character, and then the dissemination of those values throughout the whole of society.

Thus, he propounded his threefold perspective in dealing with the enemies of freedom—focusing, as he said, "first on us, then on them, and then ultimately on Him":

> At a time when liberty is under attack, decency is under assault, the family is under siege, and life itself is threatened, the good will arise in truth; they will arise in truth with the very essence and substance of their lives; they will arise in truth though they face opposition by fierce subverters; they will arise in truth never shying from the Standard of truth, never shirking from the Author of truth.[41]

It would stand us in good stead to hear and heed that sage "us, them, and Him" counsel even today.

After all, *knowing* what is right and what is wrong is not nearly so difficult as *doing* what is right and *not doing* what is wrong. Orthodoxy is a far simpler matter than orthopraxy.

Purgamentum init, exit purgamentum.[42] *Adiutorium nostrum in nomine Domini.*[43] *Qui fecit caelum et terram.*[44] *Oremus.*[45]

NOTES

Acknowledgments

1. James Matin-Longes and Kendra Povic, eds., *English Literature: An Historical Anthology* (London: Harton, 1922), II: 191.
2. Ibid., II: 34.
3. Winston Churchill, *Speeches and Papers* (London: Gallway Ltd., 1959), p. 97.
4. Before the face of God.

Introduction

1. James Matin-Longes and Kendra Povic, eds., *English Literature: An Historical Anthology,* (London: Harton, 1922), IV: 177.
2. Ibid., III: 66.
3. William J. Bennett, *The Index of Leading Cultural Indicators* (Washington, D.C.: Empower America/Heritage Foundation/Free Congress Foundation, 1993), p. i.
4. Ibid.
5. Ibid.
6. Ibid.
7. *Michigan Life News*, July 1993.
8. See George Grant, *Grand Illusions: The Legacy of Planned Parenthood* (Franklin, Tenn.: Adroit, 1992); George Grant, *The 57% Solution: A Conservative Strategy for the Next Four Years* (Franklin, Tenn.: Adroit, 1993); George Grant and Mark Horne, *Legislating Immorality: The Homosexual Movement Comes Out of the Closet* (Chicago: Moody, 1993); and George Grant, *Trial and Error: The American Civil Liberties Union and Its Impact on Your Family* (Franklin, Tenn.: Adroit, 1993).
9. G. K. Chesterton, *Fancies Versus Fads* (London: Methuen, 1923), p. viii.
10. Tim Dowley, ed., *Eerdmans' Handbook to the History of Christianity* (Grand Rapids, Mich.: Eerdmans, 1977), p. 2.

11. Ibid.
12. Michael Laughton-Douglas, *Truer Truth Than This* (London: Haverford, 1978), p. 84.
13. *Newsweek,* July 6, 1970.
14. *Church History,* February 1990.
15. James Fenimore Cooper, *The American Democrat* (New York: Knopf, 1931), p. vii.
16. Ibid.
17. "You have asked me why, if the world is governed by providence, many evils befall good men. The answer to this would more properly be given in the course of a work demonstrating the universal sovereignty of providence and the concern of God for our welfare. But since you would have me extract a fragment from the whole and resolve a single objection, while leaving the larger question untouched, my task will not be difficult, in as much as it is God's cause I shall be pleading." Seneca, *De Providentia,* 1:1.

Chapter One

1. James Matin-Longes and Kendra Povic, eds., *English Literature: An Historical Anthology* (London: Harton, 1922), V: 156.
2. Ibid., IV: 26.
3. Elizabeth Frost-Knappman, ed., *The World Almanac of Presidential Quotations,* (New York: Pharos, 1993), p. 165.
4. J. Evetts Haley, *A Texan Looks at Lyndon: A Study in Illegitimate Power* (Canyon, Tex.: Palo Duro, 1964).
5. *Nashville Banner,* January 25, 1993.
6. Ibid.
7. G. K. Chesterton, *The Common Man* (London: Sheed and Ward, 1932).
8. Ibid., p. 34.

9. Jon Winokur, *The Portable Curmudgeon* (New York: Penguin, 1987), p. 220.
10. E. J. Dionne, *Why Americans Hate Politics* (New York: Simon and Schuster, 1991), p. 9.
11. Ibid., p. 18.
12. *Remnant Review*, November 6, 1992.
13. A. James Reichley, *The Life of the Parties* (New York: Free Press, 1992), p. 22.
14. Michael Drummond, *Participatory Democracy in the Making* (New York: Carnell, 1923), p. 19.
15. Ibid., p. 22.
16. Ibid., p. 17.
17. Ross Lence, *Union and Liberty* (Indianapolis, Ind.: Liberty, 1992).
18. David Hall, *Caveat: Welfare Reformed* (Franklin, Tenn.: Legacy, 1994).
19. G. K. Chesterton, *G. F. Watts* (New York: E. P. Dutton, 1901), p. 110.
20. Eric Voegelin, *Omnibus* (Jackson, Miss.: Southern, 1969), p. 23.
21. Ibid., p. 45.
22. Horton Kael and William Loomis, *A Documentary History of Liberal Thought* (New York: Cushman, 1959), p. 163.
23. Ibid., p. 228.
24. Ibid., p. 163.
25. Ibid., p. 331.
26. *State of the Union Address*, February 17, 1993.
27. William D. Gairdner, *The War Against the Family* (Toronto: Stoddart, 1992), p. 6.
28. Ibid.
29. *The Senior American*, December 1993.
30. Frederick Bastiat, *The Rule of Law* (Irvington-on-Hudson, N.Y.: Foundation for Economic Education, 1950).
31. Ibid.
32. Ibid.
33. Ibid.
34. M. E. Bradford, *A Worthy Company* (Marlborough, N.H.: Plymouth Rock, 1982).
35. Russell Kirk, *The Roots of the American Order* (Washington, D.C.: Regnery Gateway, 1991).
36. Caroline Wilson, *The Founding Era* (New York: Pala Loma, 1955), p. 134.
37. Ibid., p. 136.
38. George Hewitt, *The Faith of Our Fathers* (Atlanta, Ga.: Heritage Covenant, 1966), p. 88.
39. Ibid., p. 91.
40. Ibid., p. 92.
41. Drummond, p. 122.
42. Ibid.
43. Hewitt, p. 109.
44. Ibid.
45. Ibid.
46. Ibid., p. 110.
47. Ibid., p. 34.
48. Ibid.
49. Ibid.
50. Ellis Sandoz, *Political Sermons of the American Founding Era* (Indianapolis, Ind.: Liberty, 1991).
51. Drummond, p. 45.
52. Hewitt, p. 88.
53. Ibid.
54. Ibid., p. 92.
55. Drummond, p. 46.
56. Ibid.
57. Richard D. Hefner, *A Documentary History of the United States* (New York: Mentor, 1952), p. 15.
58. Ibid.
59. Ibid.
60. Ibid., p. 16.
61. Ibid., p. 17.
62. Ibid.
63. Ibid.
64. Ibid.
65. Ibid., p. 24.
66. P. J. O'Rourke, *Parliament of Whores* (New York: Atlantic Monthly Press, 1991), p. 9.
67. *Forbes*, September 14, 1992.
68. Ibid.
69. H. L. Mencken, *A Mencken Chrestomathy* (New York: Vintage, 1982), p. 8.
70. H. L. Mencken, *Quotations From a Curmudgeon* (New York: Legget, 1967), p. 41.
71. *Forbes*, September 14, 1992.
72. Ibid.
73. Guinness, *The American Hour* (New York: Free Press, 1992), p. 4.
74. *Dimensions*, October 1992.
75. *Forbes*, September 14, 1992.
76. Ibid.
77. Ibid.
78. Ibid.
79. William Bennett, *The De-Valuing of America* (New York: Summit, 1992).
80. Zbigniew Brzesinski, *Out of Control* (New York: Scribners, 1993).
81. *Forbes*, September 14, 1992.
82. Ibid.
83. Ibid.
84. Ibid.
85. Gairdner, p. 6.
86. Richard Wagner, *Early Lutheran Missions* (Fredricksburg, Tex.: Wittenburg, 1971), pp. 51–52.
87. Michael Lourdes, *The Holiness Movement in England* (London: Christian Light, 1980), p. 25.
88. Ibid.

Chapter Two

1. James Matin-Longes and Kendra Povic, eds., *English Literature: An Historical Anthology* (London: Harton, 1922), 1:22.
2. Ibid., II:43.
3. Jay Friedman, *The Safety Dance* (Ithaca, N.Y.: Planned Parenthood of Tompkins County, 1989).
4. Ibid.
5. Ibid.
6. Ibid.
7. Name Tags for "Puttin' on the Condom" Game from Friedman's book, *The Safety Dance*:

   Physical attraction
   Fall in love
   Think about having sex
   Leave space at tip
   Talk about having sex
   Roll condom down penis
   Decide to use a condom
   Enough lubrication?
   Pool money . . . or more foreplay
   If no, use *KY Jelly*
   Go to a condom store
   Intercourse
   Decide what kind to buy
   Ejaculation
   Take box off rack
   Hold on to rim of condom
   Pay cashier
   Withdraw penis
   Decide where to store them
   Remove condom
   Decide to have sex
   Loss of erection (two of these)
   Need to use a condom
   Decide where to throw condom away
   Open package
   Trash it
   Penis hard?
   Feel good?
   Place condom on penis
   Partner have an orgasm?
   Wash penis
   Relax

8. Ibid.
9. Placards for "Risk Rap" Game from Friedman's book, *The Safety Dance*:

   Massage
   Oral sex on a woman with a dental dam
   Slow dancing
   Stargazing
   Fantasy
   Saunas/Jacuzzis
   Dressing/undressing one another
   Oral sex on a man wearing a condom
   Dry kissing
   Candlelight dinner
   Skinny-dipping/moonlight swimming
   Intercourse with a condom (and foam)
   French kissing
   Tender smooches
   Erotic films and magazines
   Incense
   Sex toys
   Oral/anal contact (rimming)
   Walk along beach
   Phone sex
   Body paints
   Anal intercourse without a condom
   Cruising/parking
   Fast dancing
   Anal intercourse with a condom
   Snuggling in a beanbag chair
   Showering together
   Intercourse without a condom
   Backrubs
   Eating chocolate chip cookies
   Masturbation
   Oral sex on a woman (cunnilingus)
   Eating strawberries dipped in chocolate
   Flirting
   Making out/petting
   Sensuous feeding

10. Ibid.
11. *New York Upstate*, October 18, 1989.
12. Ibid.
13. Ibid.
14. Planned Parenthood Federation of America, "1992 Annual Report," p. 21.
15. Madeline Gray, *Margaret Sanger: A Biography* (New York: Marek, 1979), p. 326.
16. PPFA, "Annual Report," p. 21.
17. Ibid.
18. Ibid., p. 19.
19. Ibid.; Also see, International Planned Parenthood Federation, "1991 Annual Report," p. 22; Also see, *National STOPP News* , November 30, 1993.
20. Planned Parenthood Federation of America, "1992 Service Report," p. 20.
21. *PPFA Insider*, April 1993.
22. "Service Report," pp. 18–19.
23. *PPFA Insider*, July-August 1993.
24. Ibid.; Also see, *National STOPP News*, November 30, 1993.
25. *New Dimensions*, October 1991.
26. Ibid.
27. Ibid.
28. Ibid.
29. *Austin American-Statesman*, November 22, 1993.
30. *Life Decisions International Caleb Report*, October 1993.
31. *Wall Street Journal*, July 19, 1993.

32. *New York Times*, June 19, 1993.
33. *U.S. News and World Report*, December 6, 1993.
34. *National Institute of Family and Life Advocates Legal Update*, July-August 1993.
35. *The Tennessean*, November 29, 1993.
36. *Miami Herald*, December 8, 1992.
37. Planned Parenthood Federation of America, "A Risky Business: Reproductive Health Care in Litigation," 1988.
38. *New York Times*, June 19, 1993.
39. Scott Somerville, ed., *The Link Between Abortion and Breast Cancer* (Purcellville, Va.: AIM, 1993).
40. *New Dimensions*, October 1991.
41. George Grant, *Grand Illusions: The Legacy of Planned Parenthood* (Franklin, Tenn.: Adroit Press, 1993), p. iv.
42. Ibid.
43. Ibid.
44. Planned Parenthood Federation of America, "1981 Annual Report," p. 16.
45. *Minneapolis Star Tribune*, October 29, 1993.
46. *National Right to Life News*, February 1993.
47. Ibid.
48. Ibid.
49. Ibid.
50. Ibid.
51. Ibid.
52. Ibid.
53. *PPFA Insider*, July-August 1993.
54. Ibid.
55. Ibid.
56. Ibid.
57. Ibid.
58. Ibid.
59. Ibid.
60. Ibid.
61. *Health Care Reform Association Newsbrief*, October-November 1993.
62. Hilaire Belloc, *The Biographer's Art: Excerpts from Belloc's Florid Pen* (London: Catholic Union, 1956), p. 33.
63. Howard F. Pallin, ed., *Literary English and Scottish Sermons* (London: Windus Etheridge, 1937), p. 101.
64. E. Michael Jones, *Degenerate Moderns: Modernity as Rationalized Sexual Misbehavior* (San Francisco: Ignatius Press, 1993), p. 9.
65. Douglas R. Scott, *Bad Choices: A Look Inside Planned Parenthood* (Franklin, Tenn.: Legacy Communications, 1992), p. 29.
66. Ibid.
67. Belloc, p. 89.
68. Gray, p. 58.
69. Arthur B. Logan and Thomas de Tilati, *Morality and the Village Elite* (New York: St. Regis, 1949), p. 63.
70. Ibid.
71. Ibid.
72. Ibid.
73. Gray, p. 59.
74. Grant, p. 53.
75. Ibid.
76. Ibid.
77. Ibid.
78. Ibid.
79. Ibid.
80. Gray, p. 280.
81. Allan Chase, *The Legacy of Malthus* (New York: Knopf, 1977), p. 81.
82. Paul Johnson, *A History of the English People* (New York: Harper, 1985), p. 276.
83. Ibid.
84. Ibid.
85. Daniel Kevles, *In the Name of Eugenics* (New York: Penguin, 1985), p. 110.
86. G. K. Chesterton, *Eugenics and Other Evils* (London: Cassell, 1922), p. 7.
87. Ibid., p. 54.
88. Margaret Sanger, *The Case for Birth Control: A Supplementary Brief and Statement of Facts* (New York: Eugenic Publishing Company, 1917), p. 3.
89. Margaret Sanger, *The Pivot of Civilization* (New York: Brentano's, 1922), p. 176.
90. Ibid., p. 23.
91. Ibid., p. 105.
92. Ibid., p. 88.
93. Ibid., p. 165.
94. Lawrence Ballard, *For God and Country* (New York: Blackpools, 1977), p. 88.
95. PPFA, "Service Report," p. 3.
96. Sanger, *Pivot*, p. 105.
97. Ibid., p. 108.
98. Ibid.
99. Ibid., p. 115.
100. Ibid., p. 116.
101. *Birth Control Review*, May 1919.
102. Linda Gordon, *Woman's Body, Woman's Right* (New York: Penguin, 1974), p. 332.
103. Ibid.
104. Ibid.
105. Ibid.
106. Ibid., p. 333.
107. Ibid.
108. Ibid., p. 330.
109. Thomas Hilger and Dennis Horan, *Abortion and Social Justice* (New York: Althea, 1981).
110. *Planned Parenthood Review*, Winter 1983.
111. Roberta Weiner, *Teen Pregnancy* (Alexandria, Vir.: Capitol, 1987).
112. Ibid.
113. Ibid.
114. Ibid.
115. Chase, p. 411.

116. Ibid.
117. *Demographics Today*, March 1983.
118. Sanger, *Pivot*, p. 177.
119. *Pro-Vita*, July 1992.
120. Ibid.
121. Ibid.
122. Ibid.
123. Ibid.
124. *Family Planning Perspectives*, May/June 1985.
125. Ibid.
126. Ibid.
127. Ibid.
128. Carl Williamson, *Limits on Fertility* (London: Carswell's, 1968), p. 37.
129. Ibid.
130. Ibid.
131. Ibid.
132. *Right to Life News*, March 28, 1985.
133. Ibid.
134. Stephen Mosher, *Broken Earth* (New York: Free Press, 1983).
135. Stephen Mosher, *Journey Into the Forbidden China* (New York: Free Press, 1985).
136. Bruce Kowlert, *Abortion and the Tax Liability* (San Francisco, Calif.: Life Memorial Research Center, 1992), p. 89.
137. Ibid.
138. Ibid.
139. Ibid.
140. Ibid., p. 101.
141. Ibid., p. 66.
142. Ibid., p. 67.
143. Ibid., p. 69.
144. Ibid.
145. Ibid., p. 70.
146. Ibid., p. 72.
147. Ibid.
148. Ibid., p. 74.
149. Ibid., p. 134.
150. James L. Batton, *The Deleterious Effects of Sexual Liberation* (Los Angeles, Calif.: St. Thomas Aquinas Association, 1991), p. 22.
151. Ibid., p. 28.
152. *Family Planning Perspectives*, September/October 1986.
153. Ibid.
154. Ibid.
155. Ibid.
156. Ibid.
157. Robert Ruff, *Aborting Planned Parenthood* (Houston, Tex.: New Vision, 1988), pp. 66ff.
158. Ibid.
159. Ibid.
160. Ibid.
161. *National Stopp News*, October 15, 1993.
162. Ruff, p. 88.
163. *Family Planning Perspectives*, January/February 1984.
164. Ibid.
165. Ibid.
166. Ibid.
167. Ruff, p. 89.
168. Louis Harris, *American Teens Speak* (New York: Planned Parenthood Federation of America, 1986), p. 6.
169. Ibid., p. 7.
170. *Family Planning Perspectives*, July/August 1986.
171. Batton, p. 45.
172. Ibid.
173. Ibid.
174. Harris, p. 7.
175. Pallin, p. 105.

Chapter Three

1. James Matin-Longes and Kendra Povic, eds., *English Literature: An Historical Anthology* (London: Harton, 1922), III: 112.
2. Ibid., III: 43.
3. William Bennett, *The De-Valuing of America* (New York: Summit, 1992), p. 42.
4. Ibid.
5. Thomas Sowell, *Inside American Education: The Decline, the Deception, the Dogmas* (New York: Free Press, 1993).
6. Bennett, pp. 42–44.
7. Ibid.
8. Ibid.
9. Ibid.
10. Ibid.
11. Ibid.
12. Ibid.
13. *Education Reporter*, November 1993.
14. Ibid.
15. *Forbes*, June 7, 1993.
16. Dan Alexander, *Who's Running Our Schools: The Case Against the NEA Teacher Union* (Washington, D.C.: Save Our Schools, 1988), p. 7.
17. Ibid., p. 6.
18. Ibid.
19. Ibid.
20. Courtney, p. 15.
21. Ibid.
22. Ibid., p. 16.
23. *The Tennessean*, November 18, 1993.
24. Sally Reed, *NEA: Propaganda Front of the Radical Left* (Alexandria, Va.: National Council for Better Education, 1984), p. 32.
25. Ibid., p. 33.
26. *Forbes*, June 7, 1993.
27. Phoebe Courtney, *Target: America's Children* (Littleton, Colo.: Independent American, 1989), p. 14.

28. Francis DelVoe, *Education in Crisis* (Denver, Colo.: Littlefield, 1990), p. 200.
29. Ibid.
30. Ibid.
31. Ibid.
32. *The Tennessean,* November 18, 1993.
33. *Tennessee Education Review,* July 1993.
34. *Forbes,* June 7, 1993.
35. Ibid.
36. Alexander, p. 89.
37. *Forbes,* June 7, 1993.
38. Ibid.
39. *Tennessee Education Review,* July 1993.
40. Ibid.
41. Ibid.
42. Ibid.
43. Courtney, p. 51.
44. *Tennessee Education Review,* July 1993.
45. Ibid.
46. Ibid.
47. Ibid.
48. Ibid.
49. Samuel Blumenfeld, *NEA: Trojan Horse in American Education* (Boise, Ida.: Paradigm, 1984), p. x.
50. Ibid.
51. Alexander, p. 101.
52. Ibid.
53. Reed, p. 41.
54. Alexander, p. 85.
55. Ibid.
56. *Forbes,* June 7, 1993.
57. Alexander, p. 88.
58. Ibid.
59. *Tennessee Education Review,* July 1993.
60. Ibid.
61. Alexander, p. 117.
62. *Tennessee Education Review,* July 1993.
63. Ibid.
64. Courtney, p. 49.
65. Ibid., p. 50.
66. *Tennessee Education Review,* July 1993.
67. Ibid.
68. Ibid.
69. Ibid.
70. Ibid.
71. Ibid.
72. Ibid.
73. Ibid.
74. Ibid.
75. Alexander, p. 127.
76. Ibid.
77. *Tennessee Education Review,* July 1993.
78. Ibid.
79. Ibid.
80. Ibid.
81. Alexander, p. 134.
82. Ibid.
83. *Forbes,* June 7, 1993.
84. Ibid.
85. Ibid.
86. Ibid.
87. *Phyllis Schlafly Report,* September 1993.
88. Ibid.
89. *Tennessee Education Review,* July 1993.
90. Alexander, p. 109.
91. *Tennessee Education Review,* July 1993.
92. *Phyllis Schlafly Report,* September 1993.
93. Courtney, p. 16.
94. Ibid., p. 17.
95. *Phyllis Schlafly Report,* September 1993.
96. Ibid.
97. *First Things,* January 1994.
98. *Tennessee Education Review,* July 1993.
99. Ibid.
100. Ibid.
101. Ibid.
102. Ibid.
103. *New Republic,* April 18, 1981.
104. *Tennessee Education Review,* July 1993.
105. *Phyllis Schlafly Report,* May 1993.
106. Ibid.
107. Ibid.
108. Ibid.
109. Ibid.
110. *Tennessee Education Review,* July 1993.
111. Thomas Sowell, *Inside American Education* (New York: Free Press, 1993), p. ix.
112. *Empowerment,* March 1993.
113. *The Advocate,* December 15, 1992.
114. Ibid.
115. James Bennett and Thomas DiLorenzo, *Official Lies: How Washington Misleads Us* (Alexandria, Va.: Groom, 1992), p. 193.
116. Ibid., p. 190.
117. Charles Leslie Glenn, *The Myth of the Common School* (Amherst, Mass.: University of Massachusetts, 1988), p. 143.
118. Ibid., p. 79.
119. Ibid.
120. Ibid.
121. *Tennessee Education Review,* July 1993.
122. Glenn, p. 80.
123. *Tennessee Education Review,* July 1993.
124. Glenn, p. 143.
125. Ibid., p. 145.
126. Ibid., p. 132.
127. Ibid., p. 183.
128. Ibid.
129. Ibid.
130. *Tennessee Education Review,* July 1993.
131. *Learning for a Lifetime,* June 1989.
132. Ibid.
133. Ibid.
134. Ibid.
135. *Tennessee Education Review,* July 1993.

136. John Henry Newman, *The Idea of a University* (Chicago, Ill.: Loyola University, 1927), p. v.
137. Ibid., p. vi.
138. Ibid.
139. C. S. Lewis, *An Experiment in Criticism* (Cambridge, U.K.: Cambridge University, 1961), p. 2.
140. Ibid., p. 3.
141. James Q. Wilson, *The Moral Sense* (New York: Free Press, 1993), p. 81.
142. *Tennessee Education Review,* July 1993.
143. Douglas Wilson, *Recovering the Lost Tools of Learning* (Wheaton, Ill.: Crossway, 1991), p. 146.
144. G. K. Chesterton, *Orthodoxy* (New York: Doran, 1908), p. 56.
145. *Tennessee Education Review,* July 1993.

Chapter Four

1. James Matin-Longes and Kendra Povic, eds., *English Literature: An Historical Anthology* (London: Harton, 1922), III: 39.
2. Ibid., IV: 199.
3. *East Anglia Commercial Review,* March 19, 1992.
4. Ibid.
5. Ibid.
6. Ibid.
7. Ibid.
8. *Chicago Tribune,* April 16, 1992.
9. *The People's Agenda,* March/April 1992.
10. *Chicago Tribune,* April 16, 1992.
11. James Lovelock, *Healing Gaia* (New York: Harmony Books, 1991), p. 153.
12. *Earthwatch,* September/October 1992.
13. *Los Angeles Times Book Review,* October 22, 1989.
14. *Harpeth Journal,* December 18, 1962.
15. *Chicago Tribune,* April 16, 1992.
16. Barbara Ward and Rene Dubos, *Only One Earth: The Care and Maintenance of a Small Planet* (New York: Norton, 1972), p. 45.
17. *The Limbaugh Letter,* November 1992.
18. Ibid.
19. Llewellyn H. Rockwell, *An Anti-Environmentalist Manifesto* (Burlingame, Calif.: Center for Libertarian Studies, 1990), p. 8.
20. Rachel Carson, *Silent Spring* (Greenwich, Conn.: Fawcett, 1962).
21. Rockwell, p. 8.
22. *The New American,* September 6, 1993.
23. Paul R. Ehrlich, *The Population Bomb* (New York: Ballentine, 1968), pp. 135–138.
24. Edith Efron, *The Apocalyptics: How Environmental Politics Controls What We Know About Cancer* (New York: Simon and Schuster, 1984), p. 36.
25. Ibid., p. 37.
26. *Ramparts,* May 1970.
27. *New York Times,* June 6, 1992.
28. Lewis Mumford, *The Pentagon of Power: The Myth of the Machine* (New York: Harcourt Brace Jovanovich, 1970), p. 413.
29. Don Henley and Dave Marsh, *Heaven Is Under Our Feet* (Samford, Conn.: The Isis Fund, 1991), p. 8.
30. Al Gore, *Earth in the Balance: Ecology and the Human Spirit* (New York: Houghton Mifflin, 1992), p. 260.
31. William Anderson, *The Green Man: The Archetype of Our Oneness With the Earth* (San Francisco: HarperCollins, 1991), p. 163.
32. *Science,* 1967, p. 155.
33. *Rolling Stone,* June 28, 1990.
34. Jonathan Porritt, ed., *Save the Earth* (Atlanta, Ga.: Turner Publishing, 1991), p. 8.
35. Callum MacQuinlin, *Civil Disobedience* (Lincoln, Neb.: Friends Center, 1977), pp. 14–18.
36. Michael Brown and John May, *The Greenpeace Story* (New York: Dorling and Kindersley, 1991), p. 8.
37. Rik Scarce, *Eco-Warriors* (Chicago: Noble Press, 1990), p. 49.
38. Ibid.
39. Ibid.
40. Ibid., p. 50.
41. Ibid.
42. Ibid.
43. Ibid., p. 51.
44. Dixy Lee Ray, *Environmental Overkill* (Washington: Regnery Gateway, 1993).
45. Scarce, p. 51.
46. Brown and May, p. 44.
47. Scarce, p. 52.
48. Ibid.
49. Ibid.
50. Ibid.
51. Ibid.
52. Ibid.
53. Ronald Bailey, *Eco-Scam* (New York: St. Martin's, 1993).
54. *British Columbia Report,* January 24, 1994.
55. Ibid.
56. Ibid.
57. Ibid.
58. Ibid.
59. Ibid.
60. Ibid.
61. Ibid.
62. Larry Abraham and Franklin Sanders, *The Greening* (Atlanta, Ga.: Soundview, 1993), p. 42.
63. Ibid.
64. *Discover,* October 1989.
65. Robert C. Balling, *The Heated Debate* (San

Francisco: Pacific Research Institute, 1992), p. xv.

66. Gore, p. 39.
67. Carl Dommer and Jonathan Terrilier, *Environmental Facts and Fictions* (London: New Earth, 1990), p. 15.
68. Ibid.
69. Ibid., p.17.
70. Ibid.
71. David Day, *The Environmental Wars* (New York: Ballantine, 1989), pp. 277–278.
72. James Garston, *Global Warming* (Cleveland, Ohio: Carvell, 1992), p. 78.
73. Ibid., p. 34.
74. Ibid., p. 35.
75. Dommer and Terrilier, p. 90.
76. Andrew Rees, *The Pocket Green Book* (London and New Jersey: Zed Books, 1991), p. 11.
77. Dommer and Terrilier, p. 65.
78. Ibid.
79. Ibid., p. 67.
80. Ibid.
81. Gore, pp. 84–85.
82. Dommer and Terrilier, p. 245.
83. Ibid.
84. Garston, p. 88.
85. Dommer and Terrilier, p. 251.
86. Ibid.
87. David Day, p. 275.
88. Bruce Mettiliz and Diane BenDarra-Pierce, *The State of the Earth* (New York: Kline and Kline, 1992), p. 111.
89. Ibid., p. 112.
90. Ibid.
91. Dommer and Terrilier, p. 77.
92. Mettiliz and BenDarra-Pierce, p. 303.
93. Ezra J. Mishan, *The Economic Growth Debate* (London: George Allen & Unwin, 1977), pp. 122–123.
94. Mettiliz and BenDarra-Pierce, p. 309.
95. Ibid.
96. Dommer and Terrilier, p. 4.
97. Mettiliz and BenDarra-Pierce, p. 307.
98. Ibid., p. 306.
99. Ibid.
100. *Brighton Journal*, May 3, 1990.
101. Ibid.
102. Dommer and Terrilier, p. 136.
103. Ibid.
104. Ibid.
105. Ibid., p. 137.
106. Ibid.
107. Abraham and Sanders, p. 133.
108. Brandon Kincaide, *Reform Movements* (London: Stockbridge, 1977), p. 78.

Chapter Five

1. James Matin-Longes and Kendra Povic, eds., *English Literature: An Historical Anthology* (London: Harton, 1922), III: 122–123.
2. Ibid., IV: 43.
3. *USA Today*, November 26, 1993.
4. *Jackson Clarion-Register*, November 13, 1993.
5. *USA Today*, November 26, 1993.
6. *Memphis Commercial-Appeal*, December 4, 1993.
7. Marcus Dunwoode, *Southern Literary Traditions* (Baton Rouge, La.: Cleburn Press, 1986), p. 134.
8. *USA Today*, November 26, 1993.
9. Ibid.
10. *Memphis Commercial-Appeal*, December 2, 1993.
11. Ibid.
12. *Memphis Commercial-Appeal*, December 4, 1993.
13. *USA Today*, November 26, 1993.
14. ACLU *Annual Report*, p. 3.
15. Ibid.
16. Jon Winokur, *The Portable Curmudgeon* (New York: New American Library, 1987), p. 12.
17. William Thayer-Noyes, *Anecdotal Evidence* (London: Charing Cross, 1979), p. 36.
18. ACLU *Annual Report*, p. 10.
19. Ibid.
20. William Donohue, *The Politics of the American Civil Liberties Union* (New Brunswick, N.J.: Transaction, 1985), p. 36.
21. Ibid.
22. Ibid.
23. Ibid., p. 39.
24. Ibid., p. 94.
25. Norman Dorsen, ed., *Our Endangered Rights* (New York: Pantheon, 1984).
26. ACLU *Policy Guide*, pp. 6–9.
27. Ibid., pp. 161–162.
28. Ibid., pp. 260–265.
29. Ibid., pp. 246–249; 267.
30. Barry Lynn, "Memo on Witchcraft Amendment to the Appropriations Bill," ACLU Washington Office, October 10, 1985.
31. ACLU *Policy Guide*, pp. 176–177.
32. Ibid., p. 261.
33. Ibid., pp. 185–187.
34. Ibid., pp. 245–248.
35. Ibid., pp. 347–348.
36. Ibid., p. 345.
37. Ibid., pp. 345–346.
38. Ibid., pp. 376–379.
39. Ibid., pp. 159–160.
40. *Conservative Digest*, December 1988.
41. ACLU *Policy Guide*, pp. 191–221.
42. Ibid., pp. 307–309.

43. Ibid., pp. 85–90.
44. *Operation Rescue Newsbriefs*, March 1989.
45. ACLU *Policy Guide*, p. 175.
46. Letter sent to the California Assembly Education Committee by the ACLU California Legislative Office.
47. *Policy Review*, September 1988.
48. ACLU *Policy Guide*, pp. 159–190.
49. Ibid.
50. Ibid.
51. Ibid.
52. Ibid.
53. Ibid.
54. Ibid.
55. Ibid.
56. Ibid.
57. Ibid.
58. Ibid.
59. Ibid.
60. Ibid.
61. Ibid.
62. *Boston Herald*, April 6, 1988.
63. *Policy Review*, September 1988.
64. Ibid.
65. Ibid.
66. Ibid.
67. *Imprimis*, April 1983.
68. *Wall Street Journal*, October 20, 1988.
69. Ibid.
70. Carl Hensen, *Life, Liberty, and Property* (New York: Paradigm, 1976), p. 233.
71. ACLU *Annual Report*, pp. 16–18.
72. Ibid.
73. Ibid.
74. Ibid.
75. Ibid.
76. Ibid.
77. *Demographics Today*, July 1989.
78. *Dallas Morning News*, March 21, 1988.
79. *New York Times*, October 2, 1988.
80. *Litigation Review*, November 1992.
81. *Washington Times*, July 7, 1993.
82. *Human Events*, May 23, 1993.
83. *Washington Action Alert*, September 1993.
84. Ibid.
85. Ibid.
86. Peggy Lamson, *Roger Baldwin* (Boston: Houghton Mifflin, 1976).
87. *Blackstones Law Review*, July 1993.
88. Ibid.
89. Ibid.
90. Donohue, p. 31.
91. Lamson, pp. 138–139.
92. Ibid., p. 141.
93. Ibid.
94. Roger Baldwin, *Liberty Under the Soviets* (New York: Vanguard, 1928), pp. 8–9.
95. Ibid., p. 10.
96. Ibid.
97. Ibid.
98. *Soviet Russia Today*, September 1934.
99. Ibid.
100. Lamson, p. 195.
101. Ibid.
102. *Review of the News*, August 13, 1975.
103. Ibid.
104. Ibid.
105. Ibid.
106. Lamson, p. 188.
107. *Review of the News*, August 13, 1975.
108. George Grant, *Trial and Error* (Franklin, Tenn.: Adroit Press, 1993), pp. 20–23.
109. Winokur, p. 92.
110. G. K. Chesterton, *Omnibus* (London: Sheed and Ward, 1936), p. ix.
111. Donohue, pp. 8–15.
112. *Washington Action Alert*, August 1993.
113. *Review of the News*, August 13, 1975.
114. *Washington Action Alert*, August 1993.
115. Ibid.
116. Lamson, p. 192.
117. Donohue, pp. 5–6.
118. ACLU *Annual Report*, pp. 12–13.
119. Ibid.
120. Ibid.
121. Ibid.
122. Ibid.
123. Ibid.
124. Ibid.
125. Donohue, p. 5.
126. Ibid., p. 4.
127. Ibid.
128. Lamson, p. 191.
129. Ibid.
130. Ibid.
131. Gardiner Spring, *Obligations of the World to the Bible* (New York: Taylor and Dodd, 1839), pp. 101–102.
132. Aleksandr Solzhenitsyn, *A Warning to the West* (New York: Harper, 1978), p. 64.
133. Dunwoode, p. 88.

Chapter Six

1. James Matin-Longes and Kendra Povic, eds., *English Literature: An Historical Anthology* (London: Harton, 1922), IV: 18.
2. Ibid., I:201.
3. *CFV Report*, November 1993.
4. *The Good Newspaper*, November 10, 1993.
5. Ibid.
6. *CFV Report*, November 1993.
7. Ibid.
8. *The Good Newspaper*, November 10, 1993.
9. *The Advocate*, September 1987.
10. Ibid.
11. Ibid.

12. Ibid.
13. Ibid.
14. Ibid.
15. Ibid.
16. Ibid.
17. Ibid.
18. *The Tennessean*, October 11, 1993.
19. *Washington Action Alert*, November 1993.
20. Ibid.
21. Ibid.
22. Ibid.
23. Ibid.
24. *World*, March 6, 1993.
25. Ibid.
26. *Quorum*, July 1993.
27. Ibid.
28. *Boston Globe*, September 5, 1993.
29. Ibid.
30. *New York Post*, August 12, 1992.
31. *Los Angeles Times*, September 11, 1989.
32. *Out*, October-November 1993.
33. Ibid.
34. *Quorum*, July 1993.
35. Ibid.
36. Simon Watney, *Taking Liberties: AIDS and Cultural Politics* (London: Serpent's Tail, 1989), p. xi.
37. *Time*, August 17, 1992.
38. *World*, March 6, 1993.
39. *Lambda Report*, February 1993.
40. Ibid.
41. *Human Events*, December 18, 1993.
42. Ibid.
43. Ibid.
44. *Lambda Report*, February 1993..
45. Ibid.
46. Ibid.
47. Ibid.
48. Ibid.
49. Ibid.
50. Ibid.
51. Ibid.
52. Ibid.
53. *Washington Blade*, March 12, 1993.
54. *San Francisco Examiner*, February 5, 1993.
55. *Human Events*, February 6, 1993.
56. *NBR Marketplace Newsletter*, February 1993.
57. *New Yorker*, November 9, 1992.
58. Ibid.
59. Ibid.
60. Ibid.
61. Ibid.
62. *Quorum*, January 1992.
63. *The E! Guide*, May 1993.
64. *The Advocate*, July 1991.
65. *Dallas Morning News*, May 14, 1990.
66. Ibid.
67. Larry Kramer, *Reports from the Holocaust*

(New York: Penguin, 1989), p. xxxi.
68. Ibid., p. xxx.
69. *Family Research Newsletter*, April-June 1991.
70. Ibid.
71. Ibid.
72. Ibid.
73. Ibid.
74. Ibid.
75. *American Spectator*, August 1984.
76. George Grant and Mark Horne, *Legislating Immorality: The Homosexual Movement Comes Out of the Closet* (Chicago: Moody Press, 1993), pp. 109–141.
77. Ibid.
78. Franklin Payne, *What Every Christian Should Know About the AIDS Epidemic: The Medical and Biblical Facts* (Augusta, Ga.: Covenant, 1991), pp. 71–72.
79. Ibid.
80. Ibid.
81. Ibid.
82. Tony Marco, *Gay Rights: A Public Health Disaster and Civil Wrong* (Ft. Lauderdale, Fla.: Coral Ridge, 1992), p. 13.
83. Ibid., p. 14.
84. Ibid.
85. Ibid.
86. *Time*, August 3, 1992.
87. *American Journal of Public Health*, December 1985.
88. *Washington Post*, June 24, 1990.
89. Frank Browning, *The Culture of Desire: Paradox and Perversity in Gay Lives Today* (New York: Crown, 1993), p. 119.
90. Randy Shilts, *And the Band Played On: Politics, People, and the AIDS Epidemic* (New York: St. Martins, 1987), p. 200.
91. Ibid.
92. Kramer, p. 263.
93. Kramer, p. 33.
94. Simon Watney, *Policing Desire: Pornography, AIDS, and the Media* (London: Comedia, 1989), p. 62.
95. Ibid.
96. *Quorum*, July 1993.
97. Ibid.
98. Kramer, p. 48.
99. Ibid., p. 171.
100. Ibid., p. 128.
101. Ibid.
102. Ibid.
103. Ibid., pp. 135–136.
104. *Dallas Morning News*, July 24, 1991.
105. Ibid.
106. Kramer, p. 292.
107. Ibid., p. 1.
108. Ibid., p. 292.

109. Ibid.
110. Ibid.
111. Nevin Lobric, *Envy* (London: Stockbridge, 1988), p. 23.
112. Ibid.
113. *Venice Rap*, May 1993.
114. *Tennessean*, October 11, 1993.
115. Ibid.
116. *Christian News-Observer*, Spring 1988.
117. George Grant, *The 57% Solution* (Franklin, Tenn.: Adroit Press, 1993), pp. 90–110.
118. Ibid.
119. Ibid.
120. Ibid.
121. Ibid.
122. Ibid.
123. Ibid.
124. Ibid.
125. Ibid.
126. Marcus Dunwoode, *Southern Literary Traditions* (Baton Rouge, La.: Cleburn Press, 1986), p. 134.
127. Ibid.
128. Ibid., p. 16.
129. Ibid.

Chapter Seven

1. James Matin-Longes and Kendra Povic, eds., *English Literature: An Historical Anthology* (London: Harton, 1922), II: 90–91.
2. Ibid., II: 97.
3. *Wall Street Journal*, November 12, 1982.
4. Ibid.
5. Ibid.
6. Marian Wright Edelman, *Families in Peril: An Agenda for Social Change* (Cambridge, Mass.: Harvard University, 1987), p. 71.
7. Charles Murray, *Losing Ground* (New York: Basic Books, 1984).
8. *Welfare Reform Journal*, April 1991.
9. Ibid.
10. Ibid.
11. Ibid.
12. Karen Hawthorne, *The Alms Race* (New York: Garden Valley, 1968), p. 62.
13. Murray, pp. 24–40.
14. Stuart Butler and Anna Kondratas, *Out of the Poverty Trap* (New York: Free Press, 1987), pp. 1–27.
15. *Welfare Reform Journal*, April 1991.
16. Ibid.
17. Murray, pp. 3–9.
18. *The New Republic*, February 15, 1993.
19. "We Are Making a Difference in Children's Lives," Children's Defense Fund, 1992.
20. Ibid.
21. Ibid.
22. Ibid.

23. *The New Republic*, February 15, 1993.
24. Ibid.
25. Ibid.
26. Ibid.
27. *Welfare Reform Journal*, April 1991.
28. Ibid.
29. Ibid.
30. *The New Republic*, February 15, 1993.
31. Ibid.
32. *Welfare Reform Journal*, April 1991.
33. *The New Republic*, February 15, 1993.
34. *Welfare Reform Journal*, April 1991.
35. Ibid.
36. Ibid.
37. Ibid.
38. Ibid.
39. *The London Statesman*, June 16, 1993.
40. *The New Republic*, February 15, 1993.
41. *Organizational Trends*, March 1991.
42. *Human Events*, February 27, 1993.
43. Ibid.
44. *Harper's Bazaar*, February 1993.
45. *The New Republic*, February 15, 1993.
46. *Human Events*, October 5, 1968.
47. *The New Republic*, February 15, 1993.
48. Ibid.
49. Ibid.
50. Robert Louis Stevenson, *Essays* (New York: Dutton, 1906), p. 12–13.
51. *The Phyllis Schlafly Report*, March 1993.
52. *Welfare Reform Journal*, June 1993.
53. Ibid.
54. Ibid.
55. *The New Republic*, February 15, 1993.
56. *Human Events*, February 27, 1993.
57. Marion Wright Edelman, *The Measure of Our Success* (Boston: Beacon, 1992), p. 95.
58. Ibid., p. 37.
59. Ibid., p. 42.
60. Ibid., p. 47.
61. Ibid., p. 54.
62. Ibid., p. 57.
63. Ibid., p. 65.
64. Ibid., p. 66.
65. Ibid., p. 69.
66. *Welfare Reform Journal*, June 1993.
67. Ibid.
68. *Measure*, p. 69.
69. Ibid., p. 65.
70. Ibid., p. 71.
71. Ibid., p. 58.
72. Ibid., p. 9.
73. Ibid., p. 61.
74. Ibid.
75. *Families in Peril*, pp. 33–34.
76. Ibid., p. 35.
77. Ibid., p. 37.
78. Ibid., pp. 58–59.

79. Ibid., p. 64.
80. Ibid., p. 99.
81. Ibid., p. 101.
82. Washington Ledger, May 10, 1993.
83. Welfare Reform Journal, June 1993.
84. Ibid.
85. Murray, p. 8.
86. Ibid.
87. Welfare Reform Journal, April 1991.
88. Ibid.
89. Ibid.
90. George Grant, Bringing in the Sheaves (Brentwood, Tenn.: Wolgemuth and Hyatt, 1989).
91. George Grant, The Dispossessed: Homelessness in America (Wheaton, Ill.: Crossway, 1986).
92. Marvin Olasky, The Tragedy of American Compassion (Wheaton, Ill.: Crossway, 1992).
93. George Gilder, Wealth and Poverty (New York: Basic, 1991).
94. Welfare Reform Journal, April 1991.
95. Ibid.
96. Ibid.
97. Ibid.
98. Thomas Sowell, Civil Rights (New York: Morrow, 1984).
99. Walter Williams, The State Against the Blacks (New York: McGraw, 1982).
100. Barry Bluestone and Bennett Harrison, The Deindustrialization of America (New York: Basic, 1982).
101. Families in Peril.
102. Welfare Reform Journal, June 1993.
103. Ibid.
104. Ibid.
105. The Phyllis Schlafly Report, March 1993.
106. Welfare Reform Journal, June 1993.
107. Families in Peril, p. 99.
108. Ibid., p. 37.
109. Ibid.
110. Welfare Reform Journal, June 1993.
111. Grant, Dispossessed, pp. 165–186.
112. Grant, Bringing in the Sheaves, pp. 53–79.
113. Vernon Carter, The New Deal and Beyond (New York: Lathrop and Harrod, 1979), p. 169.
114. Michael Harrington, The New American Poverty (New York: Holt, Rinehart, and Winston, 1984).
115. Jonathan Kozol, Rachel and Her Children (New York: Crown, 1988).
116. Ibid.
117. Murray Rothbard, For a New Liberty (New York: Macmillan, 1973), p. 86.
118. Welfare Reform Journal, June 1993.
119. Ibid.
120. Ibid.
121. The responsibility for Christians to care for the poor is stressed throughout the Scriptures: Exodus 22:25; Leviticus 19:10; Leviticus 23:22; Leviticus 25:35–37; Numbers 18:24; Deuteronomy 14:29; Deuteronomy 15:1–2; Deuteronomy 24:19–21; Ruth 2:1–23; Ruth 4:1–12; Psalm 41:1–3; Proverbs 11:25; Proverbs 14:21; Proverbs 14:31; Proverbs 17:5; Proverbs 21:13; Proverbs 22:9; Proverbs 28:27; Proverbs 29:7; Proverbs 31:8–9; Isaiah 1:10–17; Isaiah 10:1–2; Isaiah 32:6–8; Isaiah 58:1–12; Amos 5:1–27; Matthew 5:16; Matthew 7:12; Matthew 10:8; Matthew 25:31–46; Mark 12:44; Luke 3:11; Luke 6:38; Luke 9:48; Luke 10:30–37; Luke 11:41; Luke 12:33–34; Acts 20:35; Romans 12:8–20; 2 Corinthians 1:3–4; 2 Corinthians 8:1–24; 2 Corinthians 9:7; Galatians 5:6; Galatians 6:2; Galatians 6:9–10; Ephesians 5:2; Ephesians 2:8–10; 2 Thessalonians 3:6–10; 1 Timothy 5:8; 1 Timothy 6:18–19; Titus 2:11–14; Titus 3:1; Titus 3:8; Titus 3:14; Hebrews 13:16; James 2:14–26; 1 John 3:17.
122. Westminster Confession of Faith (Richmond, Va.: John Knox, 1944), pp. 95–96.
123. Charles Haddon Spurgeon, John Plowman's Pictures (Philadelphia: John Altemus, n.d.), p. 165.
124. National Reform Association Newsgram, December 1993.

Chapter Eight

1. James Matin-Longes and Kendra Povic, eds., English Literature: An Historical Anthology (London: Harton, 1922), IV: 4.
2. Ibid., III: 159.
3. Harold Frelton and Gerry Yarborough, eds., The Crisis in American Health Care (New York: U.S. Resources, 1993), p. 3.
4. Ibid.
5. Ibid.
6. Ibid.
7. Ibid.
8. Ibid., p. 4.
9. Ibid.
10. Ibid.
11. Ibid., p. 6.
12. Ibid.
13. Ibid.
14. Ibid.
15. Ibid.
16. Ibid.
17. Ibid., p. 7.
18. Ibid.
19. Brock Chisholm, ed., The World Health Organization Charter (Brussels: United Nations, 1955), p. 2.
20. Ibid.

21. Ibid., p. 33.
22. Ibid.
23. Ibid.
24. Ibid., p. 34.
25. Ibid.
26. Ibid.
27. Ibid.
28. Ibid., p. 35.
29. *American Opinion*, May 1958.
30. Ibid.
31. Chisholm, p. 33.
32. Ibid., p. 50.
33. Ibid., p. 39.
34. Ibid.
35. *Syracuse Herald-Journal*, May 9, 1989.
36. *Wall Street Journal*, May 9, 1989.
37. Ibid.
38. *Wall Street Journal*, June 9, 1986.
39. *American Opinion*, May 1958.
40. Ibid.
41. Chisholm, p. 57.
42. William Farr, *Disastrous Philanthropy* (Boston: Libertarian Praxis, 1991), p. 88.
43. Ibid.
44. Ibid.
45. Ibid.
46. Ibid., p. 42.
47. Ibid., p. 49.
48. Ibid., p. 50.
49. Ibid.
50. Ibid.
51. Ibid.
52. George Grant, *The Quick and the Dead* (Wheaton, Ill.: Crossway, 1991).
53. Farr, p. 88.
54. Ibid., p. 89.
55. Ibid.
56. Ibid.
57. Ibid.
58. *Pro Vitas Europe*, May 1991.
59. Grant, pp. 49–52.
60. Ibid., pp. 56–58.
61. Ibid., pp. 19–34.
62. Ibid., pp. 55–56.
63. Ibid., p. 54.
64. Farr, p. 101.
65. James Ricord, *The United Nations and Its Mission* (New York: Falmouth, 1959), p. 19.
66. *The Spectator*, July 31, 1993.
67. Ibid.
68. Ibid.
69. Ibid.
70. Ibid.
71. Ibid.
72. Albert J. Lee, *Imperial Peacekeeping: A History* (New York: Noebel House, 1989), p. 162.
73. Ibid., p. 139.
74. *Health Care Professional News*, June 1993.
75. Ibid.
76. Ulke Nordstrom and Javre Koss, *Health Care Reform* (London: Alliance Centre, 1992), p. 45.
77. Ibid., p. 47.
78. Ibid., p. 48.
79. Ibid., p. 50.
80. Ibid., p. 51.
81. Ibid., p. 53.
82. Ibid., p. 31.
83. Chisholm, p. 88.
84. Nordstrom and Koss, pp. 12–23.
85. Ibid.
86. Ibid.
87. *Health Care Professional News*, June 1993.
88. Ibid.
89. Ibid.
90. Ibid.
91. Ibid.
92. Ibid.
93. Ibid.
94. Ibid.
95. Terree Wasley, *Big Brother in the Emergency Room: The Hazards of Government-Run Health Care* (United Seniors Association, 1993), p. 9.
96. Ibid.
97. Ibid.
98. Ibid.
99. Ibid., p. 10.
100. Ibid.
101. Ibid.
102. Ibid.
103. *Health Care Professional News*, June 1993.
104. Ibid.
105. Ibid.
106. Wasley, p. 11.
107. Ibid.
108. *Health Care Professional News*, June 1993.
109. Ibid.
110. Ibid.
111. Ibid.
112. Ibid.
113. Wasley, p. 12.
114. *Health Care Professional News*, June 1993.
115. Grant, pp. 88–89.
116. *Health Care Professional News*, June 1993.
117. Ibid.
118. Ibid.
119. Grant, pp. 90–94.
120. Ibid.
121. Lawrence Wright, *Clean and Decent* (Toronto: University of Toronto, 1967).
122. Guy Thuillier, *Pour un Histoire de la Lessive au XIXe Siecle* (Paris: Annales, 1969).
123. Rene Dubos, *The Mirage of Health* (New York: Anchor, 1959).

124. Ivan Illich, The Limits to Medicine (London: Penguin, 1977).
125. Heinrich Schipperges, Utopien der Medizin (Salzburg: Muller, 1986).
126. David Chilton, Power in the Blood (Brentwood, Tenn.: Wolgemuth and Hyatt, 1987).
127. Illich, p. 23.
128. Ibid.
129. David M. Spain, The Complications of Modern Medical Practices (New York: Grune and Stratton, 1973).
130. Hermes Vallors, Medical Malpractice (London: Perrin, 1982).
131. Ibid.
132. Ibid.
133. Spain, pp. 33–34.
134. Ibid.
135. Ibid.
136. L. Meyler, The Side Effects of Drugs (Baltimore, Maryland: Williams and Wilkins, 1982), p. 428.
137. Ibid., p. 433.
138. Ibid.
139. Health Care Professional News , June 1993.
140. Ibid.
141. Ibid.
142. Ibid.
143. Barbara Seaman, The Doctors' Case Against the Pill (Garden City, N.Y.: Doubleday, 1980), p. 11.
144. Dallas Times Herald, January 29, 1989.
145. Ibid.
146. Health Care Professional News, June 1993.
147. Ibid.
148. Yugoslav Praemedicatum, Spring 1988.
149. Ibid.
150. The Business Outlook, November 30, 1990.
151. John Ankerberg and John Weldon, Can You Trust Your Doctor? (Brentwood, Tenn.: Wolgemuth and Hyatt, 1991).
152. Yugoslav Praemedicatum, Spring 1988.
153. Barbara DeJong, Tracing the Jewish Diaspora (Amsterdam: The English Press, 1967).
154. Nigel M. de S. Cameron, The New Medicine (Wheaton, Ill.: Crossway, 1992).
155. Illich, p. 121.
156. T. S. Elliot, The Complete Poems and Plays (New York: Harcourt, Brace, and World, 1958), p. 96.

Chapter Nine

1. James Matin-Longes and Kendra Povic, eds., English Literature: An Historical Anthology (London: Harton, 1922), 1:38.
2. Ibid., II:164.
3. William Faulkner, An Anthology of Fiction and Nonfiction (London: Carrolton, Chalmers, and Duerst, 1971), p. 34.
4. Dallas Morning News, June 28, 1993.
5. Ibid.
6. New York Times, June 27, 1993.
7. London Sunday Telegraph, June 20, 1993.
8. Washington Times, June 9, 1993.
9. Sydney Morning Herald, June 18, 1993.
10. London Sunday Telegraph, June 20, 1993.
11. New York Times, June 27, 1993.
12. Ibid.
13. London Sunday Telegraph, June 20, 1993.
14. New York Times, June 27, 1993.
15. Ibid.
16. Ibid.
17. Ibid.
18. Insider Report, July 1993.
19. New York Times, June 27, 1993.
20. Ibid.
21. Ibid.
22. Ibid.
23. Human Events, June 26, 1993.
24. Washington Post, June 9, 1993.
25. Wall Street Journal, June 28, 1993.
26. Dallas Morning News, June 28, 1993.
27. Ibid.
28. Insider Report, July 1993.
29. New York Times, April 7, 1993.
30. Ibid.
31. Washington Post, June 9, 1993.
32. Human Events, June 26, 1993.
33. Ibid.
34. Ibid.
35. Ibid.
36. Ibid.
37. Ibid.
38. Time, May 31, 1993.
39. New Republic, June 7, 1993.
40. Wall Street Journal, May 28, 1993.
41. Human Events, June 26, 1993.
42. Washington Post , May 14, 1993.
43. Ibid.
44. New York Times, June 27, 1993.
45. Ibid.
46. Eugene H. Methvin, The Rise of Radicalism (New Rochelle, N.Y.: Arlington House, 1973) p. 504.
47. New York Times, June 27, 1993.
48. Insider Report, July 1993.
49. Methvin, p. 497.
50. Michael Lerner, The Socialism of Fools: Anti-Semitism on the Left (Oakland, Calif.: Tikkun Books, 1992), p. 150.
51. Elizabeth Frost Knappman, ed., Presidential Quotations (New York: Pharos Books, 1993).
52. Michael Lerner, The New Socialist Revolution: An Introduction to Its Theory and Strategy (New York: Delacorte Press, 1973), pp. iv-v.
53. Ibid, p. v.
54. Ibid.

55. Ibid.
56. Ibid.
57. Ibid.
58. *Insider Report*, July 1993.
59. Bernard Lewis Kleinca, tr., *Zohar* (New York: Kabbala Press, 1972), p. xii-xiii.
60. Ibid, p. xiv.
61. Ibid.
62. *Kabbalism Watch*, Summer 1993.
63. *London Sunday Telegraph*, June 20, 1993.
64. *Wall Street Journal*, June 28, 1993.
65. Ibid.
66. *Nashville Banner*, January 25, 1993.
67. Ibid.
68. *Tikkun*, July/August 1993.
69. Gallup Poll, 1993.
70. George Grant, *The 57% Solution: A Conservative Strategy for the Next Four Years* (Franklin, Tenn.: Adroit Press, 1993), pp. 85–97.
71. *Tikkun*, September/October 1993.
72. Ibid.
73. Ibid.
74. *Tikkun*, May/June 1993.
75. Ibid.
76. Ibid.
77. Ibid.
78. Ibid.
79. Ibid.
80. Ibid.
81. Ibid.
82. Ibid.
83. Ibid.
84. Ibid.
85. Ibid.
86. G. K. Chesterton, *G. F. Watts* (New York: E. P. Dutton, 1901), p. 19.
87. Knappman, p. 201.
88. Tristram Gylbeard, *The Unpublished Works* (Humble, Tex.: Vorthos, 1986), p. 19.
89. Peter Jones, *The Gnostic Empire Strikes Back* (Phillipsburg, N.J.: Presbyterian and Reformed, 1992), p. ix.
90. Ibid., p. x.
91. Ibid.

Chapter Ten

1. James Matin-Longes and Kendra Povic, eds., *English Literature: An Historical Anthology* (London: Harton, 1922), II: 178.
2. Ibid., III: 108.
3. Henry L. Bell, *Under the Articles* (New York: Scribners, 1921), p. 122.
4. Ibid.
5. Ibid.
6. Ibid.
7. James Cotton, *The Legend of the Tower* (London: Pickwick, 1988), p. 16.
8. Ibid.
9. Ibid.
10. *The English Launcher*, February 12, 1991.
11. Ibid.
12. Ibid.
13. Bell, p. 49.
14. Ibid., p. 122.
15. Ibid., p. 50.
16. Ibid.
17. Ibid., p. 51.
18. Myra Ypres-Keller, *The Mood of the Nation* (New York: Princess, 1988), p. 90.
19. William Peay Johnson, *The Development of an International Party* (London: Grovenor, 1979), p. 31.
20. Patricia Hollis, *Catholic Social Policy* (Minneapolis, Minn.: Sisters of Charity, 1983), p. 46.
21. Horton Kael and William Loomis, *A Documentary History of Liberal Thought* (New York: Cushman, 1959), p. 246.
22. Hollis, p. 48.
23. Ibid., p. 50.
24. Ibid., p. 49.
25. Steven Rolle Davis, *The Southern Agrarians* (Jackson, Miss.: Southern, 1965), p. 5.
26. Johnson, p. 33.
27. Kael and Loomis, p. 244.
28. Davis, p. 5.
29. Hollis, p. 49.
30. Johnson, p. 36.
31. Ibid.
32. Hollis, p. 44.
33. Kael and Loomis, p. 249.
34. Davis, p. 7.
35. Johnson, p. 81.
36. Hollis, p. 45.
37. Ibid., p. 46.
38. Kael and Loomis, p. 200.
39. Davis, p. 7.
40. Hollis, p. xii.
41. Bell, p.122.
42. Garbage in, garbage out.
43. Our help is in the Name of the Lord.
44. Who made heaven and earth.
45. Let us therefore pray.